Communicators' Guide to Marketing

Communicators' Guide to Marketing

INTERNATIONAL ASSOCIATION OF BUSINESS COMMUNICATORS

Edited by
Clara Degen

Sheffield Publishing Company
Salem, Wisconsin

For information about this book, write or call:

Sheffield Publishing Company
P.O. Box 359
Salem, Wisconsin 53168
(414) 843-2281

Acknowledgments

We gratefully acknowledge the use of the following materials.

Chapter 5. Page 68: Sony Trinitron (TM) brochure. Reprinted with permission of the Sony Corp., Park Ridge, N.J.; page 71: 1986 Mac World Expo brochure, written by Brian Flood and designed by Michael Benes. Reprinted with permission of World Expo Company, Westwood, Mass., and CW Communications, Framingham, Mass.; pages 72, 82: reprinted with permission of United Technologies Corp., Hartford, Conn.; page 79: reprinted with permission of William Clough, Clough Management Services, Rouse's Point, N.Y.; page 90: Foremost-McKesson's *Direction* magazine from IABC's *Excellence in Communication (1983).* The photographer was Mark Tuschman. Reprinted with permission of McKesson Corp., San Francisco, Calif.

Chapter 9. Page 146: *On Target,* Target Stores, Minneapolis, Minn. Reprinted with permission; page 152: EAB, *Branch Update, Branch Marketing Notes,* and advertising examples. Reprinted with permission of European American Bank, Long Island, N.Y.; page 155: *The Bottom Line, Allstate Life,* and *Allstate Now.* Reprinted with permission of Allstate Insurance Co., Northbrook, Ill.

Chapter 12. Page 198: Reader's Digest Association, Pleasantville, N. Y. Reprinted with permission.

Contents

Foreword

An exciting part of being in communication is the changing nature of the profession. Many of us, leaving the university with our journalism or communication degrees, never imagined the range of duties we would be handling on the job.

And the profession continues to change, bringing new technologies that enable us to communicate with colleagues and media around the world, new media that force us to broaden our skills, and new demands by our organizations to find better ways to reach their audiences.

Marketing communication is but the newest tool available to communication professionals, and it is one that a growing number of practitioners in the public and private sectors are applying to their organizations.

But many practitioners fear the word *marketing* and the images it conjures up of selling and promoting business. Yet when applied with knowledge, marketing techniques can enhance communication efforts and make them more effective in reaching key audiences.

The International Association of Business Communicators has a tradition of providing professional development opportunities for its members through workshops, information sharing, a wide range of learning sessions at international conferences, and, of course, books like this one.

We hope that *Communicators' Guide to Marketing* will give an overview and foundation for understanding to help communicators develop marketing strategies and techniques for the programs and projects they undertake.

Whether the communicator is promoting greater safety on the job, asking an association's members for volunteer commitment, or supporting a company's advertising and sales effort for a new product, a communication program is much more effective when it is targeted to an audience in language it understands and accepts.

The authors of the essays in this book are all experts in using marketing within a communication context. You should find their experiences helpful guides to making marketing an effective part of your communication activities.

Norman G. Leaper, ABC
President, IABC

Preface

Studies by the International Association of Business Communicators (IABC) find that more than nine out of ten communication and public relations professionals pursue professional development activities throughout their careers. This may take the form of reading current literature—books and articles in periodicals—as well as attending and speaking at workshops and seminars and writing or lecturing before student groups.

IABC leaders strongly believe in supporting the professional development needs and desires of members. To meet these needs, the association offers services that include an annual international conference, ongoing workshops, a resource center with packets of information on a variety of topics related to the field, a monthly magazine covering news and trends, and books on relevant topics. This book, *Communicators' Guide to Marketing*, is the latest in this last-mentioned effort.

Like IABC's other books, *Inside Organizational Communication, Understanding and Using Video,* and *Without Bias,* this new book is designed to provide an overview, an introduction to the concepts and tools of marketing within a communication and public relations context.

The content roughly follows a marketing plan: reviewing and selecting appropriate research; conducting the research and evaluating results; identifying the audience and producing the right message to reach that audience. Throughout the book, the authors have tried to include examples and case studies to bring the concepts to life and to provide guidance based on experience. And, of course, all the authors have stressed the importance of setting measurable goals and objectives and of evaluating results based on those goals and objectives.

We hope you find this book helpful, another tool to make your communication efforts more effective in reaching the intended audiences and in supporting your organization's "bottom line"—whether it is to promote a product or service, reach a new audience, expand its market share, or reposition itself within its industry, community, or market.

Additional resources, books, and periodicals are cited throughout the book and at the end to help you become more knowledgeable about subjects discussed in the book.

As editor of *Communicator's Guide to Marketing*, I would like to thank a number of people who were especially helpful in putting the project together: first, the authors, who contributed so freely of their time and talents to share their expertise in marketing communication; next, the numerous reporters, editors, and magazine librarians, who helped verify publication dates, article titles, names of authors, and other information needed to complete resource data. I would like to give special thanks to Sei Tokuno, of Japan Airlines's advertising department, and Rae Hamlin, executive assistant and office manager at IABC, for their invaluable assistance; and to Gordon T.R. Anderson and Ronni Strell for their support and patience during the development and completion of this project.

Clara Degen

Communicators' Guide to Marketing

CHAPTER 1

An Introduction to Marketing: How to Apply Its Tools

Roger Haywood, ABC*

Two of the most remarkable changes in business practice in the last few decades have an extremely close link: both depend on the realization that business success comes from the public's consent, not just management's ambitions.

First, the concept of marketing has revolutionized progressive businesses in recent years. Indeed, marketing has become more than just a function or craft. It is now a way of business life, based on the simple truth that the customer is central to every organization and determines whether that organization will succeed or fail.

Second, communication has recognized that the organization is allowed to prosper only through the support of the public on which it depends. Goodwill and favorable opinions can be created both by the actions and by the communication of the organization—but not by either of these alone. This has given rise to the second change, a radical shift in boardroom thinking, which has led to the acceptance of the need for an organization to have an acceptable corporate personality and a credible ethical stance if it is to achieve any substantial success. Today, the organization not only has to *be* good, it has to be *seen* as good.

Although both marketing and communication have evolved from the common root of reputation, there does tend to be one significant difference in their areas of operation: marketing tends to be concerned with all those facets of the company that affect the customer and the customer intermediaries (wholesalers and retailers, for example); communication must influence *every* audience of significance, including the nonmarketing groups (shareholders, community residents, and so on). Marketing professionals are increasingly staking a claim to control over broader communication, with the rationale that the opinions and influences of nonmarketing audiences can radically affect commercial success.

---

*Roger Haywood, ABC, is chief executive of Roger Haywood Associates, Ltd., London. An author, lecturer, and broadcaster in public relations and marketing, he is accredited in business communication.

Communicators must understand and use marketing skills if they are to retain control over communication and public relations functions. In addition, understanding marketing techniques and applying them effectively will enhance their own efforts for the benefit of the organization. Understanding the related area of marketing also will make it easier for communicators to establish and foster stronger working relationships with marketing colleagues.

REPUTATION IS THE CRITICAL FACTOR

The communication specialist often argues that although an important part of the organization's professional communication is geared to supporting sales and marketing, it is equally important that the company respond to its other nonmarketing publics on the basis of pressures other than those of profit.

Both marketing and communication specialists agree that a good reputation is a tangible asset that takes years to build and can be destroyed in moments. Both agree that public opinion is a powerful and critical force. Both agree that attitudes are probably the most important single influence on any business decision—whether to buy from the company, work for the company, invest in the company, or supply the company with products or services.

Put a group of business communicators and marketers together and they will soon begin arguing whether communication is part of marketing, or vice versa. It is an interesting but fruitless argument, since both perceptions are partially true and partially untrue.

Marketing is much bigger than communication.

And communication is much bigger than marketing.

However, it is important for any organization to have a strong link between these two management functions. The communication function has a critical role to play in supporting sales and marketing efforts: creating awareness; generating interest in service and products; building bridges with wholesalers, retailers, and customers; establishing the reputation that helps make customers return again and again; providing an important mirror of public perceptions to help marketing executives make their business decisions, and so on.

At the same time, it is important that marketing efforts directly support the communication policies of the organization: producing products that are consistent with the organization's claims of quality or reliability; pricing products at levels that are consistent with the firm's position in the marketplace; undertaking advertising, packaging, distribution, sales promotion, and merchandising plans that relate closely to the communication stance and the corporate personality; dealing with customers, trading partners, suppliers, and consumers in a professional and ethical way that enhances the company's reputation.

It is certainly no coincidence that the companies that are most effective at marketing tend to be those that also are best at communication—probably because the two disciplines stem from the same enlightened philosophy. Good examples are IBM, Kodak, and Shell.

CONTROLLING AND COORDINATING MARKETING COMMUNICATION FUNCTIONS

Marketing communication is a very specialized and professional area within the broad field of business communication, one in which some of the highest quality standards apply. Some organizations divide marketing communication into separate functions: public relations, advertising, sales promotion, and so on. But the most effective campaigns are generally developed by organizations that have a single department to perform these functions, often reporting to an executive with overall responsibility for managing all marketing communication.

Conveying a Consistent Message

This arrangement improves the control, coordination, and consistency of the messages conveyed by the various media and the various techniques that may be used. For example, it can be disastrous to present a product image of high quality through public relations channels when the advertising is emphasizing only value for money. Such inconsistencies are at best confusing and at worst positively harmful to the marketing effort. The control of the functions by a single executive ensures that all disciplines are working toward a common goal.

Working to a Consistent Timetable

Another important consideration in this coordination is the timing of activity. As an example, when a new product is launched, many audiences within the marketing function will need to be aware of this product, its role in the product range, its features and benefits, whether it is replacing an existing line and, if so, over what period.

In addition, as noted earlier, many audiences *outside* the influence of the marketing disciplines will need to be aware of significant developments, such as the introduction of a new product. These include company employees, suppliers, financial institutions, shareholders, community residents, and opinion leaders.

The timing of such announcements, as well as the decision of when to use public relations first and when to lead off with advertising, need to be agreed upon. For example, a marketing communication program for a new product introduction might include any combination of the following elements:

Internal meetings to brief the sales force and clarify the timetable

Regional meetings for wholesalers to review details of the introduction program

A series of presentations to retailers to introduce the item

A press reception to introduce the product to trade and/or consumer reporters and editors

New point-of-sale material on the introduction to focus attention of the public in the stores

A major consumer contest to stimulate public interest

Trade advertising to reinforce the retailer/wholesaler presentations

Consumer advertising to stimulate sales

Major feature articles in key trade publications to reinforce the credibility of the organization's marketing capabilities

A debriefing of the sales force to review the introduction and to settle the product into the company's product lines

A series of press releases on features of the product to maintain public enthusiasm

Ongoing consumer advertising to stimulate sales

The incorrect timing of any of these events can seriously unbalance the program and undermine other promotional activities.

WHAT EXACTLY IS MARKETING?

Marketing is much more than a management skill; it is a business philosophy. Marketing influences every aspect of an organization's operations and becomes a powerful, driving force within every department.

The marketing-oriented organization is controlled by the marketplace, while the production-oriented organization is controlled by the factory. The difference can be stated another way: the marketing company makes what people want to buy; the production company sells what the company wants to make.

Marketing* may be formally defined as the management process of

*Definitions for the terms printed in boldface are in the glossary, page 207.

identifying, anticipating, and satisfying customer requirements profitably. In simpler terms, marketing is all about finding out what people want (or might want if it were available) and presenting this product or service to potential customers, at a price that is acceptable to them and profitable to the company.

Clearly, communication is an essential element in the marketing mix. Marketing is based on two-way communication. Before an appropriate marketing policy can be developed, the organization must discover and understand the attitudes of potential customers, it has to ask basic questions and listen to the answers. In addition, to present these products and services to the market, it has to issue information, influence attitudes, develop opinions and, in the process, create awareness, interest, understanding, and support. And the effective management of this two-way information flow is organizational communication.

WHAT MARKETING IS *NOT*

Marketing is *not* another term for selling. Selling is an essential element of marketing, but it is only a part of this broader management function. Selling is concerned with the presentation of a product or service to potential customers and the conversion of their interest into business for the company.

Marketing is *not* a fashionable management technique. It is a business way of life that must permeate all aspects of the organization. Nor is marketing optional. Indeed, marketing is essential to commercial success and was a central element in all business success stories long before the practice was formally recognized as a management discipline.

Early entrepreneurs knew what the market wanted because they were in close touch with their customers. Their organizations had not become so complex that the founders, and their employees, had become remote from the customers. Henry Ford, Isaac Merritt Singer, Howard Hughes, and Clarence Birdseye all knew exactly what made the customer tick; that is why they grew from small entrepreneurs to large entrepreneurs—though it is likely that none of them ever used the term *marketing* or would have understood any formal definition of the word. In those innocent days, marketing was plain common sense. It took generations of engineers, scientists, accountants, lawyers, and even communicators to complicate the business until the central, fundamental, and obvious importance of the customer became lost. Who could ever have imagined that whole generations would grow up thinking that business had little to do with anything as important as the customer?

ELEMENTS OF THE MARKETING MIX

Marketing as a managment philosophy is simply an orientation toward the customer. As a craft practiced in an organization, it is the combination of a number of special skills which apply almost regardless of the product or service involved. The expression generally used to cover the balance of these elements in the overall policy is "the marketing mix." Typically, the marketing mix includes such elements as market research, product development, product design, packaging, pricing, distribution, promotion, sales, budgeting, and campaign monitoring.

Market Research

Effective marketing begins long before the product exists. Some companies mistakenly believe that they have a marketing orientation when they take a product and say, "Let's market it." What they really mean is, "Let's sell it, or promote it, or merchandise it."

Marketing begins with knowing, or finding out, what the market wants—or would buy if it were available. Sound marketing decisions are based on a proper understanding of customers' opinions and attitudes, and the assessment of these is the responsibility of market research. However, while market research is important in virtually all marketing programs, it should not be the only factor in deciding product policy.

For example, even if market research had existed as the science it is today, it is doubtful that Mr. Birdseye would have had very encouraging reactions to his idea for frozen foods. The concept for his products was unknown and, therefore, there was no established market need. The market had to be created and potential customers educated to understand the benefits; from this sprang both the need and the desire.

Conversely, market research can give all the positive indicators, yet still be wrong. In the United States, the development of the Edsel car by Ford Motor Company is often cited as an example of research leading product developers down a blind alley. Market research indicated exactly what opportunities existed for a product that car-buying customers said they wanted. Yet the product developed to meet those needs did not satisfy any one particular sector strongly enough, and the Edsel was a sales disaster.

In the United Kingdom, the first nationally marketed beer was a brand called Red Barrel, which was exhaustively researched prior to the most expensive launch ever seen in Britain's brewing industry. The product achieved modest success and staggered on for a while before collapsing under a wave of public apathy. In simple terms, the research had clearly established what type of beer was likely to be least unacceptable to most people. However, the beer also had been the "most acceptable" to the *least* number of people.

The researchers had been so concerned about universal acceptability that they developed a beer that was characterless and bland and, after the excitement of the launch, the favorite beer of no one.

The moral is clear: no single car, or beer, or any other product, is likely to be acceptable to *all* the prospective customers. One of the skills involved in assessing research findings is the ability to identify the characteristics of the product that will be strongly acceptable to the proportion of the market that is necessary for commercial success.

Today, both market researchers and marketing management are more skilled at working together to ensure the intelligent application of research in developing practical marketing recommendations.

Product Development

Creating new products or services to meet identified needs in the marketplace is one of the most sophisticated areas of marketing development. It is essential that this management activity be included in the marketing function and not be allowed to become part of production or manufacturing. Too often the production engineers or the research experts can lose sight of the marketplace and find great satisfaction in innovation for its own sake.

Sir Adrian Cadbury, the chief executive of Cadbury Schweppes, the major confectionery and soft drink company, recounts the story of the amazing food breakthrough that was announced to him with glee by one of his research technologists: the chocolate-covered sardine! In overcoming the technical problems in enrobing the greasy little devils, his technologists had achieved a small miracle. But as for developing a product with market potential! . . .

New products pour onto the market in ever-increasing numbers—some destined for great success, but the majority likely to have only a short life before fading away. One major food manufacturer has estimated that some 25 potentially interesting products will be evaluated and developed to various stages for every one that eventually is marketed—and some 70 percent of those launched are likely to fail in the first year. But successful new products continue to be introduced, and they are always those that meet or create a customer need. If there is no need, there will be no product. Despite the continuing pace of developments, it is interesting to note that around the turn of the last century, the director of the U.S. Patent Office recommended that the office be closed because "everything worth inventing already has been."

Of course, product development is concerned not only with creation of new ideas but also with the improvement of existing products and services. The original television sets were massive pieces of furniture offering tiny, flickering pictures in black and white, accompanied by thin sound. They have evolved to offer stereo sound, variety in screen size from massive to miniature, portability, durability, easy servicing, pretuned push buttons, remote control, and many other improvements.

To these have been added the customer benefits that come from tape recording, home video, satellite transmission, teletext and videotext, personal messenger services, and interactive video (whereby the customer can talk back through the set to a central computer to order goods or services or vote in opinion polls). Nor does it need much imagination to see that there is still enormous potential for developments in television. The companies that improve their products to make them more attractive to customers will win tomorrow's business.

Product Design

Closely allied to the development of new product or service ideas is the specialized skill of design. Products must look good and look right, in tune with people's perceptions. Even when working with completely new concepts, designers will adapt to market trends and strive to make the new items acceptable to existing market taste. As an illustration, it is interesting to look at the early motor cars, which were built at the end of the last century. Because no one had thought of them as being much different from horse-drawn vehicles, they retained many of the same features: larger wheels at the back, smaller ones at the front; boxy, wooden bodies; high-backed seats; the engine in front, where a horse would have been. It took only 70 years or so for designers to realize that the engine could be at the back, or in the middle, underneath, or sideways!

Product design also is important in improving existing products to make them more acceptable to developing customer taste or in adapting to meet changes in the marketplace. Today, microchip-controlled, all-transistor music centers perform much the same function as yesterday's radios—and feature much the same elements. But no customers today would buy a heavy wooden cabinet with all the equipment hidden inside . . . or would they? That depends on the skill of the designer!

Packaging

The point-of-sale presentation of the product also contributes to its success. Newer materials have created new opportunities. For example, the introduction of lightweight, molded polystyrene has meant that delicate products can be distributed safely and easily; they also can be displayed attractively within their colorful containers. Transparent plastics allow customers to see the contents of packages. One- or two-piece aluminum cans have replaced expensive, dangerous, and heavy glass. Bubble-packs make it possible to package small or awkwardly shaped items, such as hinges or screws, that were once sold only loose in hardware stores and to display them easily and sell them conveniently through new outlets. A European manufacturer of furniture castors trebled sales by taking them off the shelves at the back of hardware stores and putting them into packs of four in a transparent cylindrical tube, so they could be sold at the front of the shop. The product was exactly the same, but the new packaging boosted sales.

Pricing

One area of marketing that can make the difference between success and failure is pricing. There is an underrated skill in judging the price that relates well to public perceptions of the product or service, giving the best possible return to the manufacturer. Clearly, the lowest possible price is not the best news for the supplier. But the rock-bottom price is not necessarily good news in the marketplace, either. Products can underperform if they are priced too low: the public may see them as being of inferior quality.

For example, research for British mushroom farmers found that price was never higher than sixth or seventh among the reasons cited by shoppers for not buying the product. Traditionally, growers had believed that the product was extremely price-sensitive—that is, increased prices meant lower sales and lower prices meant increased sales. However, this important finding from research enabled the growers to promote the product to increase the volume of sales and yet, at the same time, increase retail prices.

Similarly, when new management took control of Aston Martin, the sports car builder, the company had been suffering major losses and seemed destined to go the way of many other long-defunct car makers. Traditional production-oriented solutions would have included trying to reduce costs (almost impossible because of the hand-built element in these vehicles) or to increase volume (also very difficult, for the same reason). However, the new management took the intelligent, but often-neglected, step of looking at what price the product could stand in the marketplace. These cars were so exclusive and sought-after that the new management was able virtually to double the price and still sell every one of the few hundred they were able to make each year. Now, a decade later, Aston Martin is still with us (at prices that match Rolls-Royce's), while other great names have faded from the international motoring scene.

As with most areas of marketing, specialized research can help identify the factors necessary to make the pricing decision. For example, research can project the level of sales for a proposed product at different price levels. However, like all other marketing areas, market research only *helps* to clarify the options. The ultimate skill is still the judgment of the managers.

Distribution

The best product in the world will not be much use unless it can be presented to potential customers where they can buy it.

A European home-computer manufacturer developed an excellent new model, highly praised by the experts, beautifully presented and packaged, attractively priced, and stunningly advertised. Yet the company collapsed; analysts believe that the single most important factor was that not enough attention had been paid to getting the product into outlets where it could be seen, tested, and bought by potential customers.

Distribution may seem like a mechanical function, but it also can be a creative aspect of marketing. Coca-Cola pioneered the distribution of its product through gas stations many years ago, at a time when most people expected to find only a can of oil or maybe a fan belt. But the logic was so compelling (people stopped for fuel on long journeys and that is the ideal time for refreshment) that we now take it for granted.

Similarly, many appliance manufacturers expanded their sales by moving from hardware stores into food stores, where customer traffic, and therefore potential buyers, was far higher. Marks & Spencer, the famous British chain, used to sell little but clothing. Today it handles—profitably— massive sales of potted plants, books, travel arrangements, and financial services.

Promotion

A man once said, "Build a better mousetrap and the world will beat a pathway to your door." A wiser person would have said, "Build a better mousetrap, promote it well, and the world will beat a pathway to your door."

No product or service can succeed in the marketplace unless there is customer awareness of it. The most effective way of creating broad customer awareness is usually through promotion. Some very specialized products or services, such as capital goods or professional consultancies, do well through one-on-one selling, but this is the exception rather than the rule. Using the sales force to create awareness is expensive; salespeople are usually better employed in closing deals, negotiating large contracts, or selling to wholesalers or retail groups that will sell on behalf of the company.

Promotion not only is important to the introduction of new products but also plays an important role in supporting established lines. In some cases, tired products or services can be revitalized with effective promotional support.

An excellent example was the creation of a major new market in the United States by the Polyester Fashion Council, which used public relations to create an exciting new identity for the fiber. Synthetic fabrics had been enthusiastically received when they were introduced in the early 1950s, but by the mid-1970s they had become associated with cheap, tasteless clothing. Although the industry had developed more sophisticated polyesters, the public image was badly dented. In 1982 the council hired a PR firm, which undertook a major media campaign to create a new identity for the synthetic fiber. As one of the most successful elements of the program, leading designers were persuaded to create exclusive, up-market fashions using these new polyester fabrics. The result was a new fashion identity, changed public perception, and soaring sales.

In addition to public relations, the most frequently used marketing promotional techniques are advertising, sales promotion, direct mail, sponsorship, and merchandising. Some of these approaches are explored elsewhere in this book.

Sales

A company's marketing communication creates an environment in which the sales force can operate; it is up to the sales staff to convert potential business into actual business. In some organizations, sales and marketing operate as separate but parallel functions. This is usually for some historical reason, such as the power of sales management in resisting the introduction of marketing. However, sales is *part* of marketing and should not be regarded as a separate management function. The role of marketing is to identify, create, price, and package products, and to make them available where, when, and how the market will accept them. Selling is the skill of converting product interest into actual business.

Budgeting

While marketing is creative, it is essentially a management planning technique and therefore must perform to tight disciplines. One of the areas in which this is most important is in devising and agreeing upon budgets. A marketing plan needs to have both sales and expenditure budgets, and these two are closely related. The level of sales that can be achieved depends heavily on the amount of money that is expended in such areas as promotion, sales force salaries and commissions, and merchandising. At the same time, the profitability of sales depends on the expenditure budget, and all contributors to the marketing effort are expected to perform as cost-effectively as possible.

Sometimes the business communicator is asked to prepare recommendations and project costs for promotional support. First the activity necessary to make the product a success in the marketplace in terms of awareness, interest, and inquiries is determined. It is then costed out and becomes the basis of the budget calculation.

However, it is more typical for the communicator to be given a sum and asked to determine how this money could be most effectively used to achieve the sales or marketing objectives.

In planning and agreeing on a practical budget, many communicators find it helpful to use both of these simple approaches, balancing the two until a satisfactory compromise on program and expenditure can be reached.

The communicator will not be responsible for preparing sales or marketing budgets but may well be expected to contribute to such discussions. At the very least, every professional communicator should be prepared to plan his or her own program of activity, prepare the budget, argue the case for each area of expenditure and, when the final sum is agreed upon, control the activity within budget.

Overexpenditure is one inefficiency that will not be tolerated by efficient marketing personnel, or top management, who are disciplined to have the highest respect for budget control.

Campaign Monitoring

Every effective marketing plan identifies how the campaign is to be monitored so that adjustments can be made as it progresses. In some cases this may involve continuous market research designed to assess the development of awareness and the creation of favorable attitudes toward the products or services being promoted.

Simple methods for measuring the effectiveness of the marketing activity may include keeping a record of the number of inquiries, the wholesaler or retailer response, the sales level, and so on. Again, the communicator will be responsible for monitoring his or her own efforts and adjusting the activity in order to come as close as possible to meeting the objectives. The best marketing communication campaigns include quantified objectives against which performance can be assessed.

TIPS FOR COMMUNICATING WITH MARKETING COLLEAGUES

It may be helpful to conclude this chapter with a few practical suggestions on building the best relationship between communicators and marketing professionals.

The communicator is primarily concerned with creating goodwill and favorable attitudes toward the organization. These are important to marketing professionals as well, but they worry about factors of more immediate and critical importance. The communicator must always remember that marketing is effectively measured by sales and profits. The basis for a good relationship is to understand the objectives of the marketing effort, so that the communication elements can be properly identified. This helps to define the necessary communication *strategy* to support marketing colleagues.

At the same time, the objectives of the marketing effort help to define the style and approach of the necessary communication. These are the *tactics* to be used by the communicator.

To be effective in working closely with marketing people, you as a communicator must:

Learn the terminology. Understand what is meant by the terms *market penetration, point-of-sale, store traffic,* and *positioning*. (A public relations consultancy once negated a presentation to a major U.S. retailing corporation because the executive in charge of the account misunderstood the difference between *direct mail* and *direct marketing*.)

Always feed back any interpretation of a marketing objective and ensure that the communication program is understood and agreed to by the marketing team. Make sure that there is ample opportunity for discussion to eliminate later misunderstandings.

Avoid specialized jargon, which can create a rift between the two partners. Do not assume that the marketing manager will automatically understand the difference between a *media briefing* and an *interview*, or the disaster that might result from not appreciating the important difference between *off the record* and *off the cuff*.

Always agree on budgets and timetables. It is particularly important that all expenditures are clearly identified and agreed to, especially if the communication activity is to be charged to the marketing budget. The timetable for activity also can be of some consequence. For example, the communication launch plan may be very different from the communication activity required later to support the continuing sales of the product or service. At what stage should the shift in tone take place? Some elements of the communication plan may need to happen before others. (Philips, the Dutch multinational electronics company, launched a new energy control system solely through public relations activities, adding advertising at the end of the initial six-month launch period to support sales. The coordination between the advertising and public relations executives was critical; both were presenting the same story based on the same facts, but with different emphasis. In addition, advertisements were able

to feature much of the favorable press coverage that the public relations effort had generated about the introduction of the new product.)

Make sure that the marketing proposals and the actual activity are
properly presented to the marketing team. This can be done through
presentations at marketing meetings, the circulation of reports, the
inclusion of communication on sales meeting agendas, the distribution of press kits to the sales force, production of news bulletins
on the communication results, and other such techniques.

Include in every proposal an analysis of how the activity would contribute to the sales and marketing objectives. This will help answer
the questions that marketing colleagues may have. If possible, try
to quantify these so that some indication of cost-effectiveness can
be developed. It is always helpful to include the methods that are
proposed for measuring the effectiveness of this work, as well as how
you propose to monitor the performance of the promotional activity
and to fine-tune it as it progresses.

Above all, you must learn to understand (and love) the marketing function, to become very closely involved with marketing colleagues, to learn
to present your ideas in an acceptable style and language, to develop the
respect that will help marketing and communication work closely together
as mutually beneficial disciplines.

If you can win the goodwill of your marketing colleagues, you may
find that promotional support will be one of your most exciting and rewarding communication responsibilities.

CHAPTER 2

Research

David E. Clavier, Ph.D.
Donald K. Wright, Ph.D.*

Research—a word that brings peace of mind to many, yet creates much anxiety in others. Research can either be the underpinnings of successful marketing and communication programs or the most formidable barrier to such success that any professional could imagine. Viewed as an integral element of program planning, design, and implementation, systematic research provides the basis of answers to the questions, "What are we going to do?" and "Have we been successful?"

This chapter is organized to aid marketing and communication professionals to ask the right questions in the planning process. We begin with the fundamental question, "Why use research?" The answer is likely to point toward the most appropriate research method. The various methods and techniques are described, along with suggestions for successful implementation. The chapter concludes with discussions of the pros and cons of using inside resources or outside consultants when doing research, interpretation of research results, and the ethics of communication research.

Hundreds of texts and articles exist that describe the process and use of research in great detail. This chapter is intended only to give the communicator an overview—a guide to the variety and range of research methodologies available and to selection of the right one for a given project.

When practitioners approach a research question, they are often overwhelmed by the enormous quantity of material and number of sources required. Frankly, this has been, and continues to be, one of the primary unspoken reasons communicators have for not using research as part of their decision making. This chapter addresses the important questions and offers recommendations on ways of finding the answers.

---

*David E. Clavier, Ph.D., is public relations manager-Florida for AT&T in Jacksonville. Donald K. Wright, Ph.D., is chairman of the Department of Communication Arts at the University of South Alabama, Mobile.

WHY USE RESEARCH?

The most common reason to use research is to reduce uncertainty in decision making. Other reasons include: to monitor the environment, to track the ongoing success or failure of a project or product, and to measure the effectiveness of programs and activities. Although these answers appear to be after-the-fact reasons for research, they are nothing more than subsets of the basic motive, to reduce uncertainty.

Many educators and practitioners have tried to define the marketing process, the communication process, and the public relations process. A consistent element in all three—whether it is called data collection, feedback or evaluation—is research.

Cutlip, Center, and Broom, in the sixth edition of *Effective Public Relations*, define public relations as a four-step process: (1) defining the problem, (2) planning and programming, (3) taking action and communicating, and (4) evaluating the program. Research is a basic requirement in each of the four steps.

For example, in order to define a problem or situation, data must be collected to identify the characteristics of the problem. Measured past experiences form the basis of planning, while measured benchmarks are required in most programs. Ongoing research is required during the action phase of a program, and research is the key ingredient in evaluating the effectiveness of the program.

Most practitioners cite lack of time, lack of money, or lack of expertise as reasons for not doing needed research. While time and money dictate how sophisticated or extensive a research program will be, lack of expertise should not be a barrier for a marketing or communication professional. Research techniques do not need to be difficult or expensive to be effective. You can save time and money by taking the time to learn the basics of research and to identify the best sources for assistance and advice.

EVALUATING RESEARCH METHODS

When selecting a research methodology, you need to consider several factors: validity, cost, timeliness, appropriateness, and understandability.

Validity refers to the primary question, "Are we measuring what we think we are measuring?" For instance, a research project may generate results that have no bearing on "real-world" events. The researcher would need to look closely to determine whether the study itself was internally valid (that is, the methodology did not cause bias in the results) or externally valid (that is, asked the right questions).

One common mistake communicators make when considering research is drafting questions and selecting procedures without a clear understanding of budget limitations. There is, for example, a significant cost difference between an open-ended questionnaire requiring hand sorting and a checkoff questionnaire that can be keypunched for computer sorting. In addition, the same questions can be answered using many different research techniques (mail, telephone, in-person). The difference among techniques is the degree to which data from a sample can be generalized over the entire population or group being surveyed, and the cost of obtaining that data. If the methodology seems too expensive, a manager may make the common mistake of scrapping the research project. Thus, selection of methodology must include an appropriate budget in the early design of a project.

A research methodology must be sensitive to the *timeliness* of the information needs. Again, if a methodology is selected that will take several months to complete but the answers are needed immediately, a manager may make the mistake of skipping the research altogether.

Appropriateness refers to the degree of sophistication required to answer a marketing question. If the research question is to help a manager make a major decision involving a great sum of money and affecting many people, then time, care, and attention must be put into selecting the best research method. If the answers are less important, a different technique may be selected.

Finally, the *understandability* of the technique and of the resulting data is extremely important. For example, when the researcher uses an advanced research technique such as multidimensional scaling to plot movement of concepts in "psychological space," it is important that the managers using the results understand the technique as well as the results.

SURVEY RESEARCH

Perhaps the most frequently used research approach is **survey research**. The major purpose of this methodology is to discover principles that have universal application. Ideally, if we wanted to measure the attitudes and opinions of a group of people, we should survey every person in the group. However, this is often impractical, if not impossible, so instead a **sample** is selected. The sample is a special subset of the population that is observed for purposes of making inferences about the nature of the entire population.

Although sampling methods used several decades ago often produced misleading results, current sampling designs are far more accurate and, thus, more reliable. The major criterion of a sample's quality is the degree to which it is *representative*—the extent to which the sample resembles the population it is intended to represent. Regardless of how carefully a sample is selected, there is almost always some degree of sampling error, which means that a sample is seldom identical to the population it represents.

There are two basic types of sampling designs: *probability sampling* and *nonprobability sampling*. Probability methods are much more representative and permit the researcher to estimate the amount of sampling error that should be expected in a sample. Nonprobability sampling methods are generally considered less reliable than probability sampling methods. They are used frequently, however, perhaps because they often are easier and cheaper.

There are several probability and nonprobability sampling techniques. We will look at four types of probability sampling: simple random sampling, systematic random sampling, stratified random sampling, and cluster sampling. We will then consider three approaches to nonprobability sampling: accidental sampling, purposive sampling, and quota sampling.

Probability sampling
Probability sampling involves the selection of research subjects according to mathematical guidelines that allow each member of the population surveyed to have an equal opportunity to be selected.

Simple Random Sampling. Simple random sampling is conceptually the purest approach to sampling because each member of the total population has a mathematically equal chance of being selected for the sample, and this approach most easily accommodates statistical analysis.

The most convenient way to select a random sample is by the use of a table of random numbers. Many such tables have been generated by computers producing random sequences of digits. Of course, you could get a random sample by putting the name of each member of the total population in a bowl and drawing one name at a time until the sample was selected; this procedure is cumbersome, however, so most researchers use random number tables.

Regardless of how the sample is selected, you must be careful to ensure that the sample is representative of the population you are measuring. If it is not, it will be inadequate for testing purposes and you will not be able to obtain valid data that can be generalized beyond the sample. Programs and plans based on such results—and interpretations of these data—would almost surely fail.

Systematic Random Sampling. In systematic random sampling, the sample is drawn from existing lists of names. For example, if you wanted to survey the members of an organization such as the International Association of Business Communicators, you would conduct a systematic random sample by selecting every *n*th name from the membership roster. Note that it would be important to select the starting point on your list of subjects at random.

Stratified Random Sampling. Stratified random sampling divides the total population into small, homogeneous groups in order to get more accurate representation. For example, suppose you are asked to conduct a survey of members of a large country club. Looking at the membership list, you discover that 20 percent of the members live in City A, 30 percent live in City B, and 50 percent live in City C. If you suspect that the city of residence will affect responses to your survey, you would need to select a sample in which 20 percent of the subjects were from City A, 30 percent from City B, and 50 percent from City C.

A stratified sample is sometimes used to reduce possible biases of simple random sampling. Used properly, a stratified random sample can be just as representative and far less costly than a simple random sample. The characteristics of the total population, as well as the purposes of the study, must be considered carefully before a stratified random sample is used.

Cluster Sampling. Cluster sampling is an option when it is impractical to use the previously mentioned sampling methods for reasons such as geographical distribution, the infinite nature of some populations, or lack of an available list of the total population. In these situations the cluster sample may be used to draw several sample members simultaneously.

Suppose, for example, that a survey required a sample of all public high school teachers in the United States. A simple random sample would be impractical (there are about 964,000 public high school teachers in the United States). However, it would be possible to select a random sample of 20 states, and from all the counties in those states select another random sample of 50 counties. From these 50 counties all of the school districts could be listed and a random sample of 25 districts selected. It would then be a manageable task to compile a list of all the high school teachers in these 25 school districts and select a random sample of 500 teachers. This successive random sampling of states, counties, school districts, and finally individuals would be relatively efficient and inexpensive.

Cluster sampling is very popular in marketing and communication research, and it is almost essential in surveys that require door-to-door personal interviews because it reduces travel time, mileage, and other expenses.

Nonprobability Sampling
Nonprobability sampling is less reliable than probability sampling but, as we noted earlier, is used frequently because it is easier and cheaper.

Accidental Sampling. **Accidental sampling** is a nonprobability technique that relies on available subjects who happen to be at a sampling point at some specific time. This method is used by researchers when they interview shoppers at malls, passersby on street corners, or selected individuals at other locations as they walk by; the sample selects itself, rather than being identified in advance by the researcher. This is also the method used when a survey questionnaire is distributed in a college lecture class. Although it is used frequently, accidental sampling is almost never an adequate sampling method.

Purposive Sampling. **Purposive sampling** is a nonprobability method in which the sample is selected on the basis of the researcher's knowledge of various elements of the population. This method can be valuable when you wish to study a subset of a large population for which no list of members exists. In this method, subject selection differs from accidental sampling only in that the researcher selects subjects based on judgment and the purpose of the study.

Quota Sampling. **Quota sampling** addresses the issue of representativeness better than the other nonprobability methods. It is based on a sampling matrix that describes the total population in terms of various characteristics that the researcher considers important for the purposes of the study. For example, the matrix might be based on sex, race, age, and level of education. We might find that the total population of a study consists of 25 percent of white males, between the ages of 25 and 40, with university degrees. Consequently, 25 percent of any sample selected from this population should fall within this matrix. Quota sampling has a potential for sample biases, so most communication researchers approach this method warily.

Constructing the Questionnaire

Questionnaire construction is the next step after sample selection. It pays to devote considerable time and effort to design and construct the research questionnaire, since it will affect the validity of the data gathered and may influence the type of research method selected. There are two basic types of questionnaires: one is designed to be completed by subjects, usually as part of a mail survey; the other is for use by a researcher for in-person, telephone, or group interviews.

The nature and wording, as well as the format, of questions are extremely important if the subjects are asked to complete the questionnaires themselves. Questions should be phrased to make it easy for respondents to understand what is being asked and to encourage concise and accurate responses; questionnaires should be properly laid out and uncluttered.

Questionnaires normally include several categories of questions. *Screening questions* determine whether a subject meets the qualifications to be a participant in the project. Before asking a respondent for an opinion about radio advertising, you might first want to ask whether the person listens to the radio and, if so, how many hours he or she listens to the radio each week. *Substantive questions* focus on the subject of the research. This group of questions might ask whether the subject can recall advertisements for a particular company or product. Finally, *demographic questions* seek information about the characteristics of the respondents: age, sex, income, education, race, and so on.

After the questionnaire has been developed, it is wise to test it on a small portion of the sample. Such a pilot study, or pretest, permits the researcher to discover flaws in the questionnaire (misinterpretation of questions, excessive time required to complete, unclear explanations) before it is administered to the entire sample.

Conducting the Survey

Most survey research conducted for communication and marketing purposes gathers information through mail surveys, personal interviews, telephone surveys, or group interviews.

Mail Surveys. Mail surveys are popular for gathering data because they are easy to manage and relatively inexpensive. There are no interviewers to supervise, and you can conduct a nationwide survey with a questionnaire, envelopes, and postage stamps. Another advantage of a mail survey is that it provides anonymity, so subjects are more likely to provide candid answers.

The greatest disadvantage of mail surveys is that they normally elicit a low response rate. Generally, 30 percent is regarded as the *minimum* acceptable response rate, but the majority of mail surveys achieve only a 15 to 25 percent response rate, which casts considerable doubt on the validity of results. Moreover, questionnaires sent to business addresses may not be answered by the individuals to whom they are addressed. A questionnaire sent to a corporate executive may actually be answered by a junior manager or a secretary.

There are ways to improve the response rate: include a pleasant cover letter with the questionnaire, keep questions to a minimum, mail follow-up reminders to subjects who do not respond immediately, and use inducements. In one research project, for example, a U.S. dollar bill was attached to some of the questionnaires as a "reward" for the subject for taking the time to fill in and return the questionnaire. The researchers found that more than 60 percent of those who received the U.S. dollar responded to the survey, compared to a 15 percent response rate among those who did not receive the monetary inducement.

Personal Interviews. Personal interviews, when properly conducted, have the potential to be the most productive technique for gathering survey information. They also are the most difficult to supervise and the most costly. Effective interviewing is an art, and expert interviewers who can develop rapport with respondents and ask probing follow-up questions are difficult to find and expensive to hire.

Personal interviews are the most flexible means of obtaining information, since face-to-face situations easily accommodate questioning in considerable depth and detail. The interviewer also can make observations about the subject. In a home interview, for example, the interviewer might be able to record what kinds of appliances the subject owns, what radio station was playing in the background, what reading materials were displayed in the living room, and the like. This survey method also has high completion rates. Once the interview begins, it is difficult for the subject to terminate it. In contrast, in a telephone interview the subject can hang up, and in a mail survey the potential respondent can simply ignore the questionnaire.

The major question when considering personal interviews for marketing research is: Are the benefits worth the high cost? Even when the personal interview is the method chosen, concessions are frequently made in sampling to keep travel time between interviews to a minimum.

Telephone Surveys. Telephone surveys are a cross between mail questionnaires and personal interviews. In many ways a telephone survey is a personal interview, because it involves a conversation between two people. It also is easier and less expensive to conduct than a personal interview, and the questionnaire tends to be relatively uncomplicated.

Since many marketing and communication research projects are basically simple and can be handled with a few questions, the telephone survey is a popular technique. It also permits the researchers to clarify any questions a subject does not understand and to ask follow-up questions. Consequently, much information can be collected by telephone quickly and economically.

More than 90 percent of all households in the United States have telephones, so a telephone sample can be fairly representative. To reduce sample bias and allow for unlisted telephone numbers, researchers often select samples for telephone surveys by random-digit dialing. Since many of the homes without telephone service are in low-income areas, organizations interested in this audience need to use one of the other research methodologies to obtain survey data. If they are not interested in this subset, drawing a sample only from those with telephones is usually sufficient.

A major impediment to telephone research has resulted from the behavior of unscrupulous marketing and sales representatives who telephone people, tell them they are conducting "research," and then try to sell them something. This misleading sales technique has caused many potential subjects to refuse to participate in telephone surveys. In light of this, any legitimate telephone researcher should begin each interview by assuring the subject that he or she is *not* selling anything.

Group Interviews. Group interviews, conducted in what are commonly called **focus groups**, frequently are used in attempts to gauge consumer attitudes and behavior. In a focus group situation, a number of people—usually five to ten—meet with a moderator or facilitator, who leads a relatively open-ended discussion on a particular topic. The group might consist, for example, of female university students, and the subject might be casual clothing—its styling, comfort, and washability. The purpose of the group might be to discover the most important reason these students purchase a particular brand of casual clothes.

The advantages of focus groups are that they offer an inexpensive method of collecting preliminary data about a product in a short time. They also are flexible, and participants are usually less inhibited than in personal interviews, since a competent discussion leader can encourage one respondent to expand on another's remarks.

Unfortunately, focus groups have some serious disadvantages. They are difficult to conduct, and the information collected usually is neither representative nor valid in any statistical sense: results represent only the opinions of the five to ten participants. These groups almost always depend on volunteer subjects and frequently do not provide a valid measure of larger populations.

CONTENT ANALYSIS

While survey research techniques permit the observation and study of individual people, **content analysis** provides an approach to measuring the communicated message itself. Content analysis is well suited to virtually all forms of marketing communication. Messages in such formats as books, newspapers, magazines, letters, radio and television programs, movies, and so on can be evaluated.

Some research topics are more appropriately addressed by content analysis than by any other method. Suppose you are interested in discovering whether news media coverage of a particular political candidate is favorable or unfavorable. Briefly, you would first define your concepts, making certain that you are adequately defining "favorable" and "unfavorable." A good way to determine whether coverage is favorable or unfavorable might be to examine adjectives, adverbs, and verbs used by the news media in stories about this particular candidate as well as his or her opponents. Next, you would have to decide which media outlets to survey and when. Then you would start reading newspapers and magazines, watching television, and listening to the radio, noting mentions of the candidate and the context of the mentions. After completing your examination, you would analyze what you had found.

In content analysis, as in survey research, it is often impossible to observe all the news media all the time. Consequently, it is usually appropriate to sample the media. Any of the sampling techniques for individuals discussed earlier in this chapter may be applied to content analysis.

In doing content analysis, researchers usually examine both manifest and latent content. Manifest content is the visible, surface content, and latent content involves the underlying meaning of the communication.

Some marketers and communicators are interested in examining publicity pieces, or press clippings, about their employer or their client. More often than not, this information is valuable only in that it shows management that something about the organization appeared in the media. Although some publicists place considerable value on this type of research, it has minimal validity and reliability.

A form of content analysis that many people use, but do not consider research, is unobtrusive research. For instance, by quickly examining the relative fullness of a company's parking lot, a researcher can generally determine how well that company is doing financially; a quick review of the number of copies of an internal publication thrown away in the company trash bins helps a manager gauge how well the publication—and the messages in it—are received and by which groups of employees.

ADVERTISING RESEARCH

The same types of research methodologies discussed for marketing communication purposes also can be used in advertising. However, the specialized nature of advertising has led to the development of additional measuring instruments peculiar to advertising.

Audience Measurement Techniques

Audience measurement techniques are used to estimate audience size. In the case of print media advertising, newspapers and magazines can provide audited circulation figures, which give an indication of how many potential readers could have seen particular advertising messages. For broadcast media, researchers use several different methods of measuring audience size.

Although total audience size is important in advertising, more information than mere numbers is needed. Of particular importance are variables such as demographic, socioeconomic composition, sociopsychographic composition, and product usage—all of which help define target markets. The most effective advertising matches these specific target markets with specific media. This information is used by media planners in developing broadcast advertising strategy.

The cost of media advertising is based on potential audience size. Broadcast media ratings of audience size are usually expressed in percentage points. Thus, the rating of a particular TV program is the percentage of all homes with television that were tuned to that program. A national rating of 18 means that 18 percent of all television homes in the country were tuned to a particular program. National television ratings in the United States are measured electronically by the A. C. Nielsen Company, which uses a national sample of typical homes. Local television and radio ratings most frequently are measured by the diary method, where some member of a household keeps a written log of the family's program listening or viewing.

Advertising-Concept Testing

Advertisers use advertising-concept testing to plan, design, develop, test, and evaluate specific campaigns. Since the selection of the proper concepts and strategy is too important to be left to guesswork, many advertising practitioners research advertising concepts by analyzing consumer response.

Performance Tests. Performance tests measure the potential performance of finished and unfinished advertising. They include print media copy testing as well as a variety of methods designed to evaluate the performance potential of broadcast advertising.

There are two basic types of print performance examinations. Standard copy tests examine the content of print media advertising in terms of readability and understandability. Perhaps the major problem in writing advertising copy is that so much information must be conveyed in so little space. Of course, the fact that advertising is worded properly and laid out attractively is no guarantee that it will be seen, read, and understood. That is where readership recognition studies are used. Usually expensive, and involving personal interviews, these studies are based on the assumption that advertising recognition is related to effectiveness: if you are familiar with the brand, you are more likely to buy it.

Measuring the impact of broadcast commercials is more complex and difficult. To a certain extent, the factors of understanding and recognition must be incorporated, but the complexity of broadcasting, especially television, makes the research job more difficult and often more expensive, Usually these measures are called comprehension or reaction tests.

The impact of a commercial can be measured in several ways. Three of the most popular methods are day-after recall measurements, brand preference change measurements, and studies of brand allegiance shifts.

Another type of advertising performance test measures physical response to the advertising measures. These examinations assume that some response will occur in the autonomic nervous systems of people who are affected by an advertising message. Skin response measuring devices, such as polygraphs (lie detectors), are used in this type of research. At times, pupilometric measures, which examine dilations and contractions in the size of a person's pupil, are employed. Although considered effective, most of these methods are now out of vogue, mainly because of their expense.

There is considerable controversy surrounding performance tests. This antagonism pits creative people in advertising against researchers. The debate has become more strident in recent years as advertising costs have increased. Advertisers are understandably reluctant to spend thousands or millions of dollars on advertising without some assurance that the advertising will be effective. However, creative people often do not understand the potential of research, and some argue that traditional performance-testing methods do not adequately measure the emotional appeal of advertisements and may not reflect a valid response to the message. Nevertheless, most of today's major advertisers insist that their commercials be tested before they are broadcast.

Measuring Advertising Effects. Measuring advertising effects after the campaign has started is the final phase of advertising-concept testing. These tests measure direct advertising effects, including participant's brand awareness or knowledge, changes in attitudes, and changes in purchase intentions. Advertising tracking studies also can be used to assess a campaign's effects. These are telephone or personal interviews conducted to gauge the impact of an advertising campaign on consumer awareness of attitudes toward products advertised.

Corporate Image Studies

Corporate image studies measure selected audience attitudes toward an organization. Many physical and psychological variables go into the formation of all the ideas that consumers, stockholders, employees, clients, the news media, and the general public have about an organization. The image of that organization is basically the sum of all the perceptions—positive, negative, or neutral—that these various publics hold.

Consequently, an evaluation of any organization's image should consist of a study of these publics. Frequently, an organization is most interested in the image held by a particular public; thus, a corporation is primarily interested in what its stockholders or employees think, so the image study focuses on those specific groups.

Image analysis, when used effectively, can have significant impact. Companies have been known to modify or change their image with considerable success. A classic example is Marlboro cigarettes, for which Philip Morris and its advertising agency used an effective advertising campaign to change the product's image from that of a cigarette mainly for women to the image of the rough and tough, tattooed cowboy. This was done by changing the central visual element in the advertising.

OTHER RESEARCH TECHNIQUES

Many other research techniques are available to the practitioner who needs to find answers to questions. The bibliography at the end of this chapter provides a list of resources that can be used to select the appropriate technique and learn how to apply it to meet a specific research need. Experimental research, multidimensional scaling, combinations for audits, as well as more sophisticated methodologies may be used whenever the researcher has made the proper evaluation of the methodology on the basis of the criteria reviewed here.

IN-HOUSE VERSUS OUTSIDE CONSULTANTS

The determination of whether to use inside or outside professionals is made on the basis of the same criteria that are applied in selecting the technique to use. Cost and believability are primary. Organizations usually make the policy decision to staff with experts inside or to supplement a minimal inside staff with outside research consultants. This typically is a budget decision that will have a strong bearing on which resources are to be used.

Many companies hire outside researchers to investigate issues because of the general belief that a third party will be less biased and less selective in interpreting results. Believability and credibility are the cornerstones in selecting who will conduct the research.

ANALYZING DATA

Data collected through the methods described in this chapter can be analyzed in many ways. Analysis of the results of a communication research study can vary from the most simple form of descriptive analysis to the most complex statistical analysis.

Descriptive analysis procedures may be the simple listing of results or percentages of categories or the identification of indicators of central tendencies such as mean, median, and mode. More complex statistical techniques use statistical procedure to make inferences of causality or directionality and to predict results of a yet untried program.

Fundamental to the selection of a statistical technique to analyze data is a proper understanding of the types of measurement that were used to collect the data. The four basic levels of measurement, or scales, are nominal, ordinal, interval, and ratio.

Nominal scales are used to measure identity through categories. They do not indicate directionality and can only be analyzed by using the simplest forms of statistics. An example of a nominal scale would be a compilation of the numbers represented on the backs of football jerseys.

Ordinal scales reflect the rank order of individuals or objects. The scale indicates directionality of data but the measurement units are not equal. An example is a Likert-type scale, in which responses are categorized such as $1 = 0$ to 5, $2 = 6$ to 10, etc.

Interval scales are composed of measurement units that are equal. They are more powerful scales, and data collected using interval scales can be analyzed by the most sophisticated statistical procedures. An example of an interval scale is the measurement of temperature using Fahrenheit or centigrade thermometers.

Ratio scales also measure units that are equal, with the additional characteristic that the scales have an absolute zero. Measures of length, width, weight, and capacity are examples of ratio scales. As with interval scales, this type of data can be analyzed using the highest form of statistical techniques.

Analysis of data from marketing communication research projects can range from simple to very complex. The more complicated the statistical procedures, the more rules of analysis must be known, understood, and respected by the researcher. When summarizing results or findings of a research project, it is very important that you apply the appropriate level and form of analysis in order not to overstate or understate those results.

COMMUNICATION AND APPLICATION OF RESEARCH RESULTS

Since facts alone are of little value, it is crucial that results of any research project can be interpreted before they can be used. Of course, this interpretation should be conducted by people familiar with research design, data collection methods, and statistical analysis. Perhaps the most crucial phase in communication and marketing research is the point at which research results must be applied by management. Generally speaking, if the research findings coincide with prior opinions held by management, the professional will have little difficulty in selling the results to management. However, the reverse will often be the case if research results disagree with management's preconceived opinions.

Knowing how and when to use research results is one of the keys to effective communication in marketing. However, organizations that do not like the results and simply file them away are wasting time and money. Positive results reinforce an organization's marketing and communication direction; negative results indicate areas for change and opportunities for growth.

Even when results suggest a course of action incompatible with management norms, they can have considerable value. For example, not long ago a hospital in a rural area was planning a U.S. $100,000-plus advertising campaign. However, it first invested about $5,000 for a telephone interview survey with a systematic random sample of all county residents. The research indicated that for more than 80 percent of those who had been hospitalized within the past five years, the family physician was the major factor in hospital selection. The hospital then took its remaining $95,000 and designed a communication campaign targeting physicians who practiced in the county. Most hospitals would probably have spent the $100,000 on general media advertising and, in all likelihood, would have wasted their money.

ETHICS AND MARKETING RESEARCH

Ethics is an important consideration in marketing research. This branch of philosophy typically deals with matters of right and wrong. But what is right and what is wrong? Exactly where is the line between the two? These are often the major questions. The problem is that ethical considerations are not always readily apparent to marketing communicators. As a result, many plunge ahead on a project without examining ethical issues and reflecting upon their importance.

Most of the ethical issues in marketing research are subtle; some are ambiguous and arguable. They range from methodological procedures you would not use for ethical reasons to the way some samples are designed; from how certain questions might be asked to the way data are interpreted.

What is regarded as ethical in research is determined by the general agreement of many people. Not surprisingly, however, different people agree on different codes of morality. Of course, there are several absolutes which must be respected if research is to be ethical. These include honesty and integrity, as well as taking care to avoid harming research participants (as, for example, by preserving anonymity or confidentiality).

Anyone who is going to conduct marketing and communication research should be aware of the general agreements shared by researchers concerning what is proper and improper behavior in the conduct of social scientific inquiry.

BIBLIOGRAPHY

Babbie, Earl. *The Practice of Social Research*. 4th ed. Belmont, Calif.: Wadsworth, 1986.

Cutlip, Scott, Allen Center, and Glenn Broom. *Effective Public Relations*. 6th ed. Englewood Cliffs, N.J.: Prentice-Hall, 1985.

Ferber, Robert. *Handbook of Marketing Research*. New York: McGraw-Hill, 1974.

Fletcher, Alan D., and Thomas A. Bowers. *Fundamentals of Advertising Research*. 2d ed. Columbus, Ohio: Grid, 1983.

Kish, Leslie. *Survey Sampling*. New York: Wiley, 1965.

Miller, Delbert. *Handbook of Research Design and Social Measurement*. White Plains, N.Y.: Longman, 1983.

Oppenheim, A. N. *Questionnaire Design and Attitude Measurement*. New York: Basic Books, 1966.

Selltiz, Claire, Lawrence S. Wrightsman, Stuart W. Cook. *Research Methods in Social Relations*. 3d ed. New York: Holt, Rinehart and Winston, 1976.

Stemple, Guido H., III, and Bruce H. Westley, eds. *Research Methods in Mass Communication*. Englewood Cliffs, N.J.: Prentice-Hall, 1981.

Tan, Alexis A. *Mass Communication Theories and Research*. Columbus, Ohio: Grid, 1981.

Williams, Frederick. *Reasoning with Statistics*. 2d ed. New York: Holt, Rinehart and Winston, 1982.

Wimmer, Roger D., and Joseph R. Dominick, *Mass Media Research*. Belmont, Calif.: Wadsworth, 1983.

CHAPTER 3

Putting Research to Work*

Charlotte M. Vogel†

Research is not a luxury in marketing communication. It is what marketing communication is all about: *Understanding consumers and what makes them tick.*

Having a good product or service, creating a promotion that "everyone" is excited about, or producing a well-crafted press kit that media love and use may be meaningless if we are not speaking to the right consumers, with the right message, in a way that reflects their attitudes and values. Consider this example:

> A few years ago, a well-known and respected marketing communication executive noted that despite his many years of experience, research still often shows that his and his clients' assumptions about the consumer are not always right. He offered an example of a campaign that was right in every way—except that it did not work.

> Several years ago the U.S. Army developed a recruitment campaign directed toward young men, primarily minority group members, leaving high school. The advertising campaign and promotional support materials showed successful, middle-aged men reminiscing about how the Army had helped them acquire skills and experience that gave them a long-term career after they left the Army. The campaign promised a future to young men who often felt they did not have one; it was well crafted; it appeared in media the young men would see. So why did it fail? When focus groups were conducted with some of the targeted young men, the problem became apparent. These young men were not concerned with a brighter tomorrow, but with a better *now*. They wanted to know about Army food, haircuts, curfews; whether they could wear civilian clothes; how much they would be paid. For them, the Army would be an escape route from the streets. No wonder the campaign did not work. It was based on the wrong assumptions about the target audience.

As communicators, we take pride in talking the language of our audience. But how much do we really understand about how and what they think, about what drives or holds them back from our product or service?

---

†Charlotte M. Vogel is president of The Research Group in New York City.

Do we even know who constitutes our audience? Do we know whether they are listening? Do we know whether they will be there tomorrow? Do we know who is not in that audience but could be?

Research can make the critical difference in focusing all stages of a successful communication program, from planning to implementation to evaluation. Keeping an eye on the consumer can make the difference between an ordinary program and an extraordinary one.

Developing a solid marketing communication program can be compared to a lawyer's preparation for trial. A good lawyer searches out everything he or she can find about the case: where it is strong, where it is weak; who should be on the jury, who should be challenged; what biases jury members have and what areas might be open to argument; which argument and style of delivery stand the best chance in court. Thorough preparation will not guarantee a favorable outcome, but inadequate preparation can lose the case.

IDENTIFY THE BUSINESS PROBLEM
AND ITS SOLUTION

The first step in our preparation for "trial by marketing" is identifying the business problem and determining what solution we are aiming for. That may seem obvious, yet many communication plans still identify the problem and solution in terms of process—for example, "Generate publicity" or "Promote product X," instead of "Change perception of firm from X to Y by key referral sources" or "Increase trial of product 10 percent by women aged 60 or older in six cities."

The obvious fact that we cannot create effective communication unless we understand our business strengths and weaknesses is often overlooked. One place where that mistake is commonly made is in marketing our own business.

Communication agencies typically put great energy and expense into new business presentations. But how many take the time to analyze lost presentations or accounts? When two British researchers compared client and agency perceptions of the reasons clients changed agencies, they found striking differences. Agencies typically attributed lost accounts to "changes in client policy" or "fate." Clients, in contrast, cited "dissatisfaction with agency performance" and gave the specific or key events that triggered that judgment.

Communicators in service businesses might consider tracking lost accounts on a regular basis to obtain some real information, instead of relying on hunches about the kinds of clients they are serving best and the kinds they are not. A survey of current and lost clients can identify clients' perceptions and some of their reasons for staying or leaving. Agencies that have conducted client surveys typically report some surprises and the need to rethink their communication problems and solutions.

Research also can save a company from unnecessary action or programs by determining the nature and scope of a problem.

A company was the subject of negative coverage on the U.S. television program *60 Minutes* during a holiday weekend. The next morning, company executives met to determine a response. Instead of immediately issuing a rebuttal, a telephone mini poll of 300 adults was conducted overnight in major markets. Three simple questions were asked: "Did you see the show?" If they responded positively, "Do you remember the segment on *X*?" If they remembered the segment, "What is your opinion of *X*?" To management's surprise, relatively few people had seen that show; fewer remembered the segment; and only a small percentage had a negative opinion of the company. The result: The company did not make a response. Research saved it from taking action that would only have called further attention to the problem.

KNOW THE AUDIENCE

When we plan a communication program, do we know—really know—who it is for?

Identifying the prime target means more than knowing we are trying to "reach mothers aged 21 to 49." It means knowing what the group means to our product or service. Our prime target may be the largest segment of consumers or clients who have given us most of our business in the past. Or it may be an often overlooked group that is smaller than our largest segment but has more potential for sales—or for problems. Our prime target may be growing rapidly, declining in size, or being neglected by competitors. It may be those who do not know us and should or who have a misconception about us or our product. It may be those who have needs they have not identified or who know their needs but do not see our product or service as a solution.

If we do not know who our prime targets are and why they are targets, we need to do some research before going any further. That research can be as simple as studying the marketing or advertising data already in-house or as elaborate as a full-scale new survey or community study.

A simple and inexpensive postcard survey can identify how many know our product or service, who they are, and how extensive their knowledge is. One such survey sent to executives probably brought a good response rate because it was so brief. Participants were asked for short answers to four questions: "When you think of elevators, what name first comes to mind? What other names come to mind? What is your title? What is your industry?"

To be beneficial, survey findings must be put to use. A case in point:

> Soon after a rate increase, a utility in a medium-sized university town was unable to deliver sufficient residential energy to meet all needs during a severe cold spell. Although management cited factors beyond the utility's control, the local newspaper ran negative editorials and news stories. Community resentment remained long after full service was restored. The utility was not sure, but it suspected that the continued opposition came from university faculty and students. A "gunshot" communication approach might not put the issue to rest. Who should be the prime targets? A team of researchers conducted mail and telephone opinion surveys across the community (allowing them to compare opinions by neighborhoods, the university, media, and other key subgroups). They interviewed utility management and employees and did participant observation for a few days in local gathering places, such as fast-food restaurants.
>
> At the completion of the project, researchers determined that the strongest opposition came from the utility's own mid-level management and some employee groups, who believed the utility was not well managed at the top. A communication program directed toward the community, without addressing these critical internal perceptions, would miss the prime targets.
>
> Yet, after a major investment of time and money, and the opportunity to target and address a major problem, the utility did little with the findings!

The utility is not alone: Much research is wasted because no thought or commitment is given to the use of potential "unwanted" findings. If the only purpose of research is to confirm what we already want to do, why bother with it? If the research comes out "right," we don't need it; if it comes out "wrong," we won't use it.

Surveys that identify targets also may be designed to provide ideas for program content and sometimes even publicity. For example, a psychiatric hospital might conduct a survey of its service area to identify who knows about it (for example, "women aged 60 or older in the Loring Park neighborhood") and what they know about it. At the same time, the survey can ask what respondents know about mental illness and its treatment and where they get their information. Respondents also might be asked where they would go if someone in their family had a problem and whether they had a family member or friend they were worried about. Such information can be used to develop messages for target groups as well as provide publicity material about community concerns and awareness of mental health issues.

Once we know whom we are trying to reach, we need to know how they think and act, what they know about us and how they know it, and how they make decisions about the product or service we are promoting.

Consumer awareness can be measured with relatively simple structured surveys. To get inside the consumer's mind, qualitative research is typically more appropriate than quantitative or statistical research. Some examples:

A substance-abuse treatment center struggled to overcome its reputation for a controversial treatment that it had once promoted but now offered as only one of several treatments. The center depended on social-service and church-related referrals, and needed to know how these sources perceived different types of treatment and the "new" center. Two focus groups conducted with referral sources revealed their biases as well as the fact that they were not yet convinced that the center's change was "for real"—and why. Before a communication program could move forward to potential clients, a new approach would be needed to reach the gatekeepers.

When an agency landed a large fast-food restaurant account, all members of the account team, including management, spent two days working in the restaurant: in the kitchen, behind the counter, clearing tables, and cleaning up. The first-hand insight into the point-of-contact experience of customers and employees laid the groundwork for a campaign addressing their concerns and talking their language.

A clothing manufacturer wanted to promote a slow-selling new line of women's sportswear. With a low budget, either in-store promotion or media publicity could be done, but not both. Which would be more effective in influencing the purchase of these clothes? Standard research was too expensive, but information was needed on consumer purchasing decisions.

The communication counsel asked the help of six young women in different cities whom she knew personally and who, she believed, fit the target profile (executive secretaries, entry- and junior-level professionals), and could be trusted to give honest responses. They were asked to go into department stores and look at this line of clothing; observe other customers; note the other clothes sold in the department; try the clothes on; ask the salesperson for advice; judge whether the quality matched the price, and indicate whether they would buy the clothes.

Though limited in number, the six respondents' observations were thorough and consistent. The customers to whom the sportswear appealed were not primarily those to whom it was targeted; their clothing purchase decisions would not be influenced by fashion publications or other media, but by what they saw where they shopped and by what their friends wore. The implications of this simple consumer research suggested modified targeting and the use of in-store promotions rather than media publicity.

Participant observation and informal interviewing could and should be done much more often than they are. How many of those responsible for communication have spent any time working or spending time with staff in other departments or talking with salespeople and customers or clients? A gold mine of data is under our noses if we take the time to observe and systematically analyze it.

FOCUS THE MESSAGE

Knowing the consumer does not stop with identifying targets and their
needs. A good communication idea, well crafted and based on what has
been learned about the consumer, may still fail to persuade if it does not
prove the right kind of information, in the right language, in the right form
or media. Some examples:

> As recruiting by law firms becomes increasingly competitive, most major firms
> produce recruiting materials for use among law students. How could a firm
> develop a recruiting brochure that would stand out from the crowd without being
> "flashy"?
>   The first step was a content analysis. The brochures of 27 competitors were
> reviewed for content, design, and tone to determine the type of information
> they provided, how they positioned the firm, and how effectively they com-
> municated. The second step was exploratory telephone and in-person inter-
> views with 12 local law students and first-year associates in different firms to
> identify how they used the brochures, what information needs and gaps they
> perceived in brochures and other communications from law firms, and which
> brochures they found boring or too flashy.
>   These two brief projects provided immediate direction for the law firm's bro-
> chure. They also identified areas for structured research to explore later to im-
> prove the firm's overall communication program.

> A food company wanted to improve the credibility of its nutritional claims. An
> advertising campaign and an informational campaign to doctors, nutritionists,
> and home economists had not been as effective with consumers as expected.
>   A review of existing trade association and media surveys suggested that the
> target women were less likely to get nutritional information from advertising,
> doctors, or nutritionists than from daily and weekly newspapers and women's
> magazines. Focus groups conducted with a sample of women from the target
> group confirmed that while they read the nutritional claims in the ads and
> thought them interesting, the claims were contradicted by the editorial cover-
> age they read in the same women's magazines carrying the advertising. The
> campaign needed to be reslanted to reach the media, the new nutritional
> gatekeepers.

Nor should media be overlooked when assessing communication content or form. A content analysis of one year's trade and regional news coverage identified the extent and type of an advertising agency's media presence and compared it to that of major competitors. Analysis of quantity
of coverage, its tone, and key themes covered revealed each agency's media
strengths and gaps; it clarified the best topic opportunities for this agency
to position itself in the media vis-à-vis its competitors. The analysis also
provided a benchmark for annual evaluation of changes in media presence.

Surveying editors also can provide invaluable information. One organization conducted a brief, written mini-survey of 15 business editors of

major news publications, asking them how often they went to press conferences, what determined whether they went, and how they preferred to get information. The results shocked the sponsoring company into rethinking whether most (or even any) of its "urgent" press conferences accomplished as much as one-on-one visits with these editors.

Sometimes messages can be focused by applying a research "frame of reference" in shaping materials. Some advertising agencies analyze the role of right- and left-brain thinking in specific consumer product-buying decisions, and shape advertising form and content accordingly. Different approaches are demanded by a highly emotional decision and by a decision that requires weighing pros and cons based on solid information.

For example, buying life insurance typically is a highly "rational" decision based on assessment of several kinds of data and risks. Yet many life insurance campaigns appeal primarily to emotions: "Look at these kids' faces. Imagine them without you." In contrast, a doll or a plush toy may need to be seen and touched to evoke the emotional response that typically drives that kind of buying decision; communication materials for such products may be most effective using themes that touch the heart and are tied to in-store promotions.

Although agencies typically will not reveal their techniques, focus groups, in-person interviews, and participant observation can provide insight into the relative emotional and rational character of buying decisions.

After messages have been developed, pretesting can pinpoint strengths and weaknesses—especially if the material is controversial, complex, or highly technical. Even material that appeals primarily to the emotions should be tested. Often a creative idea that we are wild about does not make the impact on target groups with life experiences different from ours.

A pretest might involve interviews with four to eight members of the target group, conducted individually or in a **focus group**. Present the concept or have them read copy, and then ask them to tell in their own words what it means to them. Listen carefully to how they talk. It is not enough that they get the information; they should "get the point." If they do not get the point, would a different style work? Or is it the concept that is poorly developed?

Even if respondents do get the point, the material is still not necessarily effective. You need to assess whether they believe it and whether they care. The "don't know/don't care" factor is often overlooked in research. Copy or materials that otherwise test high for readability and accessibility and for positioning still may not persuade; although the key points are conveyed, they do not touch the consumer's values. This is less likely to happen, of course, if we have taken the time to get to know the consumer in advance.

USE RESEARCH AS THE MESSAGE

Sometimes research can persuade media to pay attention to our material. A communication manager for a camera distributor approached the editor of *Fortune* magazine's "On Your Own Time" about a column on photography as an executive hobby. The editor rejected the idea on the grounds that it would have limited appeal for *Fortune* readers. The communicator then surveyed 20 chief executives of Fortune 500 companies, asking them one question: Did they use cameras on their own time? The results convinced the editor that there were enough executives who would be interested, after all, and ran the story on camera use.

Most people, reporters and editors included, like to read about research findings, especially if the research reveals something about their own lives. Research that is related to a product or service can be an effective way to get media coverage and position the organization as a source of interesting and credible information. However, if research is not clearly related, it may be remembered, but the product or organization will not be.

Several organizations have used research to increase the visibility and to reinforce the positioning of products and services. Some examples:

> When a new hair-care product was launched, focus groups were conducted with American and European women on their attitudes and feelings about hair and hair care. Their comments were so interesting and revealed such striking cultural differences that they formed the basis of a campaign and were used directly in publicity materials.

> A trade association for pet-food manufacturers used existing market data on pet owners to obtain widespread coverage in general-interest magazines and on the lifestyle pages of newspapers.

> A computer manufacturer wanted a presence in the then-emerging office automation market. A national survey paired managers and their secretaries, comparing perceptions of office work, productivity, and office automation. The survey included questions on problems and benefits encountered in automating the office. The company wanted to position itself as a manufacturer concerned about the human aspect of office automation.

> Professional service firms often release surveys on issues of concern to potential clients and referral sources. For instance, accounting firms rate the concerns of small-business owners on economic and political issues or on the extent of retail theft. Executive search firms report patterns in salary levels and trends in the job market.

When national surveys are designed to provide regional breakouts, communicators can prepare releases highlighting local findings in the survey within a national context, adding local comments and examples.

Doing research for publicity, especially national surveys, with demographic and regional breakouts, can be expensive, although it does not always have to be. Although it can be tempting to cut corners, bad or sloppy research can backfire with negative publicity, as businesses and communication agencies have often discovered. Publicizing research is not worth the risk if the research is self-serving; if it is biased or lacks solid methodology; if it is not conducted by a respected (though not necessarily well-known) firm; or if the findings are misrepresented in the releases. Be prepared to disclose the full questionnaire or measure and details about sampling and other methodology, for example, in the United States as specified by the American Association of Public Opinion Research.

MEASURE THE IMPACT OF THE MESSAGE

Evaluating the success of marketing communication is not, as some communication professionals say, "like nailing jelly to a tree." Of course, if we have not identified a business problem and solution or used any data or research to identify our consumers—where they are in relation to our product or service, what we want them to do and to what degree—then we have no benchmark, and we are likely to agree that "communication effectiveness cannot be measured."

About the best we can do then is measure the amount of work we have done (number of releases issued, number of media called, number of invitations sent). Maybe we can count the number of media or other gate-keepers who used our material; the number of column-inches of space or minutes of air time the material received. Or maybe we can count the estimated audience: that mysterious 2.5 readers for each newspaper sold, or 2.5 listeners or viewers in homes with radios or televisions. If we want to get really fancy—and doing so is better than just counting press clippings—we can track the extent to which the exposure occurred in media or other outlets that are directed toward our target group and that carried our key messages. But we must not confuse efficiency with effectiveness. As long as we do, we are still rather like the fellow who searches for his lost keys under the street lamp "because the light is better there."

Measuring communication impact is nothing more or less than measuring how close we have come to solving the business problem we defined in our first step, "Identify the business problem and its solution." If our problem-and-solution statement was, "Change perception of the organization from X to Y by key referral sources," we must have started with a measure of the existing perception against which we can measure change today. If we planned to "increase sales inquiries in six markets by 20 percent," then that is what we measure—with the same method we used to determine the problem (existing number of sales inquiries in those six markets).

If we are concerned about documenting the impact of such communication as public relations for a product or service on advertising and other support, we might be able to test our program in one market where there is no advertising or other promotion, or we might compare four markets with advertising—two with public relations, two without.

We may find it helpful to measure our progress and adjust the program along the way. For example, the day after a speech, event, or media coverage, a short telephone survey of a small sample of targeted neighborhoods or groups can tell us how many people heard or saw the material, whether they recall what they heard or saw, and whether they have any opinions or plans to take action as a result.

We can, and should, review releases after a story has been published or broadcast by a few media to analyze how the story was played. Such analysis will give us guidelines for rewriting the story to make it more effective with other media. It also will provide guidelines for the content and form of future stories for these media.

Evaluation, however, is impossible without a frame of reference, or yardstick. Establishing that yardstick usually means research. And, yes, research takes time and costs money. Marketing professionals believe that they are contributing to bottom-line solutions and budget accordingly. If communicators believe that communication programs have bottom-line relevance to marketing, they need to stop promoting communication as a bargain-basement alternative to advertising and to commit time and money to research that will make bottom-line solutions happen.

BIBLIOGRAPHY

Accessing Existing Data

Cline, Carolyn. *Evaluation and Measurement in Public Relations and Organizational Communication: A Literature Review.* San Francisco: IABC Foundation, 1984.

Communication Bank packets on research. San Francisco: International Association of Business Communicators.

Data User News. Washington, D.C.: Bureau of Census, monthly.

"Directory of Demographic Products and Services," Ithaca, N.Y.: American Demographics, annual.

Directory of Online Databases, and updates. Los Angeles: Cuadra Associates, annual.

Information packets on research. New York: Public Relations Society of America.
pr reporter, weekly.
Reference directories. Detroit, Mich.: Gale Research.
Surveys, Pools, Censuses and Forecasts Directory. Detroit, Mich.: Gale Research,
three times a year.
Todd, Alden. *Finding Facts Fast.* Berkeley, Calif.: TenSpeed Press, 1979.
Washington Researchers, publications and workshops.

Conducting Research

Antilla, Susan, and Henriette Sender. "Getting Consumers in Focus," *Dun's Business Month* (May 1982).
Communication Bank packets on research. San Francisco: International Association of Business Communicators.
Cone, John. "Delphi: Polling for Consensus." *Public Relations Journal* (February 1978).
"Evaluation Research in Public Relations." *Public Relations Quarterly* (Fall 1983).
Focus Groups: Issues and Approaches. New York: Advertising Research Foundation, 1985.
Goldman, Elaine, and Taik Sup Auh. "Public Policy Issue Analysis: A Four-Posted Research Design." *Public Relations Quarterly* (Winter 1979).
Hunter, Bill. "Getting Things in Focus." *American Way* (November 1984).
Information packets on research. New York: Public Relations Society of America.
Lesly, Philip. "The Role of Research in Public Relations: Purposes and Types, Guidelines and Techniques." In *Lesly's Public Relations Handbook.* Englewood Cliffs, N.J.: Prentice-Hall, 1978.
Lindemann, Walter. *The Communications Audit.* New York: Opinion Research Corp.
Lindemann, Walter. "Content Analysis. "*Public Relations Journal* (July 1983).
Lindemann, Walter. "Hunches No Longer Suffice." *Public Relations Journal* (June 1980).
Lindemann, Walter. "Use of Community Case Studies in Opinion Research." *Public Relations Review* (Spring 1980).
Miskovic, Darlene. "Behind the Mirror." *Advertising Age* (17 November 1980).
Pretesting in Health Communications. NIH Publication No. 83-1493, Office of Cancer Communications.
Pretesting Television PSAs: User's Guide. NIH Publication No. 85-2670, Office of Cancer Communications.
Pride, Cletis. "Let's Take a Survey." In *Attitude and Opinion Research: Why You Need It, How to Do It.* Washington, D.C.: Council for the Advancement and Support of Education, 1977.
Public Relations Journal issues on research, annual.
Sudman, S., and N. M. Bradburn. *Asking Questions: A Practical Guide to Questionnaire Design.* San Francisco: Jossey-Bass, 1985.

Vogel, Charlotte M. "How to Recycle Your Research." *Public Relations Journal* (May 1982).
Vogel, Charlotte M. "How To Think Research." *Public Relations Journal* (September 1986).
What Is a Survey? Washington, D.C.: American Statistical Association.
"What to Expect from Focused Group Interviewing." Dallas, Tex.: Belden Associates.

Buying Research Services

Agencies and Organizations Represented in AAPOR Membership. Princeton, N.J.: American Association for Public Opinion Research, annual directory.
Directory of Marketing Research Houses and Services. New York: American Marketing Association, New York Chapter.
"The Nation's Top 40 Marketing/Advertising Research Companies." *Advertising Age,* annual.
Smith, David L. "How to Buy Research Services." *Public Relations Journal* (June 1980).
Vogel, Charlotte M. "Deflating Your Research Dollar," *Public Relations Journal* (July 1983).

Interpreting and Presenting Research

ARF Criteria for Marketing and Advertising Research. New York: Advertising Research Foundation.
Code of Professional Ethics and Practices. Princeton, N.J.: American Association for Public Opinion Research.
Huff, Darrell. *How to Lie with Statistics.* New York: Norton, 1954 and revisions.
Wheeler, Michael. *Lies, Damned Lies and Statistics.* New York: Dell,1976.
White, Jan V. *Using Charts and Graphs.* New York: Bowker, 1984.
Wilhoit, G. C., and D. H. Weaver. *Newsroom Guide to Polls and Surveys.* Reston, Va.: American Newspaper Publishers Association, 1980.

CHAPTER 4

Understanding and Applying Accountability Measures

Myra L. Kruger, ABC*

Profit squeeze, cost containment, staff reductions, divestitures, foreign price cutting and competition, changing management systems, and lower dividends are only a few of the changes organizations face continuously in their 1980s business strategies.

These are complex issues in a changing global marketplace—and they are made more complex by technological advances in automation, computer technology, and systems that quickly outdate equipment and facilities, management systems and information channels. Organizations find themselves competing in nontraditional, worldwide markets in which the buyer is strongly influenced by price, an unprecedented range of choices, and a din of pleas to favor one product over another.

In addition, the shape of corporate society is changing as a result of mergers, acquisitions, spinoffs, and takeovers. Getting the message through to the consumer is a sophisticated task that requires high levels of knowledge not only of the organization and its business, but also of society, audiences, world affairs, and finance.

In this environment, being well-versed only in the practice and techniques of communication no longer suffices. The definition of communication has changed, along with its role. Special efforts must be made with customers, the financial community, employees, stockholders, and the public to help the organization find its place within this complex market.

The purpose of activity in all aspects of organizational communication is to sell. Marketing communication is designed to help the organization sell its products, its reputation, its brand names, and its characteristics. Similarly, employee communication's primary purpose is to sell ideas—that is, to use information to promote specific types of behavior or responses

*Myra L. Kruger, ABC, is a founding partner of MC Associates in Chicago. She is a past chairman of the International Association of Business Communicators, is a member of IABC's Executive Forum and the Internal Council, and serves on IABC's Ethics Review Board. She is an accredited business communicator.

from those within the organization in order to produce a desired action or attitude.

Media relations, too, represents an effort to sell. By issuing information, responses, and position statements, the media relations communicator is selling the organization—an understanding of its actions, its positions, and its values—to the general public.

And the financial communicator is selling the strength, security, and worth of the organization to stockholders, analysts, investors, and financial evaluators.

Organizations spend huge sums in pursuit of these goals as the need to manage change and to build distinction among organizations becomes more critical. In 1986 communication expenditures by the largest U.S. and Canadian corporations alone reached an estimated U.S. $800 million. Increases in communication budgets are averaging nearly 20 percent, according to IABC's "Profile," a biennial study of trends in communication.

THE NEED TO DEMONSTRATE
COMMUNICATION'S ACCOUNTABILITY

Senior managers clearly recognize the role of effective communication in building shared understanding inside and outside the organization. Yet little is known about the results of spending these huge sums. Much of the reason lies in the planning process—or lack of it—in the communication area.

Perhaps no other area of an organization, and certainly of a corporation, functions without accountability to the extent that organizational communication is allowed to do. As a support function to the organization, communication exists solely to help others within the organization achieve specific goals. Isolating the results of the communication role is critical to demonstrating its value.

Communication programs and plans that exist to disseminate information, instead of to meet goals, solve problems, or manage issues, seldom can demonstrate their exact role in helping the organization to achieve its strategic goals. Communication departments bogged down in implementation activities spend most of their time reacting to the fires that break out or responding to issues after they have become critical. Others spend much effort trying to change perceptions among employees and the public instead of shaping them.

Marketing communication is based on the needs of the marketing plan, and the issues it deals with require a great deal of knowledge about the firm and constant monitoring of products or services, customers, competitors, the marketplace and performance.

As with all forms of organizational communication, the successful marketing communication plan—one that clearly supports the larger objectives of the organization—includes the capability of pinpointing the role that communication had in achieving the organization's goals, whether large or small, short term or long. It is possible to work in communication and be accountable. Why then are so few communicators able to demonstrate the precise effects they have had on an issue or activity of the organization?

The key to successful communication is developing and transmitting messages that produce response, acceptance, action, or change. By determining the communication implications of issues facing the business, communication plans can be developed that produce lasting, measurable results.

Strategic planning for communication is fundamentally the same as strategic planning for all other operations—with one exception: it rarely is done. The sequence of steps involved, however, is the same:

1. Gaining knowledge and collecting data
2. Identifying and defining issues
3. Setting objectives
4. Developing messages based on audience analysis
5. Implementing the messages
6. Measuring effectiveness
7. Taking corrective actions

We shall consider each of these steps in some detail.

GAINING KNOWLEDGE AND COLLECTING DATA

Planning messages based on your business issues requires close coordination between you and the executives in your organization. It may seem self-evident that communication professionals must be extremely knowledgeable and up-to-date about their organization, its markets, its executives, and its issues. In fact, most can reiterate the goals and issues, but few have a constantly evolving, intensive knowledge. At the same time, many executives have only a superficial understanding of their audiences and the perspectives and beliefs held by audience members about the organization and its issues.

Knowledge is essential to the communication process. To develop an effective communication plan that meets the needs of the organization and supports its short- and long-term goals, you must *understand* what your management wants to accomplish, what obstacles it faces, and what your management expects you to accomplish in communicating with your audiences. In turn, you must use your knowledge to help your management understand how those audiences respond and react to your messages.

Each organization has different levels of goals: corporate, group or subsidiary, business unit, major department (marketing, human resources, engineering, and so on), individual. These goals are seldom identical, but when harmonious, each builds a basis for the next level, furthering the objectives of the individual or group and the goals of the organization.

You will, of course, have detailed knowledge in your particular area of communication responsibility—human resources, investor relations, marketing—but you also need to be familiar with the "big picture," the organization's overall goals and plans. You can gain that familiarity in a number of ways. Some of the steps you will be engaged in continually; others will be specific to your planning process.

You need to know what to look for and what questions to ask. To do that, you need an understanding of what you know about the business and, more important, what you do *not* know. To help you prepare for your search, review your knowledge about the organization or your business unit and the markets it serves. Do not be afraid to admit what you do not know. No one can be expected to know everything about the organization.

Then undertake a methodical and thorough research program. Use all the research techniques, formal and informal, that are available to you. Supplement that knowledge with regular research into these topics:

Organization structure and change—various facilities and their executives, markets, and plans to expand, reduce, or reorganize

Products—what the organization sells, how those products or services are used, how customers perceive the quality, what the new developments or modifications are

Customers—who they are, what factors affect their ability and desire to buy

Competitors—who they are, how their products or services are perceived, and what their price factors, strategies, marketing techniques, profitability, and similarities or differences are

Markets—whether they are growing, shrinking, or holding steady; how large they are; what the growth history has been; what cultural, political, and social factors influence your penetration

External forces—governmental, environmental, technological, social, and so on; considerations that affect your business and its ability to meet its goals

Internal forces—internal issues (for example, employee relations, union contracts, automation, sales disincentives) that affect quantity, quality, price, and delivery.

Much of this information can be found in your organization's business and strategic plans. The business plan typically is an outline of near-term objectives, usually covering a period of 12 to 18 months. The strategic plan outlines long-term objectives for about the next five years. In most organizations these plans are highly confidential, so you may need to obtain a copy from your company's top executives. Understanding how effective communication that flows from a well-conceived plan can support those objectives will be crucial to your plan's success.

Answering questions by consulting inventory records and researching data from various planning documents will give you a solid base of facts and numbers. The final critical ingredient in your preparation comes from adding perspective to the data. That perspective can best be supplied by your senior managers and, in particular, the top executives of your organization. They can inform you about priorities among the issues and goals, show how the goals relate to one another, and explain why they are important to the organization.

There are other sources of information about the organization that should be your constant references. They include your company's annual report; speeches given by your executives before audiences such as financial analysts, the board of directors, and customers; articles about your business, competitors, and customers appearing in the general press and trade publications for the industries of which you are a part.

To determine the communication implications of the issues facing your organization, you must begin with research, both on the business and on your audiences. You must be familiar with the organization's operational information, its history and values, its goals, problems, and strategies. And you must do surveys and audits that provide the demographic and attitudinal information that will allow you to target your messages so that key audiences respond positively.

Discussion at key staff meetings, including those attended by the organization's senior staff and members of the marketing, communication, and human resources or personnel departments also are good sources of information. In addition, special meetings and task forces that the organization has set up to address key issues or business plans can provide extensive background.

IDENTIFYING AND DEFINING ISSUES

The heart of your communication program will be found in the short- and long-term goals of your unit. The annual plans addressing goals in production, sales support, employee relations, research, and other areas will be the major platforms of all your communication programs. Within each there will be obstacles working against the goals; these issues must be addressed if your program is to be successful.

Your role is to examine the implications of those issues for the organization and your key audiences. Define the issues carefully; knowing that you must emphasize quality or that international competition is depressing prices is not sufficient information on which to build a communication program. You must understand how and why a specific issue developed, what the implications of a failure to address it are, and why your audiences should care that you are addressing it.

Communication implications depend to a large extent on how specific issues affect each audience. Why should they care about the organization's issues or goals? It is important that this question be answered positively, since people rarely respond constructively to fearful or threatening messages. A positive message on international price competition, for example, will help employees understand why cost containment will help bring in work during the next contract season.

And if your audiences do care about an issue, can they do anything about it? Shareholders may be very concerned about the effect of international price competition on profitability, but they cannot do much about cost control. The message addressed to them would emphasize how vigorously the company is attacking the issue of cost control to maintain growth and profits—and to protect their investment. Customers, of course, care about cost containment to the extent that it affects price without a sacrifice in quality, and they are in a position to respond very directly.

SETTING OBJECTIVES

One of the hardest parts of communication planning is in determining what communication can and cannot do. If your activity is to be measurable and the accountability of the communication plan clearly established, measurable objectives will be at the heart of it. Clearly identifying the role communication plays allows its accomplishment to be documented, its results to be demonstrated, and its credibility to be enhanced.

Most communication objectives simply parrot business plans; few acknowledge that communication supports other corporate objectives as well.

Attainable communication objectives deal with specific assistance to help others in the organization achieve their goals. Communication alone will not solve problems of quality control, absenteeism, or errors, nor will it increase sales. It is more likely to *acquaint* the sales staff; *demonstrate* to employees; and *help* achieve other objectives.

Note the communication role in the following examples:

Organizational objectives	*Communication objectives*
Increase company sales by 10 percent.	Over the next six months, acquaint the sales staff with new product applications to help them find opportunities to increase sales.
Make employees appreciate the benefits they receive.	Within the next nine months, improve employee attitudes toward the benefits package by demonstrating how company-paid benefits enhance pay levels.
Increase market share by 5 percent.	During the next two quarters, publicize product value to key customers by demonstrating how modifications upgrade existing systems.
Increase the price of company shares by 10 percent.	In the current fiscal year, outline for investors and financial analysts how the company's growth strategy will increase profits.

In each communication objective, the activity can be documented and the results measured: Is the sales staff more familiar with product applications? Did employees' attitudes toward the benefits package improve? How many customers converted their existing systems to your products? Did investors and analysts recommend your stock?

To develop the measurable role of communication in achieving the objective, you must determine the behavior response needed from the audience—within a specified period of time—to achieve the goal.

DEVELOPING MESSAGES BASED ON AUDIENCE ANALYSIS

Audience research is critical to effective communication planning and measurable implementation. The messages you select will vary according to the audience's responsibility, expected participation, and level of influence on the outcome.

Corporate communication programs also must evaluate the different impact that messages can inadvertently have on different audiences. The reassuring and positive words issued to stockholders and analysts about the efforts that have been made to reduce debt and improve market position, for example, may contradict the messages concurrently sent to employees and the union about the dependence of continued recovery on cost containment and ongoing austerity. Likewise, the new advertising program highlighting the improvements in product quality can be seen by employees and the public as contradictions to any recent plant closing or major strike.

While consistency is important in communication, gaining the desired behavior response requires close coordination of messages aimed at specific audiences. One of the surest ways to predict those responses is through pretesting. For example:

> For years, Company A followed a traditional pattern of marketing communication. The marketing department designed a plan, the communicator developed announcements and product news releases and worked with the marketing department on direct mail. That worked fine because in an expanding economy demand for products was high and prices were driven by inflation. Loyal retail customers did little comparative shopping because they in turn could pass cost increases along to their clients.
>
> When the economy suddenly slowed and international competition increased, sales plummeted. The company spent as much again in a second, product-awareness campaign that relied heavily on the firm's reputation and history with customers and on its product reliability in order to protect its position in the face of a need for sharp price increases. Sales representatives worked hard to explain the need for the price increases in the face of the economic conditions.
>
> Company B, however, approached the situation differently. Throughout the period, it maintained its market research, monitored the competition and economic trends, and maintained a close relationship with customers to track their buying decisions.
>
> While the marketing communicators implemented a series of meetings with customer representatives, executives interviewed the presidents of the customer firms. Company B determined quickly that it was being undercut in price by international competitors, yet it had to increase prices. It also discovered a widespread misperception that its products were intended for a high-cost market. In addition, it learned that customers perceived very little difference in quality among the competing products they were being offered.
>
> Scrapping the program that focused on reliability and historical performance, Company B used meetings and interviews, as well as a series of focus groups with buyers, to test its communication messages before it launched a new marketing campaign. In short, it defined the messages in terms of the behavior sought, based on a clear understanding of the perceptions—and misperceptions—that would drive the behavior.

IMPLEMENTING THE MESSAGES

While implementation is where most corporate communication activity begins—and ends—in most organizations, to be effective it should occur only after the research, planning, and objective setting described above have been completed.

It has become widely accepted that certain media will be used in organizational communication at most times and that once in place, most messages can be sent through those media. In fact, however, the message is made to fit the media because considerable amounts of money have been spent in establishing them. Expertise grows in the design, production, and distribution of media instead of in the objectives and messages. Yet, in the highly selective marketplace, few audiences respond in the same manner to the same media.

A thorough understanding of the audiences, their patterns in absorbing information, their preconceptions about your organization and communication effectiveness, and the forces competing for their attention should be the first step toward selecting the most appropriate media for each message in the time frame specified in the objective.

In addition, one medium seldom has much impact in a world cluttered with the communication efforts of thousands of organizations. Mass distribution of information has become highly ineffective. Determining precise time frames during the objective-setting process enables you to determine how often the message must be repeated; specifying the behavior you are seeking from audiences allows you to monitor the responses closely and take corrective action before serious problems occur.

The primary considerations in implementations are the time required, the resources needed to activate the plan, the appropriate uses of media based on each audience, and the costs compared to results sought.

MEASURING EFFECTIVENESS

The next step is to measure the effectiveness of your messages. Only at this point can accountability be clearly demonstrated to your organization's management. Evaluation is one of the most widely accepted and discussed concepts in communication planning—and the most infrequently used. It is difficult to find anyone in an organization who denies the need for measurement, but it is equally difficult to find an organization that measures communication effectiveness regularly and systematically.

Why? Some of the most frequently cited reasons are the following:

Some people believe that communication is too intangible to be measured.

Many people lack the skills or knowledge required to undertake measurement.

Some measurement techniques are perceived as expensive because they require outside assistance to maintain confidentiality; as a result, the media program already in place may have to be dislodged to accommodate the budget.

Management often resists the time needed to involve employees in activities that are not directly related to operations.

People are often afraid of what they will learn about their communication efforts.

All these reasons have some validity. The main reason for failing to measure communication effectiveness, however, almost always is found in the planning process. Unless measurable objectives are developed in the issue-identification process, it is impossible to measure results. Only the "activity," often involving little more than meeting deadlines, can be measured.

Numerous techniques are available for assessing the effectiveness of your communication efforts. The appropriate time to use them depends on understanding their uses, the resources required to put them in place, and the objectives you have chosen. If it is to be reliable, the type of measurement you use for a given objective depends on some key ingredients.

First, you must determine the *standards of success* that you and your management find acceptable. Second, you must choose a *measurement technique* that fits the objectives and the desired response. Third, measurement must be practiced as an *ongoing activity* throughout all phases of your communication program. After you have the results of your measurement activities, you must revise your communication plans to correct lack of progress, improper time frames, or inappropriate messages. Thus, measurement is integral to assessing whether you have been on course and have reached your desired destination at the end of your planning process.

Developing Realistic Standards of Success

Before you can decide what measurement techniques work for a given objective and set of messages, you must determine how you will judge the success of your efforts. It is unrealistic to expect every communication program to be accepted, understood, or acted on by 100 percent of the audience.

Working with your management, you must develop standards that are an implicit part of your objectives. Your management must be involved in setting these standards, because their perceptions about the role of communication in dealing with certain issues and their expectations of what you can accomplish may well vary from yours.

Almost all other departments will have predetermined standards built into their business goals, and these can help you set realistic communication objectives. For example, the production manager will know the percentage by which errors must be reduced to maintain product quality; the marketing director will know how much sales of a product must be increased to meet sales targets. Part of your research for planning involves becoming aware of such expectations.

Standards of success also will emerge from your evaluation, especially surveys and audits. While standards should be realistic, they should not be so easily attainable that they hurt your credibility. Setting standards with your manager will help establish the appropriate level of expectation.

The standards of effectiveness you set are your measurement criteria. You may wish to set several for the same communication plan in order to track progress during the life of the program. You should not become too concerned if initially you do not meet all the standards you establish for your communication plan. Few of us are so wise that we can meet any standard without considerable experience. As you pursue the discipline of planning, you will find this step easier to complete.

Remember, the more specific and measurable your objectives are and the more they incorporate your management's thinking, the more likely you will be to achieve them.

Selecting Measurement Techniques
You should be familiar with the options available before beginning the measurement process. Not all measurement techniques need to be complex or time-consuming and expensive.

The *ongoing* measurements that you use to track your progress over the course of the program are called *micro* measurement techniques. *Macro* measurement techniques are the comprehensive studies that must be conducted at least every three years. Below are brief descriptions of the options in using these two categories of techniques.

Micro Measurement Techniques
Micro measurement activities, generally limited in scope, can be done easily with the cooperation of others in your organization. Generally, they are not statistically valid measurement techniques but informal means to test your progress during your communication program.

Interviews. The normal course of your communication work puts you in constant contact with executives, department heads, managers, and staff. It also gives you regular access to customers. Each contact represents an opportunity for you to include evaluation of the communication program simply by asking questions about recent communication materials, understanding of the messages you have been sending, or reaction to press coverage and other topics.

Interviews that are designed solely for evaluation purposes can be especially useful for programs involving controversial, sensitive, or complex communication on key issues that need to be monitored regularly and closely. These interviews require special scheduling and should not be imposed more often than every quarter.

Ongoing Sensing Groups. These are regularly scheduled meetings with changing groups of employees at various levels. They allow you to gather information from a cross section of people concerning their information needs, comments on messages, questions about issues, and so on. There are several kinds of sensing groups:

> *Pretesting groups* give participants an opportunity to help you develop messages or identify questions about issues before communication of the program begins. These groups help you ensure that what you communicate will be on target.
>
> *Communication councils* involve groups who respond to communication programs after implementation and help determine if your messages are being understood and accepted.
>
> *Communication quality circles* are formal, structured groups aimed at solving a specific communication issue. The participants serve as resource teams to the communication staff.

Focus Groups. These structured and carefully controlled meetings are used to find out why audiences feel the way they do about certain issues or topics. Unless the participants represent a reliable sample of the total population, the results will not be statistically valid. However, the discussions are an effective way to probe for information about why certain perceptions have formed or issues have developed. Even if focus groups are chosen without statistical sampling, you should attempt to select participants on the basis of the composition of the wider audience to ensure that you are getting a good cross section of opinions.

Focus groups can be used before, after, or in place of formal surveys. Focus groups produce the best results when conducted by outside consultants, because participants feel freer to comment and because it is easier to maintain confidentiality of individuals' responses (which is extremely important to the reliability of the findings).

Ongoing Upward Feedback Programs. Commonly taking the form of letters to management or upward communication, these programs identify employee, shareholder, or customer questions and complaints and help you monitor issues and prevent problems. Usually, communicators administer the programs so as to maintain confidentiality. If designed properly, these programs can be highly effective in tracking issues and reactions to particular subjects. Questions designed to elicit specific reactions to your communication plans can be fed into these programs.

Mini Surveys. Brief questionnaires are useful for gathering quick reactions on content, knowledge of particular subjects, reactions to campaigns, and the like. These types of surveys should not be viewed as reliable research on communication effectiveness; but, over time, they can provide meaningful insights into patterns and expectations and can become helpful in program design. It is important not to overuse these surveys among the same respondents. Too much use will diminish the number of respondents and may lead subjects to think that negative responses are being elicited. They should be used in combination with other methods for spot checks on particular programs.

Other Activities. Some communication programs can be evaluated as part of regular business activities. For example, one measurement technique for a program on quality improvement might be reports from supervisors on reactions or understanding among their employees. The success of a communication program introducing new products can be measured by sales reports.

None of the micro measurement techniques should be used alone. These techniques are used intermittently, between macro measurements, as part of an overall measurement effort. An effective communication plan will have one or more of the techniques in place at all times.

Macro Measurement Techniques

Unlike the informal methods just described, macro measurement devices are systematic activities aimed at developing benchmark data that describe the "big picture." Almost all studies of this nature take the form of surveys or audits. They are conducted every two to three years to evaluate a variety of subjects, including overall attitudes or perceptions about the company's image, products, and communication credibility. They require outside assistance to ensure confidential responses, reliable data, and proper analysis; and they require several weeks to complete.

Periodic surveys, image studies, or communication audits are critical to communication planning, because without this information your communication program—no matter how carefully planned—is simply incomplete.

Attitude Surveys. Attitude surveys, sometimes called climate studies or employee relations studies, measure all aspects of work life, including employee perceptions about compensation and benefits, job satisfaction, co-workers, supervisors and managers, personnel policies and practices, working conditions, and communication. The results are periodic reports on the "state of the company" from the audience's perspective. They measure morale, credibility, satisfaction, and motivation. These surveys are analyzed according to employee demographics to assess the findings based on reporting relationships, work experience, knowledge levels, and the like.

Attitude surveys measure more than perceptions, however. They also suggest the factors that influence and shape attitudes, such as emotional beliefs, habits, and assumptions—all key aspects of audience analysis and communication planning. In addition, analysis of attitude survey findings allow you to gauge the depth of issues or problems and the degree to which you must segment an issue, or the employee population, in order to plan your messages.

Communication Audits. Communication audits differ from attitude sur-- veys because they focus only on the communication climate in the company. The questions probe:

   Understanding and acceptance of organizational goals and philosophy
   The preferred and actual channels of information within the company or to and from the company and its major external audiences
   The structure and flow of communication
   The appropriateness of the media used
   The information needs of audiences
   The appropriateness of resources, staffing, and reporting relationships of the communication function.

The communication audit is the most comprehesive study of communication effectiveness available to you. The perspective it provides not only produces internal benchmarks against which to measure future efforts but also makes it possible to compare your success to that of other organizations and to accepted research in the field.

Image Studies. The purpose of conducting an image study is to take a definitive look at how key audiences perceive the firm. Those perceptions—which constitute the company's image—will vary with the type of firm, your communication effectiveness, and how you define your firm, its role, and various other factors.

Depending on the audiences to be assessed and the level of statistical sampling desired, image studies rely on techniques similar to those followed in audits and attitude surveys. Image studies can include assessments of the views held by top management, employees, customers, the consumer and trade press, the community, other firms, community, government, and business leaders, special interest groups, and the public.

Such a study provides an in-depth analysis of the firm's image compared to desired standards, the reasons perceptions are held, how communication—or lack of it—influences those perceptions, and recommendations on reinforcing or changing the findings.

TAKING CORRECTIVE ACTIONS

What do you do when you get results back from your latest evaluation and find that:

> Employees indicate a significant lack of confidence in the ability of senior management to run the business successfully?
>
> Customers say they are having service problems with a new product?
>
> Forty-five percent of your shareholders indicate they do not understand the new executive compensation plan to be submitted for approval at the next shareholders' meeting?

In some organizations, these results would be filed permanently in a desk drawer. The results of doing so, however, are clear: The problems would go unresolved and would probably get worse. Participants will be less candid in sharing their true feelings the next time you attempt to evaluate your communication program. Ignoring such negative findings is what you should *not* do with the results of your evaluation, whether they come from a full-fledged attitude audit, sensing groups, or focus group discussions.

Using Measurement Results Effectively

Evaluation techniques are used to measure the effectiveness of your communication plan and to determine the extent to which it is helping the organization meet its objectives. Generally, you do not fix something that is not broken, so if your plan is working, only minor adjustments may be necessary.

The challenge rests with those results that indicate, for whatever reason, that your audience is not responding to the program and its messages. Failure to take corrective action could do serious harm to your organization and to the credibility of your communication efforts.

For example, failure to address a deterioration in employee perceptions about management credibility could result in high turnover of people who are valuable and necessary to the success of the organization. Likewise, failure to respond to a negative reaction uncovered in a market research program can cause your organization to miss an opportunity to satisfy customer needs and to gain an acceptable return on the company's investment.

Some thought should be given to what to do with results before the evaluation begins. It is almost impossible to develop an action plan until actual results are in, but you can use evaluation results in a number of ways to improve the effectiveness of your efforts.

Decide What You Have Learned. Take time to decide what you have learned from the measurement results. Analyzing responses can be a difficult and elusive task, and it is sometimes best to get help from someone who has experience. A negative reaction to an early retirement incentive program, for example, does not necessarily mean there is something wrong with the program. It could be a matter of understanding the reasons for introducing the program, the manner in which the program has been communicated, or a reaction to other actions that caused perception problems.

Misinterpretation of measurement results can create as many problems for an organization as not communicating or taking action on results.

Compare Results. Evaluation techniques serve at least two important purposes: They tell you where your communication plan stands at a particular point in time, and they give you an idea about changes that have taken place by comparing the results of recent evaluations with those from the past.

By studying the results of various evaluation devices as well as comparing results over a period of time, you can monitor trends in behavior and understanding.

Use Results for Planning. By using the results to determine trends and patterns, you can make your evaluation techniques an integral part of your ongoing communication-planning process. The results identify which objectives are being met and which communication activity should be maintained or reinforced. They also identify which activities are marginally effective and may need minor adjusting. Those objectives that are not being met require total revamping.

Do Not Manage Only the Negatives. When results are examined, there is a natural tendency to focus on the negatives and to manage only those aspects that have gone wrong. By doing so, we often miss the lessons to be learned from what has been successful and the opportunity to apply those issues to other aspects of our communication plan. If the evaluation shows that the message was successful in conveying to analysts why the company was reorganized, for example, the techniques (media, timing, frequency, and so on) used to communicate that message should be considered for other parts of your communication program with that audience.

Establish New Standards. In addition to using the positive results as guidelines for improvement in other areas, you also can use them to establish new standards of success. If your goal was to generate a 20 percent response on a product introduction, for example, and you easily met that goal, it may be necessary to raise the goal to 35 percent. This enables you continually to improve your communication-planning process and the results of your efforts. In contrast, evaluation results may suggest that your standard has been set too high and needs to be adjusted downward.

Developing Corrective Actions

It is not uncommon in many organizations for the measurement process to stop after standards have been established, progress evaluated, and results analyzed. In these instances, managers tend to feel that knowing what is wrong is enough.

The pitfalls of taking no action were outlined previously. The real benefit of measuring communication effectiveness is developing and implementing corrective actions that allow you to put your communication plan on the right track and to keep it there if it is working well.

There are a number of answers to the questions, "What do I need to do differently to achieve greater success?" The way you answer that question will determine the success of your corrective actions. What you are trying to say, how you say it, to whom you say it, and what you expect from your efforts are at the heart of communication evaluation. If the answers cannot be found in any of these four areas, you should reevaluate your communication objectives to ensure that they are attainable.

In most cases, your answer to the question can be found in one or more of these elements of communication planning: (1) message; (2) media; (3) audience; (4) standards.

Message. Questions may have been built into your evaluation vehicle to measure audience understanding of your intended message. It is not uncommon for your audience to misinterpret the message you are sending. A story on aggressive cost controls could, for example, be interpreted by stockholders as a warning of diminished profitability when, in fact, no such change is indicated.

In another case, the message may have to be restated to be understood more clearly, or your audience may need to receive it many times and in various ways. The advertising technique of frequently repeating a message can often be applied to organizational communication. Do not make the mistake of sending a message just once and assuming that you have communicated.

Members of the audience also may attach different levels of credibility to the source of the message. Be sure to determine those perceptions before assuming that certain spokespeople are authoritative.

A final consideration is whether conflicting messages are being sent by different parts of the organization. The new corporate identity program introduced at the same time you enter union negotiations easily may be misunderstood.

Media. The communication devices used to communicate a message are often responsible for misinterpretation or lack of understanding. In assessing possible corrective action, be sure the media you have chosen to communicate your message have sufficient credibility.

The channel through which the message is delivered also can have an impact on how it is perceived. An announcement of a new-product price discount over the three-week trade fair will have little meaning to customers whose buying decisions are made in contracts a year in advance.

It is important to make full use of the communication tools at your disposal to ensure that the message is completely and effectively communicated. As much as we would like it to happen, not everyone will read the publications, releases and financial reports. Other considerations are whether the medium is reaching the right audience and whether it is available with sufficient regularity.

Audience. The audience to whom you are sending a message and the technique used to reach a particular audience play key roles in how well the message is understood. Have you sufficiently segmented and targeted your audience? Does the audience relate to the communication media you have selected?

Standards. In some cases, failure to meet an objective means that it is not attainable—that the standards are too high. Is the objective attainable? If your objective is to improve quality by 10 percent, the answer is no. Having a direct impact on product quality is not within the realm of a communication program. You must establish objectives that elicit the desired behavior response from your audience.

Similarly, is the standard within reach? If your standard is 40 percent response to a direct mail campaign, the answer is no. That simply is not a realistic objective. Depending on your organization, a goal in the range of 20 to 30 percent is more reasonable.

The logical steps to consider in developing corrective actions include:

1. New, corrected, restated, or more frequent messages
2. Additional, new, or refocused media
3. Better understanding of the intended audience
4. More realistic objectives and standards

Effective communication relates directly to an organization's potential for growth and profitability. In marketing, it is critical. When you and your management agree that you must be held accountable for specific objectives and that your communication effectiveness will be determined by clear audience research and regular measurement, the connection between your activities and the goals and issues of the organization will be clearly demonstrated.

CHAPTER 5

How to Create Persuasive Marketing Tools*

Karen C. Wilson, ABC†

It is 9:00 a.m. on an overcast Wednesday in July. The phone rings.
"Clough Management Services."
"Hello. I just this minute got your brochure in the mail. Who can I talk to?"
"Well, you can talk to me. What was your reaction to the brochure?"
"Good. In fact, very good. And I'll tell you something. If your product is as good as your brochure, and it *really* does what you say it does, you've sold me already. But let me be right up front—I'm a tough customer."

Sound implausible? Well, it's not. In fact, this phone call happened in my office just as I started this review of persuasion skills in marketing.

The caller? The president of a multimillion dollar chemical company in Linden, New Jersey.

The product? Software for chemical manufacturers and distributors that helps reduce costs and increase profits.

The mailing? A two-color, no-photograph, no-nonsense, 8½- × -11-inch brochure, with a one-color cover. And a personally typed and signed letter offering a free set of reports.

The strategy? Use a carefully pinpointed, well-combed mailing list of high-probability prospects in a tight geographic area and direct a benefit-oriented brochure to get the hottest potential buyers to raise their hands and ask for the next step in the selling process, the thick book of reports.

The letter and brochure had a terrific burden, persuading a busy man to take the time to read eight pages, then pick up the phone to call for more reading.

But then, this is the burden of all marketing communication—to persuade so successfully that our prospect actually becomes willing to give up

*Copyright 1986, Karen C. Wilson, ABC.
†Karen Wilson, ABC, is president of Marketing Momentum, in Springfield, Massachusetts. She is the recipient of a Gold Quill Award of Excellence for sales promotion materials and is on the Accreditation Board of the International Association of Business Communicators. She is an accredited business communicator.

something dear: attention, time, cash, commitment, even the temporary luxury of indecision.

PERSUASION: MEETING HIGH STAKES

Sometimes the stakes in the persuasion process are high, as when huge advertising and promotion budgets figure prominently in aggressive competitions to attract customers to fast-food outlets operated by McDonald's, Burger King, or Wendy's. Other times, the stakes may seem almost as large but the budgets are smaller, as in the meticulously planned effort to persuade the citizens of Palm Beach County, Florida, to support the local United Way charity campaign.

Whatever the budget or the stakes, the art of persuasion remains the same. The tools, skills, and basic ingredients must be carefully managed and orchestrated. When they are, the impact can be long-lasting.

A classic example of the positive impact of persuasion inside the workplace was described in a recent cover story in *Forbes,* a U.S. biweekly business magazine, which outlined the contrast in attitude, environment, and expectation of workers at two automobile manufacturing plants in the midwestern United States. At one factory, shop floor personnel were clearly unsupportive and uncooperative, nearly obstructionist, because they feared automation. But "at Honda, workers are persuaded that automation will not eliminate jobs by improving quality control, with the result that workers see it as an investment in their own job security. Thus many new automation ideas at Honda come right from the factory floor."[1]

Of course, the reasons that any particular group of people are persuaded to do anything are enormously complex. The workers at Honda may be the beneficiaries of a superior work environment, one that has paved the way for the persuasion process to be successful.

The point is, someone set the known tools of the persuasion process in motion. Using basic techniques and concepts of selling an idea, someone convinced a group of workers to break out of their rut and support something new. Other examples might be a computer visionary selling radically new ideas in computer architecture to a venture capitalist, or a longtime vendor of automotive products attempting to convince its skeptical distributors that shipping and fulfillment problems will be solved.

THE ART AND SCIENCE OF PERSUASION

The process of persuasion is both an art and a science, requiring creativity and disciplined use of long-researched and proven tools. Communicators and marketers need to review for themselves the books and articles that have been written on persuasion, including some of the best-selling books on selling.

No Such Thing as a Captive Audience

The starting point in the persuasion process is admitting to ourselves that there is no such thing as a captive audience. Changing employee and customer loyalties, the inventiveness of the human mind, and the constantly evolving perceptions of our world guarantee that people are not sitting around, awaiting our every word. Far from it. *People are active,* moving around, doing what they want to do or must do. They are too busy to be told, and cannot be told. They must be won over.

Three Hurdles: Time, Clutter, and Sameness

There are at least three huge hurdles standing in the way of winning anyone's attention: time, clutter, and sameness.

Time. The more your prospect has of it, the less likely you are to want his or her attention; the more important your prospect is, the less time he or she has. You are fighting for awareness, seeking to grab attention in a matter of seconds. While your prospect is scanning the newsstand looking for interesting cover stories, flipping channels on television, walking briskly through a building, or skimming through a magazine, you have only 5 to 8 seconds to catch the eye and ear and perhaps 20 seconds or less to say exactly what you want the reader or listener to do!

And yet, to be successful, you must stop the individual. You must get him or her to see or hear your message *when you want it read or heard, not days or weeks later.* Unless you are read or heard right away, you may not get the funding or the sales or the cooperation you need when you need them.

Clutter. Another obstacle in the persuasion process is the growing clutter: proliferating channels of communication, which call upon the persuader to find some way to stand out from the pack. Our prospect is inundated with attractions and excitement. But how often do we remember this? Somehow we think our four-color specification sheet for plastic-injection molding equipment is must reading. Somehow we are convinced that the same employees who read a personality-oriented magazine and watch fast-action sports actually want to stop and read all about the new benefits program. The fact is, too many other interesting activities and subjects compete with ours.

Sameness. A third major hurdle is the boredom that people feel when they see the same thing over and over again, presented in the same, nondescript, copycat communication process. Yet organizational communicators persist in producing a vast sea of gray blocks of type surrounded by predictable photographs and voguish corporate jargon. They spend millions on advertising programs using visual and verbal clichés, accepting "the way everybody does it" as *the* way to do it.

I am reminded of two competing advertisers in the diesel engine business who ran nearly identical advertising campaigns targeted at the diesel engine distributors who provide parts and service to heavy-duty equipment users. One advertiser used single-page ads, the other spreads. But the two ads used nearly identical layouts: the same white-space areas, nearly identical four- to six-word headlines, photos in the same position, and blue logos with boxed symbols or words in reverse on the left and corporate names on the right. Instead of informing readers about the differences between the two products and organizations, the companies were communicating sameness, even down to the nearly identical blue logos!

The unfortunate aspect of such sameness in advertising and communication is that the intelligent people to whom these large corporations wanted to sell really wanted to be sold. Research by one of these two companies uncovered a customer base outspokenly demanding more product literature, sales, and company information. The heavy-duty equipment dealers knew that their distribution business depended on a better understanding of product and delivery and urged a communication overhaul. In effect, the customers said, "We need you to break through this sameness and clutter and help us sell the farmers and truckers who depend on us."

USE KNOWN SELLING TECHNIQUES TO BREAK THROUGH

Whether you are selling a product or an idea, through personal selling, print, or audiovisual media, the persuasion process is fundamentally the same: catching attention and holding it until the sale is closed. The following basic steps in creating persuasive marketing tools are essential for breaking through and selling your ideas and products:

Six Steps to More Persuasive Marketing

1. Attract attention
2. Excite, arouse interest and desire
3. Inform and explain why
4. Satisfy concerns, answer objections
5. Ask for a commitment to action
6. Protect your credibility

The rest of this chapter will discuss some of the techniques involved in maneuvering through each of the six steps.

Step One: Attract Attention

To attract prospects and get them to read or attend to your message *when you want them to*—not hours, days, or weeks later—requires creative energy and discipline. From the start, you must have only one overriding, simple message; reject the impulse to save money through multiple objectives. For one reason, people cannot remember multiple, rapid-fire messages without help. For another, conveying one idea alone is tough enough; why compound your difficulties by adding one or two more?

You must concentrate everything—every word, symbol, picture, sound, and emphasis—on that one message. Everything extraneous to the message must be deleted.

You must focus on only one basic idea, enhancing it with reinforcing demonstrations. This is true whether you are giving a speech or preparing a data sheet on a product. In fact, if you get across the same idea in multiple ways and in multiple dimensions, your likelihood of success soars.

A brochure for computer owners says on the cover:

"Two little words that will forever change the way you look at computer monitors . . ."[2]

We look inside the first fold, and two simple words stand out on a black background:

"Sony Trinitron"

Then we look inside the next fold. The theme of improved vision is reiterated, reinforced, and proven.

This focus on one overriding message and objective works for one communication piece as well as for an entire communication program. Every marketing tool, every message, must echo the same melody. The entire orchestra of communication—from speeches by top officials to envelope stuffers—needs to reinforce the same message or theme, or the impact is lost. Instead of unity and power, there is disconnectedness and weakness.

Next, you must vigorously choose and prepare the atmosphere of your communication. The basic law behind this is the law of similar response. You smile, he smiles. You are friendly, she is far more likely to become a friend. Some of the most effective television advertisers understand this phenomenon and use it with great success. Soft-drink commercials are upbeat, warm, and friendly pastiches of life as people would like it to be. A wonderful mood is presented, and the viewer is swept toward the assumption that the product is an essential part of the scene.

Sell Benefits, Not Features. The attraction process requires that you sell benefits, not features. People want something to make life easier, happier, more satisfying, friendlier, less expensive, less confusing, less difficult. They do not want to have to think of a product in terms of metal that will eventually rust, plastic that will break, or anything to inventory, dust, wax, repair or make payments on.

Look at the Sony brochure (Figure 5.1). The inside spread of the brochure reviews the reasons "Trinitron monitors make any computer look its best" and gives "six ways Sony Trinitron™ improves your vision":

Bright colors
Sharper characters
Reduced glare
Viewing comfort
Fuller, flatter screen
Input flexibility

Each point is buttressed by illustrations. We are convinced we will actually see a much-improved computer screen; the quality of our work or leisure hours will be better. Basically, we all want things to be improved; we want to feel good.

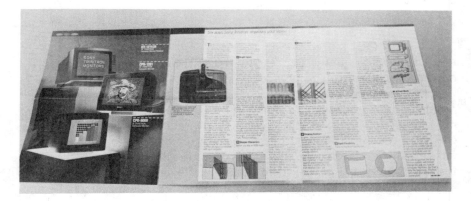

Figure 5.1. The purchase of a color monitor for your computer is not only a considerable expense, but it involves a great deal of learning about viewing differences and comfort. The entire discussion in this brochure revolves around the reader, not the Sony Corp. or the hardware features.

This fact has not escaped the attention of one of the largest manufacturers in the United States, the General Electric Company. When persuading prospects to buy its household appliances or its billion-dollar jet engine programs, advertisements or commercials always end with the slogan "GE . . . we bring good things to life." Eventually, unless you have a bad experience with one of GE's products, countless positive impressions will lodge in your memory, and your good feelings about GE could last a lifetime.

The International Association of Business Communicators also understands the principle of selling benefits. Developing a membership marketing campaign, board members asked for a new way to convince potential members to join. Research—formal and informal—showed that the main reason people joined IABC, or any professional association, was not for the chance to go to international meetings or to buy books or to meet experts, but primarily to grow professionally. Implied in the desire for professional growth were the satisfaction, prestige, and financial remuneration that would come from climbing the career ladder. The seminars, meetings, professional

Figure 5.2 Consistency of message through direct mail, envelopes, reproduction slicks, brochures, and other collateral materials continually reinforces the primary benefit of joining the association.

colleagues, and so on constituted the features. The benefit was the boost in professional growth that those features could provide.

Accordingly, a new tag line was created: "Grow with Us." This slogan was used on all selling materials and reinforced by inducements directly relating to professional growth. The theme has helped IABC become the largest international communication organization in the world.

Of course, the organization's growth was not created by the tag line, but the slogan helped. The organization had the benefits its prospects wanted; the communication was an essential, excellent, attractive mirror. Remember, people do not buy things, they buy what things can do for them. You must make your appeal so attractive that they will want your product more than what they have to give up in order to get it. And you may need to describe many benefits before you overcome the "no" in their minds.

Strive for Impact. Just presenting the benefits is not enough. The message must be presented so compellingly that it breaks through the clutter and boredom. In order to achieve this impact, the marketer must know a great deal about what makes for impact in each medium. It is not just a matter of color, although knowing which colors advance and which recede no doubt helps. It is not just a matter of size, although, in fact, full-page advertisements have 181 percent more impact than smaller advertisements.[3] And it is not a matter of bleed (with photos and background filling the entire page or touching one or more of the page edges), although a McGraw-Hill study shows that advertisements that bleed attract 21 percent more attention than those that do not.[4]

Often, impact is a matter of surprise, of being different. You must be different in every medium you choose, even when color, size, or shape of communication imposes constraints.

One of the most successful advertising campaigns ever to appear in *The Wall Street Journal* was a "strikingly untraditional" campaign that United Technologies Corporation introduced in 1978. Harry Gray, chairman of the board, offered the reason for the success of these advertisements:

> Five years ago, when some of us at United Technologies decided we needed to let the business world know more about our corporation through advertising, we had a choice to make. We could launch the traditional sort of ad series to explain our product lines, our research investments, our operating philosophy, our financial results. Or we could take a flier on a strikingly untraditional series of messages which would discuss life in general instead of life at the corporation. . . .[5]

The copy-only advertisements have persuaded more than half a million busy *Journal* readers to send a 22-cent letter to Gray himself, asking for reprints. The goodwill, name recognition, and friendship this series has created will go a long way toward supporting the future of the company.

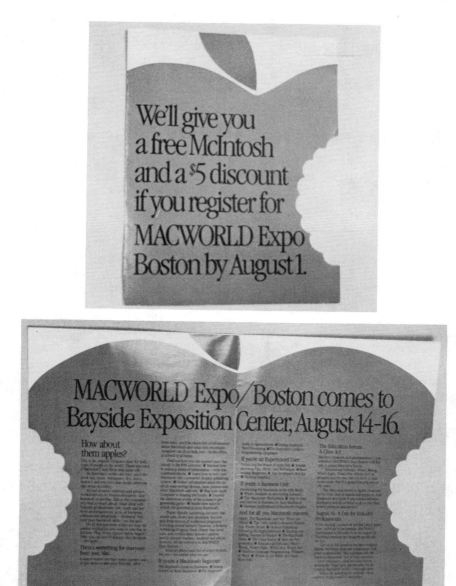

Figure 5.3. This flier, for an exhibit designed to draw users of Apple Computers, successfully used a die-cut design, candy-apple-red ink, a humorous tone, and an instantly recognized theme to single out and attract the target audience. (CW Communications and World Expo Co.)

Little Things

Most of us
miss out
on life's
big prizes.
The Pulitzer.
The Nobel.
Oscars.
Tonys.
Emmys.
But we're
all eligible
for life's
small pleasures.
A pat
on the back.
A kiss
behind the ear.
A four-pound bass.
A full moon.
An empty
parking space.
A crackling fire.
A great meal.
A glorious sunset.
Hot soup.
Cold beer.
Don't fret
about
copping life's
grand awards.
Enjoy its
tiny delights.
There are plenty
for all of us.

Figure 5.4. United Technologies Corporation's advertisement, "Little Things," generated 26,184 letters. It is one in a campaign series that has generated more than 500,000 requests for copies.

Later, in remarks to United Technologies corporate communicators, Gray said, "The campaign has been a bell ringer. People are talking and writing about it. They're asking for reprints by the basketfull. . . . This is the sort of distinctiveness and originality we need more of. . . . No other company can sign its name to these messages. They're ours and ours alone."[6]

Of course, there were several reasons why this advertising was successful: Its message was reader-oriented, instead of organizational chest-thumping. Its simple writing struck home. And its breakthrough design immediately caught attention.

Know How to Differentiate Your Product. Being different is good, but differentiating your product is even more important. Your prospect must instantly know *why* your idea is better. Just saying that it *is* better will produce yawns, because everyone else says the same thing, but showing and proving how and why it is better will produce sales.

Are you selling software for accounting? Then you need to convince me *instantly* why your package is better than the rest. Do not tell me it is better, show me it is better. When you determine what it is that separates your product from all the rest, you must get that benefit into a compelling headline. Headlines count for half of a letter's success in direct mail and test out at 50 to 75 percent of the success of an advertisement.[7]

Does the headline have to be short? No. You can read the following words:

Introducing a New Beeper

in about the same amount of time that you can read:

Introducing a New Beeper
for Your Freedom and Security

The importance of reader-oriented benefits clearly differentiating a product or service in a well-written headline is covered extensively by Philip Burton in the usefully illustrated textbook *Which Ad Pulled Best?*[8] Throughout, he displays side by side two advertisements for the same product or service. In every case we can see exactly why "the winning ad gives the reader a clear idea in the illustration and headline of what is being offered."[9]

Step Two: Excite, Arouse Interest and Desire

In one stunning ad, delicacies served by Japan Airlines are spread out before us showing "How to Fly, Japanese Style." Captions at each plate or platter fascinate and compel our attention. A coupon offers quick response to the mouth-watering creative. As Burton writes, "The picture-caption technique. . .leads the reader through the various parts of the illustration and the presence of the coupon may have drawn more eyes to the advertisement."[10]

Exciting and arousing our prospect's interest and desire, step 2 in the persuasion process, means catching the eye and moving it where you want it to go. The writers understand that if you are writing for English-speaking readers, you must keep in mind that they most often read from left to right, and top to bottom. This does not mean your plan must be identical to everyone else's; it just means that going against the grain (bottom to top, for example) is a tougher assignment.

Draw the Reader into the Material
But eyes do not move smoothly over printed matter. Professor Jack Sissors of the Medill School of Journalism at Northwestern University (Evanston, Illinois), has researched how the eye moves. He points out that the eye "makes four fixations a second, or about 240 a minute. The duration of these fixations is about 1/500th to a full second, depending on the kind of material being read, ability of the reader, interests and habits of the reader. Type style and arrangement also affect the number of fixations made. The objective should be to minimize the fixations in order to speed the reading process."[11]

After you have minimized the number of fixations, you need to plan where the fixations will lead. And guide the process as much as possible. Whether you are writing an ad, editing a feature story for a magazine, or planning a direct mail letter, you must think where the eye will go. Your readers are not going to start at the top and move in perfect order down the page. They will go to the following items before they read the body copy:

> Headline first
> Blurbs or callouts
> Charts, graphs, tables, diagrams
> Subheads
> Captions
> P.S. at the bottom of a letter
> Sidebars
> Response cards
> Well-known bylines
> Bullets

These are the well-used tools of editors, advertising copywriters, art directors, and direct mail specialists—the talented professionals who must produce sales through their writing. These are the tools that should be thoroughly understood by organizational communicators.

Studies have shown that sidebars, response cards, photographs, and well-known bylines are powerful in their impact on readership for an employee magazine. William Savage, ABC, and Tessa Gaston conducted a study for the IABC in 1981 that found that

> between straight text and text plus sidebar, participants preferred the sidebar approach by a margin of 93 percent to 7 percent. . . . Text with a response card was preferred over straight text by a margin of 73 percent to 27 percent. . . . Desire for a chance to participate while reading was the expressed preference of 84 percent for quiz and text. . . . Participants overwhelmingly preferred an article bylined by a well-known personality to the same article with no byline. The margin was 93 percent for the byline, 7 percent for the anonymous artricle."[12]

The effort to draw the reader into the material will, of course, fail if the writer lets the material become dry and lifeless. The impact of writing on reader interest was studied by Professor Lewis Donohew of the Department of Communication at the University of Kentucky (Lexington). Donohew tested the effects of eight news stories, each written in three styles. All stories written in a narrative style generated significantly greater physiological arousal than those written in traditional news style. Traditional news story formats (summary leads, followed by more detailed information) yielded the lowest arousal ratings.[13]

Tap Human Emotions. To excite the audience and arouse their desires, we simply must touch them emotionally, giving them some reason to keep their eyes traveling over the material. This important emotional factor was first exploited in advertising decades ago by N. W. Ayer, an advertising agency for DeBeers diamonds. Because of the advertising campaign alone, which teamed diamonds with fine art and public personalities, sales of diamonds soared 55 percent in the United States. Ayer himself noted, "There was no direct sale to be made. There was no brand name to be impressed on the public mind. There was simply an idea—the eternal emotional value surrounding the diamond."[14]

Easy, you say. Anyone can make a diamond romantic and exciting. But is that really so? Is not the diamond—a clear, small jewel—rather pale in comparison to the drama and brilliance of an opal swirling with a brilliant rainbow of colors? Good marketing gave the diamond its "color."

Compare these two potential leads for a story about coal haulers, prepared for an energy company for publication in a marketing magazine:

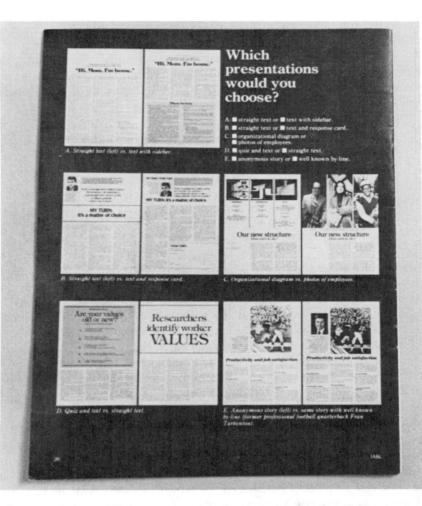

Figure 5.5. In this survey, 93 percent of readers preferred the text with the sidebar on the left. Only 3 percent chose the straight text. (Journal of Organizational Communication, IABC, 1981/3.)

[Lead 1] The Long-Airdox Company of Oak Hill, W. Va., successfully operates coal mines from Pennsylvania to Utah. Besides that, more than half of all conventional chain-and-belt conveyors in U.S. underground operations were built by the company.

[Lead 2] They remind you of giant reptiles out of a movie about creatures on Mars. But they're on our side. Actually, they're a unique breed of coal haulers.[15]

The first lead is what you would expect: every press release and news story seems to start that way. But the second lead, which the editors used, has a surprising hook, drawing you into the story. And the good writing in this story did not stop with the lead. A photo caption reads:

> Bullet-shaped carbide teeth on a feeder/breaker's rotary drum will crack big chunks of coal into small sizes so they can be fed evenly onto conveyors.[16]

Will your article on donations to the United Way produce a yawn? Will your sales presentation on advances in materials research produce doodlers in the audience? If they do, you are not giving your audience something to be excited about, and you probably should not be wasting their time.

Sell the Offer, Not the Product. Even more important, if your audience does not know exactly what you are offering and what you want them to do to take advantage of the offer, you have probably lost your sale.

The offer is the product, service, or benefit you will give me if I sign up, or join, or call, or buy, or do what you want me to do. A free car wash with gas fill-up; lifelong vision if I wear safety glasses at the milling machine; free service for a year if I buy a four-color copier now.

The most often used direct mail technique offers some reward rather than just describing something: "Order here to get 12 issues for half price." "Call for a demonstration today and get a free saucepan."

Inducements have been used as long as people have tried to barter or sell. Smart organizational communicators recognize the power of inducements and rewards in the persuasion process: prizes for the largest donation; plaques for outstanding suppliers; parties for team winners; trips for top sales personnel; cash gifts for cost reducers.

Like the law of similar response, the principle of reciprocation goes into effect as soon as the offer is accepted. We are "obligated to the future repayment of favors, gifts, invitations, and the like."[17]

Let Nothing Interfere with the Selling Message. The book by Philip Burton discussed earlier illustrates another important point about selling in print. You must make it easy for your reader to read.

Reverse type in lower-readership advertisements, printed over pictures, nearly defies you to read the ads. "Reverse printing (or white letters on a black background) slows reading about 11 percent. Reverse printing therefore should be limited to very small areas.

Do nothing to slow readership. Do not use all capital letters, or you will reduce readership by 12 percent. Do not print on nonwhite stock unless it is very light in color and contrasts strongly with the color of ink you are using. Do not use typefaces that are hard to read.[19]

Keep the attention and the eye moving, so as not to let the reading momentum slow down or stop even for a minute. Are your paragraphs ending with the most boring words on the page? Remember, the reader's eye is scanning for tidbits of interest and will probably see the last words in your paragraph before it sees the words in the middle! The end of the paragraph is where the benefits you are offering should be most visible.

The one-page direct mail letter shown in Figure 5.6 was sent to about 700 chemical company presidents. It produced 14 strong replies, leading to on-site demonstrations of the integrated software package. This letter is an excellent example of persuasion at minimum cost with profitable payback. The primary benefit—increased profits—almost leaps off the page, even though there are no pictures to illustrate it.

Are you using more than one page in your printed piece? Then make sure your page turn becomes a cliff-hanger of sorts. At the bottom of the page, stop a curiosity-arousing sentence in midair so the reader will want to turn the page for the rest of the story.

Why do anything, even for just a second, that will lose a prospect? You are already losing readers rapidly anyway, and each one is important. The fall-off in readership of anything—whether it is a feature article, an advertisement, or a letter—is extremely rapid. The chart shown in Figure 5.7, presented by James E. A. Lumley in his book *Sell It by Mail,*[20] shows the stages of decline in readership of a direct mail package. The decrease in attention is similarly rapid for speeches, lectures, and radio or television commercials.

An audience listens in chunks or fragments of time. Their minds wander, tuning in and out, flitting to the speaker and away again. It is insensitive to assume that our listeners are attuned to our every word. It is not enough to come on stage and start to speak. To be heard so that we can be persuasive, we must avoid attention loss and do everything we can to keep listeners' interest: present provocatively interesting ideas; change the pace; raise or lower the decibels of speech and the kinds of sounds; gesture; pour a glass of water to achieve a dramatic pause; chalk our main points on a board; add color, excitement, and drama with pictures.

Add Excitement with Pictures. A good picture is worth hard cash in marketing. Why? Because more than 90 percent of memory is visual. It would be hard to forget the tempting delights spread out in the Japan Airlines advertisement. Pictures not only add the excitement and realism that the

CLOUGH MANAGEMENT SERVICES
4 MONTGOMERY STREET
P. O. BOX 625
ROUSE'S POINT, NEW YORK 12979-0625

WILLIAM A. CLOUGH
PRESIDENT

TELEPHONE
(518) 298-4350

April 29, 1986

WXXGeorgexParker
president
CobkXXXBUNNXPAINIXCORP
157XXbkSXthXStreet
NewarkxXNJXOIIDI

DearXMrXXParkers

Three years ago, in my mid-forties, I was able to turn over the day-to-day operations of my company, Clough Chemical, to my management team. This was because the entire operation had become much easier to control and, as a result, so much more profitable!

A complete business and production management system I'd been developing for eighteen years, with ideas from fifty other chemical companies, had really paid off. I could relax, knowing the system would keep me thoroughly informed and my managers increasingly successful.

I'll be glad to tell you how I keep on top of what's important in my chemical business simply by using half a dozen, to-the-point, short exception reports. Also, I'll be glad to let you in on how my system, which enables rewards based on profitability, has helped Clough attract the best representatives and consistently increase sales and profits without a raise since 1969.

To date I've installed the program, which operates on IBM PC XT's, AT's and compatibles, for a number of other chemical specialty companies. They'll tell you this system will make your organization much easier to operate and control. They'll also tell you that the savings and profits it helps you build will quickly pay for the hardware and software many times over.

Since we are engaged in similar enterprises, you may be interested in learning about my business system in greater detail. I'll be happy to share my ideas with you at no cost or obligation and at your convenience. Just mail me your card using the enclosed envelope or call me at (518) 298-4350 and let's get together.

Sincerely,

William A. Clough

Figure 5.6. Notice how the New York office of this Canadian firm skillfully used paragraph endings to give product benefits great visibility in a direct mail letter to chemical company presidents.

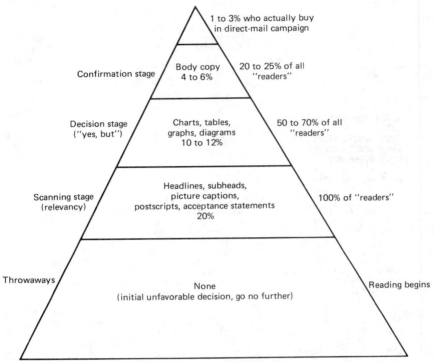

Figure 5.7. Only 20 percent of the direct mail recipients who scan the package go on to the supporting materials, which have great impact on the decision stage.

sales message needs, but they give human beings something to tie the words to (see Figure 5.8).

The Importance of Simplicity. Does this mean that in order to keep attention the marketer must add a jumble of color and activity to make the message more persuasive? No—far from it, in fact. Simplicity of purpose and design is absolutely essential. One photograph has been proved to have more effectiveness in advertising than many. Complexity of symbols and design (let alone message) distracts, tires, and confuses the eye.

If you want to make a point about the clear tones of a flute, you must use the whole orchestra sparingly—or maybe not at all—when you demonstrate. If you have an offer to make, you must not overwhelm the presentation of the offer with a cute, distracting picture. Arguments and ex-

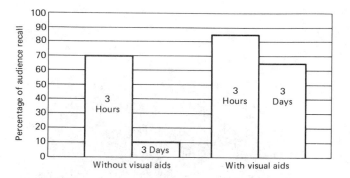

Figure 5.8. Recall lasting more than three days is improved more than 50 percent when visuals are added to the presentation. (From *Small Business Report,* August 1983.)

planations about benefits must build overwhelmingly, but with unswerving purposefulness. Resist every temptation to add even one element that can distract even one prospect from the selling process.

Strive for Memorability. This process of exciting the reader and arousing interest in the message requires the creation of symbols and vivid presentations that will have lasting impact on the memory. This is very important when your sale involves several contacts with the prospect and when repeat business is important.

The human memory is fragile, requiring repetition and symbols to help it work best. Logos, tag lines, and constantly recurring themes should be developed and consistently used to help the prospect fix on which product and which company he or she should remember.

A decade ago, a Chevrolet dealer in Cleveland (Ohio), used a rousing theme song in radio commercials. The words "Sha-a-a-ke Hands with Hugh Gibson, at Central Chevrolet" were repeated so often and with such a memorable refrain that strangers would stop Gibson on the street just to shake his hand. New and used car shoppers carried the message in their minds when they walked into Central Chevrolet's showroom, and many of them seemed to get great satisfaction out of remembering the song when the deal was closed and Gibson shook their hands.

Although Walter P. Margulies (Lippincott & Margulies, New York), and other skilled practitioners in corporate identification have often proved that updating and changing identifying symbols can be very successful, marketers should make such changes with extreme care. The investment in memorability and positive associations is won at great cost and over a long

Figure 5.9. Pratt & Whitney Aircraft's Government Products Division in West Palm Beach, Florida, wanted a symbol for its 25th anniversary. More important, it needed a message and theme that would spotlight its long-standing partnership with free world defense agencies. A seal was created for the event and combined with a well-conceived plan for communicating Pratt & Whitney's pride and respect for its customer. A subtle 25 in the waving flag added a sophisticated depth to the symbol designed by Ron Caron.

period of time. After all, the persuasion process requires credibility. If we change our tune, we risk losing our followers.

Get Your Audience to Take Part. If you have ever attended a county fair, you may have watched someone hawking a simple kitchen device like a vegetable peeler. With spellbinding speed, hypnotic words ensnare an audience, and sooner or later someone in the crowd has been persuaded to step up and participate in the demonstration. Enthusiasm grows as freshly peeled carrots and apples are passed around for tasting.

Audience participation in the sale is a long-used device in direct mail as well as personal selling. More and more, editors of magazines use it to increase reader involvement.

Once you have elicited a reaction, you not only have gained attention but also have created a confidence in exchange, an expectation of further benefit. Successful direct mail pieces ask readers to "place this silver decal in the spot marked A to set your subscription in motion" or "punch out the *yes* sticker, moisten the back, and attach here." Successful sales meetings ask sales personnel to "take the quick test at the end of the day and win 50 silver dollars." Successful advertisements often ask readers to "return the coupon today for a free booklet on 'The Seven Ways You Can Increase Your Profits.'" Successful charitable organizations often put potential major contributors or fundraisers on a committee or a board. Marketers know that participation means cooperation and mutual attention and signifies that the prospect is responsive.

Step Three: Inform and Explain Why

Once you have attracted attention and excited interest, you must build a solid case—one that will prompt an exchange, persuading the audience to give up something to get your offer. This means a careful stitching together of all the reasons why someone should buy. And it is at this point that many people ask, "Shouldn't my copy be short, to keep people from getting bored?"

The answer is usually "yes and no." Yes, if your copy is boring, because you will lose your readers and need not waste time trying to persuade. But no, your copy should not be short if it is interesting to the person you want to reach, the one who needs to make an informed decision about your product or your organization. In the latter case, long copy may make a great deal of sense.

John Caples, a distinguished advertising copywriter, is an advocate of research on scientific methods of testing advertising effectiveness. He champions long copy in his book *Tested Advertising Methods:*

> Advertisers who can trace the direct sales results from their ads use long copy because it pulls better than short copy. For example, the book club advertisers, the record clubs, the correspondence school advertisers, and the makers of various items sold by mail use ads that contain 500 to 1500 words of copy. Also you will find that real-estate advertisers, patent medicine advertisers, and classified advertisers put as much selling into their ads as the space will allow. These people cannot afford to run so-called "reminder copy." They have to get immediate sales from every ad.[21]

The messages you develop—whether you are president of a growing business announcing a new product, head of a small service firm, or a writer urging improved safety procedures in the operations department of a large industrial organization—should have as much urgency and need for response as these advertisers have. If not, perhaps the messages are not worth sending.

Be Specific. To be persuasive, you must give facts, many specific facts that apply to your product but not to anyone else's. The requirement to be specific in writing is stressed at great length in every book on effective writing skills, but it is most important in advertising and marketing. Herbert L. Kahn offers a handy guide that he calls "The Pocketknife Rule."[22] He reasons that if you can intelligently put the word "pocketknife" in place of the name of your product in the material you are writing, then the sales message is so general and vague as to be worthless.

In the Sony Trinitron brochure discussed earlier, we read that typical TV sets give "a very coarse dot pitch: 0.60mm . . .[but] Sony's CRT designers have brought dot pitch down to a mere 0.25mm. As a result, the CPD-1201 and CPD-9000 have the highest horizontal resolution of any monitors in their price class. You get crisp, vivid character displays with incredible sharpness."

Like Sony, we must make sure that generalities get pared down to specifics: "Reduces the time to operate" should be changed to explicit measures of performance: "cuts machine operation time at least 45 percent." "Huge cost savings" should be changed to the more concrete "Customers have saved $300,000 and more a year with just one of these new cutting machines." "Increased profits" should be thrown in the wastebasket and replaced with something more specific: "The savings in reduced downtime and the 37 percent increase in goods processed can increase profits by 200 percent or more." "Many reports" should be changed to "33 reports."

The reason specifics are so important is that most people have, at one time or another, responded to flaky claims and false advertisers and thus are understandably suspicious. Grand statements and sweeping generalities have all been heard before. The audience's frame of mind is "show me, prove it to me, tell me the real story."

Persuade Multiple Levels of Supervision When Necessary. When you are selling in an organizational environment, the sale is often not completed until several individuals have agreed to it. This is true for anything that takes employee time or company funds. With great salesmanship or luck, you may be able to reach all decision makers at once. But more often you reach each one, one at a time. For example, when you make a successful presentation, your prospect will internalize your ideas and pass them to the next level of management (or to the controller) for approval. You must help by giving your prospect the tools needed. This is the only way you will get the funding or resources you need.

This concept is often misunderstood by presenters, who do not fully realize that the visual and oral presentation is the tool used to send the information up the chain of management.

If the presentation includes slides and reprints of these slides, the visuals should be much more than statistics. The statistics need explanation and reference. Compare these two sets of data:

	Widget Marketing
30% increase in sales	New Packages Make Major Impact
17% more orders	30% more sales
89% fewer returns	17% more orders
	89% fewer returns

The "slide" on the left is good on statistics, but will the audience remember what is being talked about? The "slide" on the right not only tells what is being talked about but also enhances the message. If the new packaging resulted in the sales increases, you will want to make sure everyone knows it—especially senior management.

Be Personal. If you have attracted your prospect and sustained his or her interest so that many benefits of your ideas are being discussed, it is important that you do not lapse into a "we, the company" formula. Nothing is more boring than hearing about "the company" in its collective wisdom.

In contrast, nothing is more interesting to the prospect than the prospect. Everything should be couched in terms of benefits to "me." For example, I yawn when you proudly announce that "we have been in business since 1948." But I take more notice if you tell me, "You can be confident in our ability at National Acme to deliver widgets because more than 73,400 satisfied customers have been served since 1948."

The idea is to think along with your prospective customers. Imagine yourself in their shoes, sitting at their desks, or standing at their machines. Enter their private world. Try to understand how life looks to an individual prospect, using every manner of research possible to get a complete understanding of probable likes, dislikes, needs, wants, concerns, abilities. How else can you speak directly and persuasively to your prospect?

The effectiveness of this personal, one-on-one tone was once described by David Ogilvy, founding partner of Ogilvy & Mather and a member of the Copywriters Hall of Fame:

We, for some years, did the advertising for Helena Rubinstein. I wasn't very good at writing that myself, because I'm not terribly interested in lipstick and face powder. You see, the posture I always take when I finally close the door and have to write the ad is this; I always pretend that I'm sitting beside a woman at a dinner party, and she asks me for advice about which product should she buy and where should she buy it. So then I write down what I would say to her. I give her facts, facts, facts. I try to make them interesting, fascinating if possible, and personal—I don't write to the crowd. I try to write from one human being to another human being in the second person, singular. And I try not to bore the poor woman to death and try to make it as real and personal as possible.[23]

People will become more involved in what you are saying if you address them this way. Gary A. Miller and C. Winston Borgen, in their book *Professional Selling: Inside and Out,* tell us that we should express benefits in personal terms: "This hammer will last a long time" is revised by the authors to "You will never have to buy another hammer."[24]

It is true that explanations of the people and the philosophy of the company are often quite important to the growing esteem you are creating. But you must still put these messages in the form of customer benefits versus company prowess. The slick phrase "Acme is dedicated to customer service" is much more believable when couched in more specific, personal language: "You can pick up the phone and reach a department of 12 customer service experts who will dispatch service specialists within two hours."

Use Appropriate Vocabulary. While constructing your case, you must speak in a language that the reader understands. Write in his or her vernacular, not yours, being careful to avoid terms and phrases that are not easily understood. This may sound obvious, but it is painfully clear that a great percentage of speeches and organizational presentations are beyond the comprehension of listeners. Even more important, technical presentations are often beyond the understanding of decision makers!

Engineers, technicians, computer scientists, chemists—specialists in highly technical fields—often feel that their prospects and colleagues know and understand exactly what they are saying. This may be true. But why speak in such technical terms that you risk shutting out *any* listener or reader who might affect the decision to use your product? Perhaps the controller, who approves all the organization's expenditures, does not understand. Or maybe the technician is now in administration and has not kept up with technical changes and terms. Yet these are the people who also must be persuaded.

The same is true for financial experts and personnel administrators: too much professional jargon will lose your reader or listener. Words can be either obstacles or facilitators. They can open minds and keep them open or set jaws in resistance and raise don't-try-to-sell-me hackles.

Obstacle Words	*Facilitators*
problem	issue
price	investment
cost	value
contract	agreement
buy	own
fix	solve

Use Natural Language. By the same token, if your attempt to persuade becomes mired in stuffy, pompous, and awkward phrasing, the same result will ensue: lost readers or listeners. You must speak real language, as if you are speaking face-to-face with someone you know. A good exercise is to read your material out loud to make sure the words would read well to your audience:

The Read-It-Out-Loud Test

If the phrases are not comfortably said,

If it makes you sound officious,

If you feel awkward or embarrassed,

If the sentences take longer than one breath,

If the promises are slick and slippery,

If they are boastful and empty,

change them, make them believable.

Phrases like "the best," "unique," and "the finest" are not believable. Readers of such hyperbole will stop reading.

Step Four: Satisfy Concerns, Answer Objections

Step four in the persuasion process is tricky. Objectivity is your strong suit, because you make a far more persuasive case if the reader believes you have been fair and honest in your presentation.

You can state your case in a positive way, but do not bring up objections in print. Why mention something your prospect may not need to consider? Lumley, author of *Sell It by Mail,* cautions writers of direct mail literature against wasting valuable copy space answering objections. He points out that "80 percent of recipients are the ones with serious objections and aren't reading anyway. Since you are writing to the 20 percent that already have an interest, you don't need to counter the objections. Bringing up an objection only succeeds in bringing it to the prospect's attention.[25]

How do you then deal with resistance from the prospect? By removing concerns through guarantees. The more complete these guarantees are, the more powerfully they will move your prospect to consent. An expert in placement of workers in the automotive industry knew exactly how to put it in this letter to car dealers:

> Our service is 100% GUARANTEED. You pay only 10% of the estimated annual earnings of the ACPC candidate you select. We will bill you on hiring. If there is any reason for separation in 90 days, you will receive— no questions asked—all your money back. Period. No strings attached.[26]

One wonders how anyone could resist that!

If you anticipate objections ahead of time, your selling words should cover all the bases in a positive manner before the objections can even be raised.

Use Third-Party Endorsements Whenever You Can. You can do more to strengthen your case: you can use third-party endorsements. Prospects have a natural desire to feel that they will not be "had" and have a normal disposition to follow intelligent leaders and colleagues, people who have been there before. This helps to mitigate some of the worries about making a commitment to something new.

So promote new members of your organization and tell me what they get from belonging, if you want my membership. Share a customer name or two—or, better yet, show me customer pictures—and tell me what they like about your product. Tell me why Sam Sanders likes being a cost reducer in the purchasing department. Good testimonials impress.

A brochure for Mitimite Software prominently displays the following testimonials, giving the name, job title, and company of each testifier:

> We had another package installed. Finally we found Mitimite; it's a good fit. . . . We've doubled our sales in three years . . . I give a lot of credit to Mitimite. . . . Now that it's installed, we are still impressed.[27]

Step Five: Ask for a Commitment to Action

You have attracted, excited, even convinced your customers. Now you must ask for the order, right? Well, that is partially true. Experts in direct mail recommend asking for the order immediately, even on the envelope. ("Send this important coupon in today") or at the beginning of the letter ("Send in this coupon for 50 percent savings"), and as often as five to six times more in the letter. If that is still not enough, use a postscript at the end to restate your case, enticing with one more inducement.

If you do not make your offer right up front, but wait until the middle of the last paragraph, you have a high probability of losing the sale. Only a few of your prospects will read the entire letter—even if they are buyers.

This is true for personal selling, as well. "A study made by a midwestern university several years ago found that 46 percent of all sales people asked for the order only one time. However, studies show that the professional salesperson asks for the order three to five times in a single transaction."[28] Making the assumption that a prospect will at some point be ready to buy, the professional seller asks for the order as many as six times, because five "no's" and one "yes" add up to "yes."

Do you want your prospect to make a deposit today? Ask for it. Do you want approval of your plan from management? Ask right away. Do you want employees to sign up for a new training program? Ask them to— right in your headline, because they may never read the article.

Employee newspapers are used to announce new programs, yet most readers do not know what the organization wants them to do because they read only the headlines or lead paragraphs, often not getting the message buried in the story. The action request should be in the headline.

In every marketing communication, make the required buying action crystal clear and easy to do. Give the audience postage-paid return envelopes, a toll-free number to call, an employee hotline number, a drop box, a prominently displayed local phone number, coupons that are easy to clip.

Asking for the order is the fundamental difference between communication in general and marketing communication in particular. In communication we exchange ideas or transfer information from one person to another. To be successful, some purists add, communication also requires the exchange of understanding. The communicator tries to take facts or ideas and somehow transfer them to the other person so that the other person gets the basic message. However, in marketing communication, there is a requirement for commitment in the exchange of information, and the object or prospect of our attention is expected to end up in co-ownership of the idea (or the product). In marketing communication, we expect the prospect to buy in to the message by buying our product, investing in our business, signing up for a cause, or committing time and effort.

The process of marketing communication often requires the receiver of the information to give up something dear: cold, hard cash; already limited hours; the temporary escapism of indecision. This challenge of persuading the prospect to give up something is what makes the marketing communication process so difficult and what makes proven selling techniques so important to learn and use.

Step Six: Protect Your Credibility

The objective of the persuasion process is to build credibility. This is critical to the success of the project. Everything you say will be judged against what the product or organization delivers.

First impressions are lasting impressions. If the brochure is weak, sloppy, out of focus, arrogant, or puny, that will color how your product

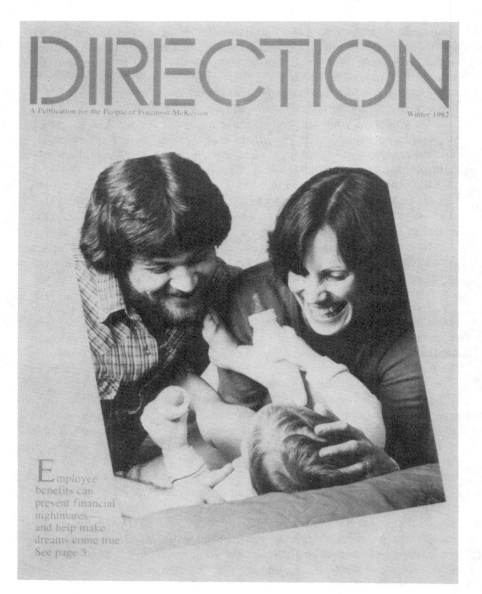

Figure 5.10. Here is an excellent example of persuasion for an internal audience. The rare quality photo and the "dreams come true" copy convince you even before you look inside that the benefits offered by Foremost-McKesson are designed to make dreams of the good life come true. (IABC, *Excellence in Communication,* 1983, p. 30)

or your organization will be perceived. High-quality products should be matched by high quality in marketing communication. A sales presentation for advanced computer technology in use on the manufacturing floor should not use 1940s technology to create the charts. A brochure explaining the outstanding quality of the organization should feature an outstanding printing job. Unless you are trying to telegraph that your service is cut-rate or discount, it pays to look prosperous.

Be able to substantiate everything you say. Give proof. Research. Confirm. "Assertions are easy. Support is more difficult," Peter Jacobi wrote recently in the *Ragan Report.* "Assertions without support lack meaning, import, impact. They are not likely to be remembered, either. You can say Azzaz Corporation is the most progressive outfit in all of the Southwest, but unless you can provide evidence, the assertion amounts to an empty boast.[29]

Consistency is everything. Do not convey the wrong image of your organization by carelessness or inattention to detail. For example, you say in your visitors' brochure that precision drilling and quality forming are hallmarks of your manufacturing skills; but while visiting the plant, customers notice litter in manufacturing aisles, haphazardly placed tools, and dirty work stations. Little pride in workmanship shows. You say in your annual report that customers are your most important asset, but the only people pictures are expensive looking, stiff and unsmiling head shots of the top three officials. You say in your plant newspaper that employees are the most important asset, but the employees have just received this year's slick annual report, which boasts how customers are your most important asset. To make matters worse, the internal newspaper is printed on flimsy stock, poorly written, and filled with items that have little perceived value to the employees.

If your marketing communication is strong, impressive, and substantial but the product is not, and customers see the disparity, you have another problem: nothing you say in the future will be believed. Ad agencies know that nothing can kill a product faster than good advertising. As the chemical company president said in the phone call described at the beginning of this discussion: "If your product is as good as your brochure, and it *really* does what you say it does, you've sold me already. But let me be right up front—I'm a tough customer."

NOTES

1. John Merwin, "A Tale of Two Worlds," *Forbes,* 16 June 1986, 101.
2. Brochure, Sony Communications Products Company, Park Ridge, N.J.

3. On the average, spreads have 60 percent more impact than single-page advertisements, and research shows that people rarely miss them entirely.
4. "Bleed Ads Attract 21% More Attention," *Folio,* November 1983, 30. McGraw-Hill Study, Laboratory of Advertising Performance.
5. Harry H. Gray, *Gray Matter,* United Technologies Corporation, 1983.
6. Harry H. Gray, remarks at a United Technologies Communications Workshop, 1983.
7. John Caples, *Tested Advertising Methods* (Englewood Cliffs, N.J.: Prentice-Hall, 1974), 17.
8. Philip Ward Burton, *Which Ad Pulled Best?* (Chicago: Crain Books, 1981), 77.
9. Philip Ward Burton, *Which Ad Pulled Best? Teacher's Guide* (Chicago: Crain Books, 1981), 12.
10. Ibid.
11. Jack Z. Sissors, "Suggestions for Improving Publications' Communication through the Use of Type and Design" (Evanston, Ill.: Medill School of Journalism, Northwestern University).
12. Tessa R. Gaston and William Russell Savage, "What Do Readers Want? How Do You Know What They Want?" *Journal of Organizational Communication* 10, no 4. (1981), 20.
13. Lewis Donohew, "Reader Arousal: It Makes a Difference How You Write It," *Journal of Organizational Communication* 9, no. 2 (1980), 9–10.
14. Edward J. Epstein, *The Rise and Fall of Diamonds* (New York: Simon & Schuster, 1982).
15. Tom Mahr, "Movers for Miners," *Oilways* no. 4 (Houston, TX: Exxon Company U.S.A., 1983), 12.
16. Ibid.
17. Robert B. Cialdini, *Influence: How and Why People Agree to Do Things* (New York: Morrow, 1984), 29.
18. Sissors, "Suggestions for Improving Publications' Communication."
19. Ibid.
20. James E. A. Lumley, *Sell It by Mail* (New York: Wiley, 1986), 54.
21. Caples, *Tested Advertising Methods,* 138.
22. Herbert L. Kahn, "Your Own Brand of Advertising for Nonconsumer Products," *Harvard Business Review* (January/February 1986), 25.
23. Denis Higgins, "David Ogilvy Talks about How He Writes Copy," *Advertising Age,* 15 March 1965, 126.
24. Gary A. Miller and C. Winston Borgen, *Professional Selling: Inside and Out* (New York: Van Nostrand-Reinhold, 1979).
25. Lumley, *Sell It by Mail,* 80–81.
26. Direct mail letter, Automotive Career Placement & Counselors, Springfield, Mass., 1985.
27. Brochure, Mitimite Systems, Clough Management Services, Montreal, 1984.
28. Miller and Borgen, *Professional Selling,* 218.
29. Peter P. Jacobi, *Ragan Report,* 12 April 1982.

CHAPTER 6

Healthcare Marketing: Challenges and Opportunities

James E. McHaney*

Healthcare is often called the last frontier of marketing. Formalized healthcare marketing began in the early 1970s and was of necessity disguised as community relations by a few forward-thinking pioneers.

As healthcare has matured, it has gone through the classic sequence of maturing products: manufacturing or simply meeting demand, encountering financial constraints and demands, and finally becoming market-driven and thus subject to the laws of supply and demand.

Payment for services in the United States in the 1960s and 1970s was on a "cost plus" basis, which allowed the proliferation of glaring supply and demand inefficiencies under U.S. Medicare/Medicaid legislation because there was no upper limit on reimbursement. Currently, demand for traditional inpatient care is down—and decreasing—and supply, including new outpatient treatment options and locations, is at an all-time high and increasing.

Thus a need arose for professionally trained marketers and state-of-the-art marketing programs. Sadly, too many healthcare marketers do not match, either in training or in position, the requirements to direct marketing for healthcare institutions, companies, or individual physicians faced with tremendous market pressures. In fact, most of what has been called healthcare marketing calls to mind the wagon train of stupid travelers who drew their wagons into a circle—and pointed their rifles inward.

MARKET PRESSURES ON THE HEALTHCARE SYSTEM

In any well-researched marketing strategic plan the environments of the past and present are assessed and the future predicted in the light of various

---

*James E. McHaney is chairman of Magliaro & McHaney in LaJolla, California. He is a member of IABC's marketing council and has won several awards for marketing campaigns, including IABC's Gold Quill.

options. Before we look at the past and present problems inherent in health-care marketing and decide what we can correct in the future, we should explore certain market pressures. These pressures apply primarily to health-care delivery systems based on a free-enterprise model, not to those which are operated solely by national governments.

In order for healthcare providers to determine their proper position, marketing thrust, and service mix in tomorrow's market, they must first clearly understand the direction in which healthcare is moving in their mar-ketplace. In the United States the major social, technological, economic, and political forces that are affecting and will continue to affect the health-care system are: (1) an aging population; (2) medical applications of bio-logical and physical scientific research; and (3) increased competition among healthcare providers and deregulation and privatization of healthcare de-livery.

Aging of the Population

The graying of America has been widely discussed in the popular press and in public policy debates about the cost and the capacity of the United States to finance social benefit programs for its older citizens. Recent and pro-jected growth in federal pension and health benefits since the U.S. Social Security Act was expanded to include Medicare and Medicaid is shown in Table 6.1.

Elderly Americans spend between three and four times more per person on healthcare (estimates vary among the American Hospital Association, the Health Care Financing Administration, and the U.S. Senate Committee on Aging) than those younger than age 65. The proportion of persons 65 years of age or older is expected to increase from 11 percent today to 20 percent in 1990, so these expenditures are likely to increase—especially with

TABLE 6.1. FEDERAL PENSION AND HEALTH BENEFITS AS A PERCENT-AGE OF GNP AND THE FEDERAL BUDGET (1985-2040)

Year	Pension programs % GNP	Health programs % GNP	Total programs % GNP	Total programs % budget
1965	4.1	0.3	4.4	24.90
1980	6.5	2.3	8.8	38.20
1990	6.6	3.1	9.7	40.40
2010	6.0	4.7	10.7	44.60
2040	7.0	7.5	14.5	60.47

Source: Adapted from J. L. Palmer and B. B. Torrey, "Health Care Financing and Pension Pro-grams," in John L. Palmer and Gregory B. Mills, eds., *Federal Budget Policy in the 1980s* (Wash-ington, D.C.: Urban Institute), 124. Copyright 1984 by the Urban Institute.

the projected quadrupling of the "old old" population (85 years or older) during the first half of the twenty-first century.

Technological Advances

Advances in medical technology stem from scientific research in both the biological and physical sciences, such as genetic engineering to equip monoclonal antibodies with radioactive isotopes to attack oncogenes, using the body's own cells as medical "magic bullets" to fight cancer. Adaptations of physical science breakthroughs have generated new technology using lasers, magnetic resonance, and ultrasound waves for new machines and procedures that have dramatically changed the practice of medicine in recent years. Most have reduced in-hospital time or eliminated the necessity for inpatient care, while at the same time requiring heavy expenditures for equipment purchase and staff training.

Increased Competition and Deregulation

In the United States the economic and political forces of competition and deregulation are a reflection of the current preference for free-market solutions to social problems. Healthcare cost containment is achieved not by limiting capital facility expenditures, but by encouraging competition for limited healthcare funds.

These social forces, individually and together, will continue to change the practice of medicine as they have in recent years. Healthcare for an aging population is already a major proportion of most community hospitals' service focus. The increasing elderly population also will mean an increased demand for "new parts" for aging bodies—fueled by parallel advances in immunology research and transplant techniques. Technological developments also will increasingly affect where care is delivered, as advances in high technology make it feasible to bring healthcare to the consumer at home or in outpatient settings.

CURRENT TRENDS IN HEALTHCARE DELIVERY

Considering these social, technological, economic, and political factors in terms of their current effect on the healthcare delivery system brings three trends into focus: (1) declining inpatient services and physician visits, (2) increased use of fixed-payment systems, and (3) more direct involvement by the major purchasers of healthcare in cost-containment activities. The excess capacity of the healthcare system has received extensive attention in the popular media and in business publications in the United States. Thus, a recent *Harvard Business Review* article estimated that there are at least

25 percent too many hospital beds today and forecast a nationwide physician surplus of 70,000 by 1990.[1]

Decline in Hospital and Physician Visits

Pressures to control costs and changing technology are reducing hospital use dramatically; many hospitals will have to make extensive changes to survive. In a poll of U.S. hospital administrators conducted by National Research Corporation for *Modern Healthcare* magazine, two-thirds of the respondents reported a decrease in occupancy from the prior year. Fifty-two percent reported less than 60 percent average annual occupancy for 1985.[2] In the first nine months of 1985, total hospital admissions fell 5.1 percent compared to the same period in 1984. Average length of stay declined 7.9 percent, from 6.3 to 5.8 days.[3] Hospital admissions in the United States declined from 6.6 million in 1980 to 5.8 million in 1984, according to the American Hospital Association.

Visits to physicians also have decreased significantly during the past 10 years. In the United States the mean weekly total of patient visits per physician declined from 130 in 1975 to 119 in 1984.[4] The average number of weekly office visits declined from 95 in 1974 to 75 in 1984 (see Figure 6.1).

Both hospitals and physicians are losing patients to new, specialized outpatient centers for surgery and minor emergency treatment. The number of freestanding surgery centers increased from 212 in 1982 to 330 in 1984; emergency clinics (also called *emergicenters* and *urgent care centers*) grew from 260 in 1981 to 2,500 in 1985.[5]

Increased Use of Fixed-Payment Systems

Much of the recent decline in hospital use and revenues is the result of a fundamental change in payment policies—specifically, a trend away from

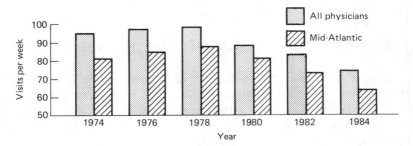

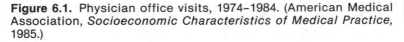

Figure 6.1. Physician office visits, 1974–1984. (American Medical Association, *Socioeconomic Characteristics of Medical Practice,* 1985.)

retroactive fee-for-service reimbursement to fixed-price payment systems under which the hospital *shares* financial risk. Medicare's Diagnosis Related Group (DRG) system pays on a combination of illness and length of stay. Health Maintenance Organizations (HMOs) provide comprehensive prepaid care, charging a set monthly fee for a comprehensive set of services. Preferred Provider Organizations (PPOs) most commonly offer prospectively negotiated per diem rates, generally less than usual and customary charges, with the implied promise (but no guarantee) of volume referrals.

Health Maintenance Organizations grew more rapidly from June 1984 to June 1985 than during any previous year, according to the latest HMO census conducted by the InterStudy organization of Excelsior, Minnesota. Between 1981 and 1985 HMO enrollment nearly doubled, from 10.2 million to 18.9 million members. The number of HMOs grew markedly as well— from 243 in 1981 to 393 in 1985. By 1990, the number of HMO plans is expected to exceed 800, with total enrollment forecast at 53 million.[6] The growth of HMOs is likely to continue at a high rate as Medicare capitation contracting, which builds in limits on the amounts to be repaid, increases. The U.S. Tax Equity and Reform Act of 1982 authorized the Health Care Financing Administration (HCFA) to contract with federally qualified and state-licensed HMOs or other qualified plans (called Competitive Medical Plans) to serve Medicare beneficiaries; however, the payment structure and administrative regulations were not adopted until January 1985. In just one year, HCFA had contracted with 100 health plans to serve nearly 1 million Medicare patients.[7]

As one might expect, physician affiliation with HMOs is increasing, particularly among younger doctors. A 1983 American Medical Association survey found that 39 percent of physicians under age 36 were employees rather than owners of their practices, compared to 23 percent of those between the ages of 36 and 45. HMOs offer larger starting salaries than a new physician can usually earn in private practice; however, 1984 median pretax income for all self-employed medical practitioners in the United States was $100,000, compared to $74,000 for physician employees.[8] HMOs contain costs primarily by controlling inpatient use of facilities.

Health Insurance Cost Containment by Businesses

In addition to governmental health policy changes, businesses are shaping the future of healthcare by becoming more aggressively cost-conscious purchasers of healthcare coverage. More than 150 business health coalitions throughout the United States are devising new strategies and policies to decrease employers' share of cost by imposing higher copayments and deductibles (patients' share of medical costs) and by offering more managed care programs, in which one source has responsibility for all healthcare.

Major employers today are likely to be self-insured—about 62 percent of those with more than 500 workers in 1985, according to a recent survey of business insurance agents.[9] Insurance industry analysts and claims administrators are predicting that the real growth in self-funding will occur in small businesses, now that market forces have motivated insurance companies to provide stop/loss protection (which limits an insurer's risks by putting caps on payments) against high individual or total claims.

In summary, physicians as well as hospitals are experiencing a vastly changing healthcare environment. Constraints on use and payment are expanding. Alternative delivery systems are growing and fostering these forces. Healthcare buyers (government, insurance companies, and employers) have strengthened their roles in healthcare decision making. Competition among providers has increased and will continue to do so. Marketing communicators are already faced with meeting such effects on hospital patient and revenue volume as:

A decrease in inpatient tests, number of surgeries, and average length of stay

A shift of services to ambulatory care providers

An increase in severity of inpatient complaints and illnesses

An increase in "brokering" patients to appropriate points in the healthcare system

An increase in competition among physicians, hospitals, and corporations

A forced realignment of organization mission

A life-and-death dependence on financial controls and marketing

TRADITIONAL HEALTHCARE "MARKETING" AND WHY IT WILL NOT WORK IN THE FUTURE

Marketing of healthcare has traditionally been based in public relations—volunteer teas, "Aren't we wonderful!" events, and all the gushy, warm stories in the media. That is the typical way that healthcare has been presented to the American public—not from the supply-and-demand standpoint. Several people have dubbed this approach "Golly Gee." In the past, hospitals' annual reports never discussed healthcare as a business; they focused on how many pounds of laundry they processed and how many warm meals they served.

Golly Gee has a cohort named "Glitz," which is simply the "Aren't we wonderful!'' approach taken a step further: "If you are going to have open-heart surgery, you ought to have it here because we have valet parking and we put flowers in your room." While a favorable image is necessary, hospitals and physicians will not survive solely on the basis of good community relations or even consumer-based advertising. Yet that seems to be the major strategy of many so-called marketers. Any marketer worthy of the title will realize that the key element in marketing any product or service is the distribution channel. To date, very few have paid attention to how patients enter and move through the healthcare system. To cite an example from the food industry: If you were Kellogg and you were going to introduce a new cereal, you could spend great sums of money merchandising the cereal to the general public—but if the grocer won't put it on the shelves, the consumer can't buy it. This is the way healthcare marketers must start thinking. If the doctor does not sell the services of the hospital, if he doesn't "put it on the shelf," it is not going to do you any good to spend marketing or advertising money to promote your services. In a recent editorial *Modern Healthcare* magazine commented:

> In fact, it probably is more efficient for hospitals to support physicians' marketing efforts than it is to spend money on consumer advertising. That's because the physician remains the key player in determining consumers' selections of healthcare providers. Physicians make more than 80 percent of the hospital selections for patients not in managed care plans (one provider for all care), yet hospitals spend less than 15 percent of their marketing budgets to attract and assist them. It just doesn't make sense.[10]

Also, traditional healthcare marketing has not segmented or targeted audiences. As a result, for example, people who are 65 years old are getting information about obstetric services from hospitals through direct mail or other targeted media. Hospitals have not segmented their audiences so that messages about specific services reach prospective patients who can really use the services; consequently, they spend vast sums of money reaching people who can never use the service.

Of course, there is a simple reason for this: Hospitals and physicians want additional patients just like the ones they already have. However, too many cannot tell you, for example, the average age of their obstetric patients. How do you find more just like your patients if you do not know who they are? There also has been an unsophisticated use of existing bases and little effort to define available products or services. Often a thing has been done because "it's sexy" or it has "sizzle" or the staff wants to do it or, worst of all, the other hospital in town is doing it. Hospital public relations staff told administrators 10 years ago that they were really product managers and they should start acting like it. Many administrators did not like hearing this and certainly didn't adapt, but anyone who is a good product manager understands the market and the potential for a product before introducing it into the marketplace.

Another key problem is a strange use of strategic planning—or lack thereof. The hospital administrator says to the marketing person, "We have problems in the emergency room," and the marketer says, "We'll do a brochure." No strategies—just go right to the tactics, to the brochures. That is typical of past healthcare marketing.

Yet another key issue whose solution has eluded many service organizations is that they truly are not customer-oriented. Healthcare providers for years have treated patients like sacks of wheat moved around at will—and then have wondered why people complained about the impersonal care they received. An amazing number of hospitals in the United States pay no attention to patients once they are discharged. A personal example: I was in a hospital for a week; the bill was quite large, but the service had been good and I left with a good feeling about the hospital. About two months later, I received a letter from the hospital's foundation addressed to "Dear Occupant." The letter asked for a contribution to help the hospital buy some new equipment. If the hospital had managed our relationship well, I would have contributed because I was favorably disposed toward the hospital. Instead I was irritated that despite my week-long stay, I was treated like a stranger the hospital did not know or care much about.

In fact, traditional healthcare marketing can be compared to the gentleman farmer who moves from a large city to a rural area to raise chickens. He does not know much about it, but he knows that you need baby chicks if you are going to have a chicken farm. So he goes to the nursery, buys 1,000 baby chicks, and takes them home. Two weeks later he returns to the nursery. The nurseryman (who is delighted to see him, because of the high volume in two weeks) asks, "How are the first 1,000 doing?" And the gentleman farmer says, "Not good. But I have the problem solved. I think I either planted them too close or too deep." This is where healthcare marketing has been. It has not heeded the basic commandments of marketing strategies.

HEALTHCARE MARKETING IN THE FUTURE

A major change in healthcare marketing in the future will be in the amount of financial and human resources allotted to this area of marketing. In 1986 only 10 percent of the hospitals in the U.S. had more than a $1 million marketing budget, with most budgets falling between $50,000 and $150,000. In the future healthcare marketing budgets are likely to be formulated as a percentage of sales—and those budgets will rise continually. One of the nation's midsized hospital chains has set aside at least 4 percent of sales for marketing for each of its hospitals—a major change in direction.

Another trend will be a heavy reliance on trend analysis and market information obtained from physician practices. Most hospitals do not know **demographics**—characteristics such as age, sex, race, educational level, and occupation—of their clientele until patients walk in the front door. How can they influence consumer decisions if they do not know who their consumers are? Physicians' patient bases offer tremendous potential for healthcare marketing. This base allows for demographic analysis and for establishing a potential customer base for many hospitals. Many doctors are now willing to share this demographic data for marketing purposes.

Another change for hospitals that have identified strategies is that value will rest with rapid execution and implementation. An example: Several years ago a Houston hospital decided it could gain a 10 percent share of the existing market for emergency care with an aggressive marketing campaign. For a year and a half staff members planned their campaign. By the time the campaign was launched, the hospital's market share was down 5 percent, the anticipated 10 percent gain was gone, so the hospital was now behind 15 percent. The hospital would have been better off doing nothing rather than spending a year and a half on planning.

There also will be extensive product segmentation—high-tech for the inpatient and consumer-driven for the outpatient. John Naisbitt, author of the bestselling *Megatrends,*[11] says that the high-tech aspect of healthcare in hospitals has made everyone want to return to the friendliness of the family physician or the neighborhood clinic. He makes another excellent comment about segmentation: Just as highways have given us more cars, computers are going to give us more and more segmentation, and marketers are going to be in the forefront. Communicators will need to follow if we are to ensure that promotional funds are spent wisely.

Future healthcare will be noncompetitive with the physician. Much of previous healthcare advertising and marketing has thought: "The physician doesn't count. It's really up to consumers, and we're going to influence those consumers. They're going to read our ad in the morning paper and say, 'I think I need an appendectomy,' and check right in at ten o'clock." This may seem a little far-fetched, but many marketers did think along such lines. Moreover, this antagonism was sometimes fueled by doctors. About five years ago physicians, when approached about marketing, reacted with the ferocity of Attila the Hun. They would not share their patient lists because they feared that hospitals were trying to steal their patients.

The CEO of a large southwestern U.S. hospital makes the point that he feels that hospitals will join with physicians or with insurance companies to control healthcare. However, if hospitals join with insurance companies, they will still need to work with physicians because it is physicians who control patients' selection of hospitals.

The next major trend, already surfacing, is that of managing customer relationships. Leonard Berry of Texas A&M University (College Station), 1987 president of the American Marketing Association, says that "attracting, maintaining, and enhancing customer relations is what relationship marketing's about,"[12] and that service marketing really thinks of marketing not only as acquiring new customers, but as *having* customers. That is the difference; healthcare marketers have not thought about having customers. Our healthcare providers treat patients when they come in for episodic care, then forget about them until they come in again—and do nothing in the meantime to encourage them to come back. Berry says that servicing and selling existing customers is just as important to long-term marketing success as acquiring new customers. In other words, managing the patients you already have is just as important as trying to attract new ones.

Any business person knows that it is much cheaper to do more business with existing clients than it is to find new ones, but that axiom has not been applied to healthcare. Berry also notes that good service is necessary to maintain relationships. In effect, marketing aimed at acquiring the new customer is just the first step in the relationship; the key to creating closer relationships is the service component, and perceptions of service—which are a function of expectations—are all that really matters. Winners in healthcare marketing emphasize customer expectations and research needs; relationships are strengthened by increasing the frequency of professional interaction, by broadening the service line, by offering a unique service, and by building a core service.

SUMMARY

In the future, healthcare marketing will make more use of classic marketing strategies such as the *push/pull strategy*—do you "push" a patient into a hospital through an access point such as a physician or "pull" him or her in through image marketing or advertising. Hospitals will seek to control the distribution system; they will try to move patients to the access points and then capture them, and they will try to better manage long-term relations with patients.

Marketing advertising funds will probably be split somewhat evenly between image advertising and access-point advertising—once again following the practice of industry. The American automobile companies are excellent examples: They spend funds both on creating product image nationally and on moving customers into their local dealers for purchases.

First-rate segmentation technologies involving computer tools will be used to spark word-of-mouth advertising, which is the primary way physicians obtain referrals. Hospitals and physicians will use marketing in a manner approaching the fine tuning of marketing services done by financial organizations 10 to 15 years ago.

Formalized patient relations will be a big-line item on the budget. Most one-time consumers will never complain about healthcare services; if they are unhappy, they will simply not come back.

Sophisticated tracking mechanisms will add credibility to marketing efforts. Several years ago in the Dallas area, some hospitals were spending $12.60 for each new patient attracted to the emergency room through a marketing campaign. The question arose whether this cost was too high. Follow-up research revealed that 30 percent of new hospital users had to be hospitalized, and about 30 percent of them did not have a personal physician. So the expenditure actually turned out to be a low investment for a high return. If you know what you are paying per new patient, and what the long-term value is, you can justify your marketing budget.

Such research provides an opportunity to develop extensive demographics, and the most effective marketing is based on extensive demographics—on knowing exactly who prospects are and how to deliver the proper services to them.

Healthcare marketing is shedding its "last frontier" mentality, as professionals in the field accept the need to consider the forces of supply and demand when developing strategies for their facilities. And they will continue to learn from their colleagues in advertising to meet changing pressures and demands in the healthcare field.

NOTES

1. D.C. Coddington, L.E. Palmquist, and W.V. Trollinger, "Strategies for Survival in the Hospital Industry," *Harvard Business Review,* May/June 1985, 131.
2. Joyce Jensen and Ned Miklovic, "Declining Censuses Plague Hospitals; Administrators Expect Further Drops," *Modern Healthcare,* 16 August 1985, 86–87.
3. American Medical Association, *SMS Report,* 1985.
4. American Medical Association, *Socioeconomic Characteristics of Medical Practice,* 1985.
5. D. Grady, "The Cruel Price of Cutting Medical Expenses," *Discover,* May 1986, 26.

6. *Hospital Management Review,* October 1985, 4.
7. *San Diego* (Calif.) *Tribune,* 20 January 1986.
8. *Wall Street Journal,* 13 January 1986.
9. *Blue Shield Short Shots,* March 1986.
10. "Physician and Hospital Administrators Team Up," editorial in *Modern Healthcare,* 21 November 1985.
11. John Naisbitt, *Megatrends: Ten New Directions Transforming Our Lives* (New York: Warner Books, 1982).
12. From a speech by Leonard Berry at a conference of the American Marketing Association, February 1986.

CHAPTER 7

Marketing a New Product or Service

Wilma Mathews, ABC*

Numerous studies show that marketing is becoming a key concern of communicators for several reasons. First, marketing is an important business tool, and communicators find it necessary to know more about business in order to do their jobs well and move into management. Second, to create the most effective messages, communicators need to target their audiences, and marketing research is an effective tool for this purpose. Third, to be a part of the decision-making team, communicators need to understand the goals of the organization and how application of marketing tools to their communication programs will help organizational goals.

Interest in marketing is developing among communicators in the profit sector (large and small companies) and in not-for-profit institutions and associations, as well as among freelance public relations specialists interested in promoting their services not only to other businesses and the general public but also to such special audiences as employees, opinion leaders, top management, and volunteers.[1]

Some years ago, when AT&T was gingerly putting its big toe into the vast waters of the marketing ocean, each of us in public relations was starting to think about what our roles would be in the "new" AT&T; few if any of us had ever had to think about marketing. For years we had been the only game in town when it came to telecommunications, and the very thought that we would have to *sell* our products and services was anathema to us all.

An early internal paper on marketing[2] talked about the "augmented product"—that is, "what companies add to their factory output in the form of packaging, services, customer advice, financing, delivery arrangements, warehousing and other things people value—all the benefits buyers *think* they receive when they buy the product. By definition, the 'augmented product' is whatever the customer *thinks* it is."

This anonymous author continued: "So, the first step in managing our

---

*Wilma Mathews, ABC, is manager of public relations for AT&T in Morristown, New Jersey. She is first vice chairman of the IABC Foundation and an accredited business communicator. She is also co-author of *On Deadline: Managing Media Relations*.

customers' perceptions of us is to manage the image we project, starting with the physical appearance of the products we sell. The next step is to manage our *reputation*, keeping in mind that our customers buy more than our products—they buy the company that makes them.''

In short, then, it is the *company* that we in public relations are selling. Our communication strategy is not specifically product- or service-based. It is directed at defining what we want our ultimate customers to think of the company. Products are offered as examples, as proof that the organization's desired reputation is deserved.

For the marketing-communication professional, therefore, marketing a product or service is not a one-step process dealing with a singular item. It involves a mix of the marketing and public relations processes, ideologies, skills, talents, tools, and missions.

While marketing deals with primary constituencies (those people who may actually buy a product or service), communicators deal with tertiary constituencies (people in the financial community, the employee body, the shareholder community) who may not buy the product or service but who will buy the image of the company.

For the communicator who wishes to become a marketing-communication professional, the merging of marketing and public relations functions can be awkward at first. But a look at how the two operations mix, an understanding of how to position a product or service and then advertise it, a grasp of the relationship between advertising and publicity, and, finally, a mastery of the many tools available will make the communicator an integral part of the marketing–public relations team.

THE MARKETING AND COMMUNICATION MIX

Of the nearly 250,000 communication professionals in North America, fewer than 11 percent are now working in departments where they use marketing techniques regularly. This is a gain of 3 percent over just two years ago, though it is far below the proportion of communicators who have indicated an interest in the use of marketing techniques.[3]

This growth in marketing brings a predictable confusion about terms, turfs, and titles. While there are differences between marketing and public relations, there is one thought that many professionals subscribe to:

> Marketing and public relations are complementary functions, but their objectives are different. One oversimplified way of looking at them is that marketing is something you *do* and public relations is something you *have*. You can stop doing marketing and your customers will dry up. You can

stop tending to public relations but nothing will dry up except your good-will. You will continue to *have* public relations—your public will continue to form opinions about you. . . . [4]

The Differences between Marketing and Public Relations

One of the basic differences between the two groups is that, for the most part, "marketing has always been a very quantitative discipline, where[as] public relations and communications have been very qualitative."[5]

This difference starts in college, where marketing is taught as a part of the business school curriculum; public relations and communication are taught principally in journalism and mass communication schools. In business, marketing and public relations appear in different slots on the organizational chart, increasing the perceived difference between the two groups.

Another significant difference is the way each group relates to the bottom line of the organization. Marketing personnel can point directly to the contributions they make to the company: the numbers of products sold, the numbers of people who have chosen a service. For many years, public relations practitioners have been unable—some say unwilling—to relate their effort to the bottom line. While this is changing, marketing has several credible years' head start on the public relations groups.

Another problem is the perception of public relations and what it can do for a marketing program. One author suggests that marketing public relations is not considered up front in the discussion of objectives and strategies "for a lot of reasons having to do with the visibility and understanding of what public relations is and does, but probably more likely because public relations doesn't command big marketing dollars and therefore, in the eyes of the marketing manager, can't be very important."[6]

The Advantages of Combining Marketing and Public Relations

Such problems aside, there is a growing awareness that marketing and public relations are becoming intertwined, and for good reasons. When the strengths of the two specialties are combined, the resulting talents, strategies, and objectives are of significant value to the bottom line of the organization.

Both marketing and public relations attempt to persuade people to *do* something. That persuasion may be directed toward getting a person to buy a product or enroll for a service or simply think well of the organization, but both marketing and public relations are in the persuasion business.

And both bring strengths to the union. Public relations can bring cost effectiveness, its ability to extend the reach of advertising, its power in increasing the credibility of the sales message, its use as an inexpensive way of discovering new markets or of measuring interest in a new product, its ability to generate leads, its usefulness in prescreening advertising media, and so on.[7]

Public relations also can "build a market. It can inform people that they are within the market for a specific product or service. Particularly in the launch of a new product or service, information about the new entry into the market can be legitimate news."[8]

Other contributions of public relations may include " . . . assistance in creating strategy and advertising themes; developing publicity in appropriate media; and, strictly in the PR domain, communicating suitable information about what's being marketed to employees and, in the case of publicly owned businesses, the stockholders and the financial community."[9]

Marketing brings to the union the sound business principles of research, forecasting, and budgeting that public relations needs. Each group needs to expand its capabilities, however. For example, marketing needs "closer identification with the corporate mission and the franchise built around it [while] public relations needs a more businesslike approach, particularly including quantitative evaluation, as well as leading-edge communications capabilities for better messages to new audience configurations through changing media."[10]

Just as marketers should not expect advertising to bear the weight of selling, so should they not expect public relations to bear the weight of the image-building process. Conversely, communicators should not expect marketing to be *the* solution to the effective selling of products or services.

Communicators can do a number of things to become an integral part of the overall marketing and communication mix of an organization:

They can help from the beginning by assisting in creating strategy for the overall marketing campaign. Just as other disciplines are brought into the early strategy sessions, so should public relations/communication; it is no less a part of the planning team than legal, manufacturing, or finance.

They can and should share some of their own work with marketing, such as results of surveys, opinion research efforts, and public affairs concerns. By sharing information, both groups learn to think beyond their traditional boundaries and to question whether or not an action in one area will have an effect on another area.

They can serve as a conscience to marketing, just as they do to other parts of the business. For example, are you marketing a product or service in a way that does not reflect the social conscience of the organization? Are the messages you impart through advertising in conflict with those your CEO gives in a speech? Is what you tell employees about a product or service the same thing you tell your customers?

They can help assure that the short-term marketing messages about a specific product or service are easily woven into the organization's longer-term public relations messages.

They have an obligation to make sure that their marketing counterparts are well-informed about the public relations function, that there is clear understanding on both sides that the goals of each are often the same, even though the strategies may differ.

One voice speaking in a joint marketing–public relations campaign is louder and clearer than two voices shouting disparate messages.

POSITIONING A PRODUCT OR SERVICE

"The one-two punch of public relations in the marketing sense is to position first, followed closely by or in some cases simultaneously with product publicity—then advertising. This sequence is important, because to move first with advertising is to pay dearly for stealing your own thunder."[11]

While there are exceptions to this generally accepted practice, exceptions are rare and for good cause or unusual circumstances.

A smart organization manages its image and its reputation, making the marketing of an offered product or service easier. IBM, to cite an overworked but nonetheless valid example, uses all the visual means available to reinforce a style that locks the firm into the world of modern business technology. From computers to typewriters, IBM products have a certain style that sets them apart. Any new product or service introduced into the IBM family automatically carries with it the IBM image and reputation.

"In deciding what your promotional mix and thrust will be, you can find out what position you hold in the public's mind and work to improve it. If needed, develop a new plan for positioning your company. Once you figure out what your position is in the market, or public's mind, stick to your plan to improve it."[12]

Identifying your organization's position in the public view and creating a plan to improve it is not difficult or complex. A marketing communication program can be structured to provide the vital nuggets of corporate excellence on which customers can build positive generalization about the organization. Such a program would use all the tools available: advertising, media relations, exhibits, seminars, executive appearances, and direct mail.

There would be nothing new about all this except that these tools of marketing communication would be employed to forge a common strategy. And that strategy would not be directed at supporting a specific product, but at repositioning the organization.

Working with your marketing counterparts, you can identify your position with a few activities. Start with an audit of your organization's existing product or corporate identity programs. Compare your organization's programs with those of other major organizations in the same industry. Look at design, messages, implementation, disparities. Prepare a recommendation for change in your organization, if necessary.

On the basis of your findings, prepare the communication strategy for repositioning. Identify roles for the principal communication operations—advertising, exhibits, community relations, executive support, media relations, and investor relations. Set objectives in terms of an attitudinal change.

Develop a system that will enable you to measure progress in achieving communication objectives as you implement the plan. Be sure to monitor your customers' attitudes toward your organization as well as toward your competitors' major communication activities.

Positioning applies to both product and service offerings. For example, Republic Health offers its commodities like consumer goods, says Michelle Salazar, director of product management. "Nabisco, for example, doesn't advertise the Nabisco name, it advertises Ritz crackers. So, we pulled out five or six surgical specialties and began marketing those as products." The result is that plastic surgery is called "You're Becoming" and cataract surgery has become the "Gift of Sight." These and other surgeries are advertised in such media as women's magazines and Sunday newspaper magazines.[13]

AT&T, upon entering the competitive arena, found difficulties because of lack of positioning. One advertising manager likened the drastic changes in AT&T's image to that of an oil company suddenly deciding to go into the milk business.

One of the difficulties was that AT&T had positioned itself too well and was still carrying its older image. "On the surface, AT&T says it is ready to do business in the highly competitive systems marketplace, but there seem to be remnants of the sluggish, bureaucratic and monopolistic Ma Bell that appear to be hampering AT&T's effectiveness in a very intense business."[14]

The "Ma Bell" image is still being positioned in its proper historical context, and the company is still being repositioned as AT&T.

Positioning an organization and then managing that image and reputation are essential before marketing a product or service. As one writer put it: "On closer inspection, it seems that names aren't necessarily worth anything. Reputations are worth a great deal, but they are easily lost."[15]

THE RELATIONSHIP BETWEEN ADVERTISING AND PUBLICITY

There is an axiom that says a product or service can be introduced only once; after that, it can only be publicized. Unfortunately, this axiom often gets lost in the rush to "introduce" a six-month-old product at a trade show or to take advantage of an executive speech to "introduce" a new service. Complicating matters are disagreements about what constitutes a "new," "enhanced," or "improved" product. Also in the equation is the role that advertising plays in this game.

As with any program, simplicity is best. And the simplest approach for a product or service involves: (1) issuing product/service announcements; (2) advertising; (3) continuing with publicity programs.

An advertising program is more credible to an audience *after* the merits of the service or product have been announced and discussed on the editorial pages or on a news show. This is because the audience knows that an advertisement is created and paid for by the sponsoring organization; the editorial material is seen as objective. Making the best of these two worlds calls for smart thinking. Creating powerful, believable corporate advertising and getting it through a gauntlet of approvals is more an art than a science, and the kind of media relations required is based more on nurturing relationships with editors than on churning out news releases.[16] And because advertising and publicity are each one part of an overall campaign, product managers should not expect advertising to bear the weight of selling or expect one article to turn the tide in consumer understanding or perception. Both advertising and publicity need careful planning, enough time in which to accomplish objectives, and a clear understanding of each other's roles.

Sometimes advertising may be the way to start on a program, however. This is true for small, new businesses that do not have a public relations program or perhaps for service industries. For example, when a lawyer who had been a public defender wished to start private practice, he had no positioning power, no built-in clientele, so he decided to advertise. Such professional-services advertising should meet guidelines for generally accepted practices, according to Irwin Braun, author of *Building a Successful Professional Practice with Advertising*. He suggests:

> Determine what aspects of your practice will distinguish you from the competition and stress them in your ads.
> Analyze the demographics of your location to get an idea of what services will be most appealing and affordable to area customers.
> Watch TV, listen to the radio and comb newspapers, magazines and direct mail to see what your competition is doing.[17]

Even in the normal relationship between advertising and publicity, some general dos and don'ts apply:

1. Do check with your advertising agency or in-house advertising managers to see which media they recommend for advertising. They will obviously not spend the organization's money on media that do not reach the targeted audience.
2. Do work out a timetable with advertising so that a product or service announcement appears before the advertising launch. The two may be separated by only a few days, but the timing is critical.
3. Do make sure that the wording in an advertisement and the wording in the news releases and other material say the same thing. They may say it in different ways, but the overall message, or promise, must be identical.
4. Don't use the pressure of advertising to get an editorial piece into print or on the air. Not only is this considered unethical within the public relations profession, but reputable reporters and editors do not allow their editorial decisions to be influenced by the advertising might.
5. Don't play games with introduction dates of a product or service. There are many ways to gain publicity without resorting to "announcing" a product or service several times over a period of months. It will not take reporters long to realize what is happening, and then you will have lost your credibility.
6. Don't promise more than you can deliver with your publicity campaign. It is easy enough to say that you will place 12 stories on a product, but it is difficult to deliver because placement of stories is dependent on an editor's decision, not yours.

Achieving the most from an advertising and publicity mix often depends on how you take advantage of the many tools available to both.

TOOLS OF THE TRADE

There is an unfortunate perception that the primary publicity tool is the news release announcing the new product or service. Since, as we noted earlier, a product can be announced only once and publicized thereafter, an announcement has limited value.

However, there are numerous ways to spread the word about a product or service and keep it in the public eye. Following are discussions of some activities that can help you further the marketing effort for your product or service. Keep in mind, however, that these public relations techniques, while individually worthwhile, should not be used in a haphazard way. They should be integrated into a well-thought-out marketing program, complete with timetable and measurement capabilities.

Press Kits

The press kit, a staple of the publicist's trade, is often misused and poorly prepared. The material in the kit is likely to be sales material, rather than news releases and feature articles. Worse yet, the kit may contain reprints of the material issued months before, when the product was introduced. Sometimes design and presentation of the kit itself are at odds with the material it contains.

At trade shows and other special events the press kit often must be able to speak for itself, because it is on a table with dozens of other kits, each of which is attempting to catch a journalist's eye. G. A. Marken, president of Marken Communications, Inc., once reviewed the press kits available at a trade show of information/communications vendors. He lamented the absence of true information in a kit:

Very few exhibitors identified:
What the company was all about.
What products were being shown at the show.
That they had done anything special for the show.
Where they could be located during the show or [where reporters could] obtain additional information.[18]

In preparing news releases for press kits, or for any other occasion, never assume knowledge on the part of the audience. There will always be one reporter who is attending the trade show or press conference or product demonstration for the first time, and it is for the novice that you prepare your material.

There are some basic pieces which can be included in almost any press kit. The following list was compiled by Carole Howard, APR.

The main news release. It usually need not run longer than two pages.
More-detailed technical information, such as fact sheets, for the trade press.
Related feature stories. These can be customer testimonials or unusual manufacturing processes.
Black-and-white photographs or drawings, with cutlines attached or taped to the back. Include color slides for TV. Offer color prints to magazines and newspapers with four-color capability, and offer network-quality videotape or film to TV stations as background footage, if you have it.

Photos and biographies of key speakers.
A basic fact sheet, annual report or other background on your company.
The person to contact for additional information.[19]

Be sure that you include a local phone number where your contact person can be reached during the duration of the show as well as the phone number at the office, for follow-up after the trade show or exhibition ends. Remember, the press kit leaves with the reporter and will keep speaking to that reporter long after the event is over. Take care that the first impression the kit gives is the best one, from design to content.

News Releases

The news release introduces your product or service when you do not use a news conference or trade show display. Here again, publicists often fail to listen to the repeated pleas of editors about the ideal news release for their purposes. Editors receive hundreds of releases every day and throw most of them away because the releases fail to do their job. A news release is not intended to take the place of a reporter; a news release functions as a "for your information" memorandum to an editor or reporter about a particular product or service. The editor or reporter then chooses to follow up on that memorandum by requesting more information or by writing a story based on the material provided in the release.

If a news release functions primarily as a memo, it stands to reason that it does not need to be more than two pages long to include the essentials of who, what, where, when, why, and how. Remember, no Pulitzer Prizes are given for news releases.

Some other basics to bear in mind: put the date on the release at the top of the page, and include a contact name and telephone number(s), a summary headline, and a dateline. News releases should be in a format that is easy to read. They should be printed on one side of the sheet, on original letterhead (not photocopied so that a color logo comes out in black and white). The type should be easy to read; fancy typesetting does not ensure readability—in fact, it often prevents it. Releases should be written with the proper audience in mind: reporters and editors first, customers second. Releases should not be written for management.

Product Releases

The product release, which announces the product, provides a brief description, tells a reader how to get more information, and supports the advertising program. When preparing such a release, the communicator should not be bound by the "one-product, one-release" rule. Because almost every product has more than one feature, benefit or application, it can sustain a series of releases, each one devoted to a particular product characteristic. This fact enables the PR practitioner to develop a long-term release program for every product and enables the company—even with a limited product line—to keep its name before the public on a continuing basis.[20]

The same principle applies to the service industry. A service may have different applications or different audiences. The public relations practitioner can schedule a service release program timed to the program and its advertising campaign, if any.

Feature Releases

The feature release can be a part of a press kit or it can be sent as a follow-up release after the announcement. This release takes one aspect of the product or service and describes it in a way that appeals to the mass media. For example, you might create a feature release detailing one woman's use of the services provided by a shelter for battered women. The combination of the personalization of the service through one woman's plight and information about the services available to that woman (and others in similar circumstances) makes for an interesting story.

Unusual applications of products also serve well. If your product has a generally accepted use but you can describe an unusual adaptation such as a case in which a picnic cooler was used to transport a donated human organ for a transplant, you have given the product a different exposure while enhancing the messages of quality workmanship, dependability, and so on.

Customer Application Releases

The customer application release is almost always a good tool for the publicist. The biggest drawback is that such a release generally must come long after the installation of the product or the beginning of the service, in order to ensure that all the bugs are out of the operation before boasting in public about its capabilities. Work on this release is best done jointly with the customer so that you can bring out both the best of your product/service offering and the customer's wisdom in selecting it.

These releases also make excellent case studies for specialized publications in your particular industry. A hotel that installs a new communications system to handle alarms, wake-up calls, billing, and maid service, is a good candidate for a case study for publications in both the hotel/motel industry and the communications industry. These case studies often are written by the technicians involved in the actual installation, with gentle massaging of the text by the communication staff.

How-To Releases

The how-to release is interesting, has visual appeal and—depending on the process involved—can be sent to just about any medium. Whether it explains how fiber for telecommunications systems is made from glass or how a political candidate manages to mail tens of thousand of "personalized" letters or how you can raise a pig as a household pet, this type of release has an automatic hook. People are just plain curious about how things get done. For the communicator, the how-to release is one of the best of the many tools available because every product or service has a beginning, a way it is manufactured/organized, and a way to be sold or distributed or installed.

It is easy to fall into the trap of producing only press kits and news releases, but several other effective tools are available to communicators.

Factory Tours

For many trade journalists, the factory tour is a highlight of the business. Writing about a product solely on the basis of interviews, releases, and photographs is competent work, but it is not complete. You can arrange a tour of the factory that makes your major products and invite the reporters who cover your industry. The tour, which should take less than a day, could include talks from an executive in your marketing department, a case study, an overview of your company, and a question-and-answer session, as well as the actual walking tour.

The memory of actually having seen how cosmetics are packaged or how suits are cut or how lasers are used will stay with the reporters for many stories to come. You can reinforce that memory by following up the tour with quality color photographs for the reporters' files.

Media Breakfasts

Service industries can make effective use of media breakfasts. In these sessions, editors and reporters meet with a key executive or organization representative to discuss a single topic or a variety of issues in an informal but on-the-record setting. Such breakfasts are useful in the healthcare industry to explain the rising cost of healthcare or the need for new kinds of care; in the food industry to demonstrate and explain the changing tastes of consumers; in the legal profession to explain new trends in jurisprudence; in the computer industry to discuss consumer expectations and how they are being met. In short, these sessions can be used to present a wide variety of topics.

Product Fairs

Product fairs also are a great way to show and tell reporters, as well as customers, employees, and investors, about what your organization produces. Fairs can be held over several days in order to reach various audiences. They provide hands-on demonstrations of your organization's latest products. Attenders have a greater recall of the products after actually using them. Fairs can be a lot of work, but the joint efforts of the marketing and communication groups can produce professional, entertaining, and informative events.

Individual Briefings

If you deal with only a few reporters, you may want to consider individual briefings. These sessions, although seemingly informal, require considerable planning. Each reporter should be guided through a half-day or full day of company overview, product/service specific information, hands-on demonstrations (if applicable), a visit with the chief executive officer or other high-ranking manager, and an open-ended question-and-answer session. These detailed briefings serve to keep a reporter fully informed and also help cement your relationship with that reporter.

Newsletters

A newsletter for reporters and editors can often make the difference between journalists blotting you from their memories and writing articles about your product or service. The newsletter should be written specifically with the journalists in mind, to provide them with information about your company, not-for-profit organization, or industry.

It is crucial to understand that the purpose of the newsletter is not to generate articles, but to keep the journalists informed. Do not be surprised, however, if items in the newsletter ultimately result in stories. It is the nature of the journalist to take a small piece of information that he or she thinks will interest readers and develop it into a story.

Material for the newsletter can be information about people, products, or services. It can tell of personnel changes, new department names, small contracts that were not considered big enough for news releases, talks given by professional or technical members of your staff. Only nonproprietary material should be put in the newsletter, and it should be clearly understood that any item in the newsletter can be developed into a story by the reporter.

If you do not have the staff or the time to create a special newsletter, then add reporters to the mailing list for your employee newsletter. Much of the same information discussed above is covered in an employee publication. Reporters who cover your company cover all of it, not just the selected information you give them through news releases.

Trade Shows

Making special arrangements for reporters at trade shows is always a generous gesture. For example, you might make arrangements for reporters to show up a few hours prior to the show's opening for a private tour of your display. This gives them time to talk with the demonstrators without jeopardizing crucial customer demonstrations later.

You also can take advantage of the large numbers of reporters attending a trade show by announcing a new product or service at this time. The one drawback is that other companies may be doing the same thing, so reporters may be too busy covering several product/service introductions to give yours the same coverage that it would get if introduced alone.

Press Seminars

For technical or scientific industries, you might consider sponsoring seminars on a particular product, technology, or aspect of research. Seminars require the assistance of the organization's specialists, and the rewards are worth it to those key reporters who cover this highly specialized beat. The seminars might carry a broad theme, such as organ transplants and might present several speakers on various aspects of the topic: organ procurement, transplant research, advances in control of organ rejection, and so on.

Videotapes

When reporters cannot get to seminars, product fairs, or trade shows, take the information to them through videotape. Many of these events are videotaped anyway, for other uses. Working with your marketing counterparts and the audiovisual department, plan ahead to videotape the key speakers, products, and demonstrations. Combine these elements with a narrative that gives the reporter the feeling that he or she attended the event. Keep the videotape short and to the point.

SUMMARY

The marketing-and-communication mix still has its stumbling blocks and points of confusion for today's communicator. However, the mix is essential if an organization is to thrive in the face of domestic and foreign competition.

Publicity is not hucksterism. It is an integral part of the marketing-communication program. The person who professionally manages a publicity program in concert with the marketing campaign can take pride in the work he or she does. "Further, announcing a new product can be as professionally stimulating and newsworthy as announcing a modern office complex or writing a speech for your president—as long as you direct your message to the right audience via the right media at the right time."[21]

Applying Communication Tools to Marketing Objectives

Susan Lightner-Blume*

If you do not know a product life cycle analysis from an electrocardiogram, the talk of mixing public relations and marketing may make you nervous. Compounding this anxiety are stories that communicators, with their bachelor of arts backgrounds, cannot cut it in the tough business area; that communicators are ill equipped to be market driven on demand since their work normally deals in such nebulous areas as "creating goodwill"; that communicators are slow to respond, while marketers have a predisposition to action; that communicators simply do not have any knowledge about or understanding of marketing.

As a communicator, you might question how, without a background in marketing, you can support sales. How do you hold your own with marketing and sales groups? How do you become an equal, contributing member of the management team?

The reality is that communicators have, for many years, studied client needs and adapted traditional tools to meet these needs. The difference is that now the "client" is the marketing and sales group.

When developing communication programs for other areas of the organization, did you really need to become an expert in each? Did you have to understand all the ins and outs of the manufacturing process to create public relations programs for a plant? Did you have to be as versed in the technical details of your organization's products as the engineers? Did you have to actually perform surgery to create a program for your hospital?

Communicators are specialists in communication. That is the skill you bring to the management team. As a professional, you already have all the tools necessary for sophisticated, market-driven sales support programs. Marketing support requires only a new outlook, a new focus to developing public relations programs. The tools, however, remain the same.

Communicators have been selling and marketing for years. Reflecting the functions of marketing, you have analyzed your clients' needs, identified and produced products—public relations programs—to meet those needs, set objectives,

*Susan Lightner-Blume is the public relations manager for the AT&T Network Systems Group.

and developed means to measure and ways to track results. In the sales area, you have taken your product—public relations plans—and sold it to management. You have taken the messages and, applying different tools, have sold them to employees, to the media, to the financial community, to stockholders, to the community in which your organization is located.

Now, you are being challenged to bring a new market awareness to the traditional functions of employee relations, public affairs, and media relations. You are being asked to integrate these functions into overall marketing support plans. You are challenged to find ways to support marketing objectives in these traditional areas. And you are being asked to think of new ways to use traditional public relations tools to directly support the marketing effort.

You are valuable because of your mastery of these tools. You are even more valuable when you are able to review traditional skills and imagine new ways to use them. By really understanding the objectives of the marketing department, and being aware of the strategies being used to achieve them, you can add to the effort in many ways.

For example, you can use information tools to show employees where they fit in the marketing and sales effort. You can explain goals, outline ways the company hopes to achieve specific goals, then explain how each employee supports achievement of those goals.

You can use community relations efforts to position executives with key customers. Look at each community relations activity, event, and expenditure with an eye toward facilitating a relationship between your oraganization and your customers—that is one focused way of using an old function or tool.

Develop a more aggressive media relations program by creating and placing stories directly in support of scheduled sales promotions as a more sophisticated integration of media relations and the sales effort. Be sure, however, that stories have news value and are not advertisements disguised as public relations materials. Evaluate media on specifically targeted purchase decision makers and develop a program to reach that media group. Encourage your customers' internal media to cover the purchase and placement of your organization's products as a new way to support sales.

By understanding what your marketing and sales departments are trying to do, and by forging an agreement on priorities, you can focus your skills on developing plans to support these priorities. This will make you a resource to be called on to solve problems, not just someone to call to execute the ideas of others.

NOTES

1. "A Communicator's Guide to Marketing," a prospectus, IABC, Winter 1985.
2. "Marketing Corporate Perceptions and Marketing Product Perceptions," Western Electric paper, 1980.

3. Robert Kendall, "Public Relations Employment: Huge Growth Projected," *PR Review* (Spring 1984).
4. Lew Riggs, APR, "Public Relations and Marketing—Partners in Survival," special reprint from *Health Marketing in Communications Briefings* (March 1985), 8b.
5. Sunshine Janda Overkamp, APR, interview in newsletter of the IABC Marketing Council, 1, no. 1, January/February 1986, 2.
6. Kenneth Lightcap, "Marketing Support," *Experts in Action* (White Plains, N.Y.: Longman, 1984), 9.
7. Jordan Goldman, *Public Relations in the Marketing Mix* (Chicago: Crain Books, 1984), 9.
8. Alan K. Leahigh, "Marketing Communications: If You Can't Count It, Does It Count?" *Public Relations Quarterly* (Winter 1985), 23.
9. "PR Strategies for Marketing," *PR News* case study collection, study of A. T. Cross Company, public relations aspects of a successful new-product introduction.
10. Merton Fiur, "Where Public Relations Is Going," *Experts in Action* (White Plains, N.Y.: Longman, 1984), 129.
11. Lightcap, "Marketing Support," 129.
12. Notes from an AT&T seminar, New York, N.Y., 27 June 1980.
13. Nancy L. Croft, "Marketing," *Nation's Business*, April 1986.
14. Tom Henkel, "AT&T Marketing Strategy: A Failure to Communicate?" *Computerworld*, 8 July 1985.
15. Robert McGough, "Death of a Brand Name," *Forbes*, 19 May 1986, 35.
16. "Marketing Corporate Perceptions and Marketing Product Perceptions."
17. Quoted in Croft, "Marketing."
18. G. A. Marken, "The Ultimate, Final Word on Press Kits—Part II, Too Much Costly, Misguided Noise," *Computer Advertising News*, February 1985.
19. Carole Howard, APR, "Integrating Media Relations with the Marketing Mix," *Business Marketing*, December 1985.
20. Goldman, *Public Relations in the Marketing Mix,* 16.
21. Carole Howard, APR, and Wilma Mathews, ABC, "Marketing Communications Is Not Hucksterism," *Public Relations Quarterly* (Winter 1985), 17.

CHAPTER 8

Marketing in Not-for-Profit Organizations

Sunshine Janda Overkamp, APR*

One day Japanese warlord Nobunaga learned that his enemy's army was 10 times larger than his. Rather than defending his castle, he marched his army out to attack. He was confident of victory, but his troops were not. He announced that he would seek an omen to predict their destiny. After praying at a shrine, Nobunaga emerged to reveal the sign: he would toss a coin. Heads, they would win; tails, they would lose. He flipped the coin. Heads! With a great cheer, the army went on to an easy victory. Later an attendant gushed, "It's wonderful how we can foresee what destiny awaits us." Nobunaga nodded, showing him the coin with heads on both sides.[1]

Like Nobunaga, not-for-profit organizations can create the future they desire, rather than just letting it happen. Marketing, used correctly, can be a powerful force in helping not-for-profit organizations create their own future.

The use of marketing principles and techniques in the not-for-profit sector is relatively new. At first there were some basic questions: Could ideas, culture, social services, and social behavior be marketed like toothpaste, hamburgers, and automobiles? Is marketing in bad taste or crass commercialism in a sector that involves values, the imparting of knowledge, and "doing good"? Or, worse, is marketing manipulative, a form of hucksterism that will mar an organization's integrity and credibility?

Then, as demographic and economic realities began to hit universities, museums, churches, and philanthropic organizations, the questions changed: Is marketing the salvation of managers, fundraisers, and communication specialists in not-for-profit organizations? If so, how do you do it? How do you take marketing, a product-oriented sales promotion tool, and turn it into a people-oriented tool for promoting messages, ideas, and programs that deal with health and social issues?

---

*Sunshine Janda Overkamp, APR, is senior vice president for the United Way of Texas Gulf Coast, Houston, Texas. She is past chairwoman of the Marketing Council of the International Association of Business Communicators and is accredited in public relations.

These questions have frequently been asked. The answers evoked have then been explored, dissected, and often heatedly discussed. Having listened to this fray—and at times having jumped into it—I propose that the answer seems to be: *Yes, but. . . .*

Yes, marketing's organizational disciplines—use of quantitative methods, identification of target market opportunities, matching product design to market needs, use of coordinated and comprehensive strategic plans and actions—can benefit the not-for-profit field. These disciplines will help those in not-for-profits to be more scientific and better organized, to manage more effectively and use more meaningful evaluation techniques. And, as James Gregory Lord notes, marketing offers not-for-profits "a systematic way of thinking about institutional development and a technology to implement that technology."[2]

But . . . there are some basic differences between profit-making package goods marketing and not-for-profit marketing. Marketing is not directly transferable from the commercial world to the thousands of not-for-profit organizations operating in countries all over the world. In the United States more than 500,000 not-for-profit organizations are registered with the Internal Revenue Service. The basic principles of marketing are the same for profit and not-for-profit organizations, but there are many of what William D. Novelli calls "nuances of differences"[3] and what Philip Kotler calls "new and challenging settings for the application of these principles."[4] Novelli and others expand on this point, saying that not-for-profit marketing can be much more complex, require more exercise of personal and professional sensitivities, and be more difficult to accomplish. Before discussing these differences and how they affect marketing in the not-for-profit field, it might be appropriate to first discuss the differences among not-for-profits.

CATEGORIES OF
NOT-FOR-PROFIT ORGANIZATIONS

Organizations in the not-for-profit sector—often called the independent sector or the third sector, because they are neither business nor government organizations—vary widely. The historic stately church on the corner and the community's new zoo are both not-for-profits, as are your father's fraternal organization, your professional association, and women's rights groups. Political parties, lobbying groups, universities, consumer groups, and social welfare agencies also are not-for-profits. These groups tend to carry out a social purpose, are more experimental and change-oriented, and depend on donations of money and volunteer time. Kotler groups third-sector organizations as follows:

1. Religious organizations
   a. Churches
   b. Church associations
   c. Evangelical movements
2. Social organizations
   a. Service clubs
   b. Fraternal organizations
3. Cultural organizations
   a. Museums
   b. Symphonies
   c. Opera companies
   d. Art leagues
   e. Zoos
4. Knowledge organizations
   a. Private grade schools
   b. Private universities
   c. Research organizations
5. Protective organizations
   a. Trade associations
   b. Trade unions
6. Political organizations
   a. Political parties
   b. Lobbyist groups
7. Philanthropic organizations
   a. Private welfare organizations
   b. Private foundations
   c. Charity hospitals
   d. Nursing homes
8. Social cause organizations
   a. Peace groups
   b. Family planning groups
   c. Environmental groups
   d. Racial rights groups
   e. Consumerist groups
   f. Women's rights groups
   g. Anti-vice groups[5]

Ten percent of the workforce in the United States is employed in the third sector. Of white-collar professionals, about one of every six is a not-for-profit employee. Between 1972 and 1982, more new jobs were created by not-for-profit organizations in the United States than all jobs existing in either banking or insurance in 1982. Not-for-profits in the United States spend about $150 billion annually, pay out more than $65 billion in wages and salaries, and own about 10 percent of all real property in the country.[6]

Henry B. Hansmann has identified four categories of not-for-profit organizations (see Figure 8.1).[7] First, he uses an organization's income source to designate some as "donative" and others as "commercial." Donative organizations receive most of their income from grants and donations, whereas commercial not-for-profits receive most of their income from fees for their services. Second, Hansmann looks at who controls the organization. He designates organizations controlled by patrons "mutual" and those controlled by professionals "entrepreneurial." Some organizations, of course, fall into more than one category. For example, universities and most community cultural organizations depend on both user fees and donations.

These distinctions in revenue sources and control become important as you look at the differences between profit and not-for-profit marketing and as you select the right marketing techniques for your not-for-profit organization.

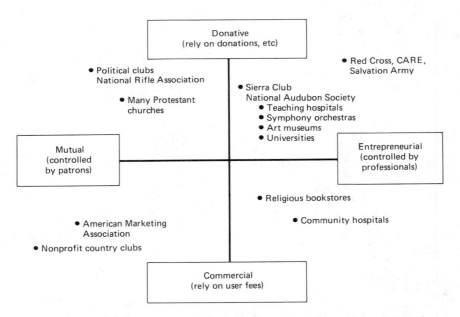

Figure 8.1. Categorization of nonprofit organizations by source of funds and nature of control. Adapted from Hansmann, "The Role of Nonprofit Enterprise," *Yale Law Journal* 89 (April 1980), 842.

DIFFERENCES IN PROFIT AND
NOT-FOR-PROFIT MARKETING[8]

Profit-making organizations normally offer either tangible goods or services with simple, well-defined benefits. Not-for-profits usually provide services that are intangible—hard-to-define "products" such as mental health, expanded self-knowledge, self-respect, hope, conservation, family and community linkage.

Just as product in not-for-profit marketing is often intangible, so price is often nonmonetary. Benson P. Shapiro notes that "it can include many things more personal than money, such as time, effort, love, power, prestige, pride, friendship, and the like. Alcoholics Anonymous, for example, charges a very high price—commitment not to drink and public admission of one's problem."[9] Not-for-profits may receive monies through user fees: tuition, ticket sales, charges for services. These funds, however, seldom provide all the revenue an organization needs to meet its financial needs.

For-profit organizations use marketing in a direct two-way simultaneous exchange that includes resource allocation (the goods or service) and resource attraction (revenue). Most not-for-profit marketers, however, must develop two separate marketing programs: one to meet the organization's mission through resource allocation and one to attract funds so that it can accomplish its stated goals and objectives.

In business, goods and services are focused on a single end user, the consumer. Not-for-profit marketers have two "first priority" customers—donors who will provide the resources and funds and clients who will use the resources. It is not uncommon for these audiences to have different focuses, needs, and expectations.

For-profit marketers rely heavily on research to determine what their potential customers (the market) *want* and will go to great lengths to prevent a decrease in sales. Not-for-profit marketers, in contrast, must take into consideration what their communities *need* to function effectively, and sometimes this means deliberately including unpopular services because they fill a need. Christopher H. Lovelock and Charles B. Weinberg call this a tension between mission and customer satisfaction:

> The declared objective of many social-behavior marketing programs is to stop people from doing things that appeal to them (like driving fast, smoking, or using drugs), or to do things that do not initially appeal (volunteering time to help a charitable or political cause). Nutritional foods are not necessarily tastier than "junk" foods; the withdrawal symptoms resulting from giving up drugs, smoking, or drink are often quite unpleasant; putting one's litter in a trash can, fastening a safety

belt, or recycling bottles can be a nuisance; driving at 55 miles per hour on an empty highway or performing physical exercises can be tedious and time consuming.[10]

A goods marketer controls all aspects of size, shape, and color of the goods. The time involved in delivery also can be controlled. Business service providers have similar control. Because they rely on volunteer support, however, not-for-profit marketers have much less control over the end product and the time and manner of delivery. This is particularly true when a marketing plan includes donated labor, goods, or services (gifts-in-kind). Contributors of this type of support often do so with either implicit or explicit control attached. Thus the development and execution of marketing plans may rest on consensus rather than command.

In the hands of a sensitive communicator, this constraint may represent an opportunity instead of an obstacle. John A. DiBiaggio says that

> the net effect of any decision is a factor of its quality, times its acceptance. You might come up with an idea that's a ten on a scale from one to ten, walk in and say, "Boy, have I got a great idea we're going to implement immediately" and then have the folks sitting there say, "Like hell" and sabotage it. On the other hand, if you can bring people together you can arrive at a decision that on a qualitative scale is a six or seven but it is accepted by everyone and the net effect is going to be great.[11]

In other words, volunteers add a dimension foreign to general marketing.

Another difference between for-profit and not-for-profit marketing, according to Lovelock and Weinberg, is "the large number of fingers in the managerial pie or management in duplicate or triplicate"[12] in voluntary organizations. Multiple, elaborate layers of both volunteer and staff decision makers can make the development of a comprehensive, coordinated marketing strategy difficult and time-consuming.

The major objective of for-profit marketers is to make a profit. Since by definition not-for-profits do not make a profit, they normally have multiple objectives, most of them nonfinancial. It can be difficult to formulate strategies and tactics to satisfy these differing objectives. Evaluation or measurement of success also can be harder to achieve. The fact that an organization is meeting campaign goals does not mean that it is attaining its goals for servicing people or fulfilling its mission.

When business marketers introduce a product, the company usually has a short exclusive franchise, one that lasts only until a competitor can offer a lower-priced comparable product. This competitiveness influences much for-profit strategy. Most not-for-profits, however, have a long, non-exclusive franchise. A person may have a warm, long-term relationship with the YMCA after having learned to swim there. Or a person may have an abiding gratitude toward the Boy Scouts or Girl Scouts for having taught him or her leadership skills. Moreover, exclusiveness is not usually a consideration for many "helping" not-for-profits. In the 1800s Bertha Suttner said, "After the verb 'to love,' 'to help' is the most beautiful verb in the world." Not-for-profit organizations do not have a corner on helping people; nor do they want one, since there are usually more people who need help than any one organization's resources can encompass.

Marketers in the private sector are guided by the marketplace in their decisions about product, price, place, and promotion. This is not always true in the not-for-profit sector. Legislative or regulatory actions, funding source budgetary decisions, accrediting bodies, professional or trade associations, or the reality of a political environment may influence the decisions of not-for-profit organizations.

Today almost all organizations are subject to public attention—usually in the form of media coverage. However, because of the expectation that organizations that "do good" must "be good," not-for-profits are often watched more closely. Practices that are considered part of doing business in the private sector—including some marketing practices—would cause "disappointment" if discovered being used by not-for-profits. One third-sector executive says that when making any decision, he reflects on how the public would react to it if it appeared on the front page of the local newspaper.

Another difference is the limitation on operating funds faced by not-for-profits. As George Wasem points out, exceed the marketing budget in a bank and you go into deficit financing. Exceed some not-for-profit agencies' budgets and they go out of business.

There are other differences between the two sectors that affect not-for-profit marketing. Key among these are the difficulties involved in implementation, use and control of distribution channels, and communication strategies. Novelli notes that it is "a thousand times harder to do social marketing than to do package goods marketing."[13] And he warns not-for-profits to avoid people who assume that selling ideas, social services, and social behavior is *exactly* like selling other goods and services. "Watch out for these people. They're wrong and they can cost you time, money, and good will."[14]

Having identified major differences, out next step is to describe appropriate marketing techniques for not-for-profits—some can be adopted and others adapted.

MARKETING TECHNIQUES THAT CAN BE ADOPTED OR ADAPTED FOR NOT-FOR-PROFITS

Written Marketing Plan

A written marketing plan is a must. A well-thought-out plan is a working document that enables your organization to focus on the following questions: Where are we now? Where do we want to go? How do we get there? What resources (people, time, money) will it take? Who is in charge of the various actions to get us there? When will we get there?

Once written, the plan should be used to monitor progress. It should be an often-consulted road map, not a filed-away historical document. Here is a format for a typical marketing plan developed by Lovelock and Weinberg:

Executive summary
Situational analysis (where are we now?)
  External
    Environment (political, regulatory, economic, social, technical, etc.)
    Consumers
    Employees
    Funders
    Distributors
    Competition
  Internal
    Objectives
    Strengths and weaknesses
Problems and opportunities
  Momentum forecast
  Identify gaps
Marketing program goals (Where do we want to go?)
  Specific (quantifiable)
  Realistic (attainable)
  Important
  Prioritized
Marketing strategies (How are we going to get there?)
  Positioning
    Target segments
    Competitive stance
    Usage incentive
  Marketing mix
    Product
    Price
    Distribution
    Marketing communication
  Contingency strategies

Marketing budget (How much and where?)
   Resources
      Money
      People
      Time
   Amount and allocation
Marketing action plan
   Detailed breakdown of activities for each goal or strategy
   Responsibility by name
   Activity schedule in milestone format
   Tangible and intangible results expected from each activity
Monitoring system[15]

Customer Identification

Identify your customers and give attention to their needs and wants. Part of the preparation for writing your marketing plan will be to identify your various publics. As mentioned earlier, not-for-profits are unusual in that they have two primary customers—the client and the donor. Beyond these primary customers, however, are other audiences being served. For a university, for example, the major customers may be students and benefactors, but the institution is also involved with parents, alumni, faculty, staff, trustees or regents, the local community, the national academic community, and others. Just as satisfied customers are the key to business success, they are paramount to a not-for-profit's continued good health. What happens when a customer is dissatisfied? In the United States, the White House Office of Consumer Affairs conducted some research and found that:

Of unhappy customers, 96 percent never complain.

However, 91 percent of the noncomplainers will no longer patronize the business that offended them.

The average unhappy customer will share the story with at least nine other people; worse, 13 percent will tell more than 20 additional people.

As not-for-profits have discovered marketing, many have focused on their product and its promotion to the exclusion of their ''customers''— those people who give an organization its reason to exist. As Peter Drucker notes, ''The purpose of the company is to create a customer.''[16]

Organizational Audit

Audit the organization to find opportunities and obstacles, strengths and weaknesses. Take a step back to look objectively at your organization; this is an integral part of any marketing plan. This also is part of a marketing

audit—a periodic, comprehensive examination of an organization's marketing performance. Relatively new to this technique of marketing is a concept called **vulnerability relations.** Instead of dealing with organizational strengths—a relatively easy thing to do—this process deals with "alleged or actual weaknesses in a company, its products or its operations that can affect its relationships with its publics."[17]

Market Research

Yes, a not-for-profit can afford to do research. In fact, it cannot afford *not* to do it! As Gabriel M. Gelb explains, "Learning how to exercise the undersized ear may be more important than paying further attention to the oversized mouth."[18] Information can be obtained from the kinds of internal and external existing sources, voluntarily submitted communication, and formal research listed below:

Collection from existing sources
    Organizational records
    Photography files
    Reference books
    Public records
    Trade journals
    Newspapers
    Public opinion polls and voting records
    General magazines
    Libraries
    Colleges and universities
    Associations
    Personal experience
    Demographic publications
Voluntary inbound communication
    Personal contacts
    Mail
    Reports
    Advisory committees or panels
    Performance records
    Suggestion systems
    Study of opinion leaders
Research (attitudes, beliefs/values, motivation expectations)
    Surveys
        Mail
        Telephone
        In-person

Focus group interviews
Project techniques[19]

Primary data are gathered for an immediate, specific study; secondary data are statistics gathered for some reason other than the immediate problem.

Once gathered, research should be used—even if it tells you things you do not want to know. Perceptions are reality, and reality is what you need to deal with when you use your research for decision making.

To hone your research skills, read about the latest techniques: geography as illustrated by Garreau's *The Nine Nations of North America*; PRIZM, a segmentation scheme by the Claritas Corporation that is based on what people are like and where they live; psychographics as illustrated by SRI's Values and Lifestyles Study (VASL); **involvement studies,** which determine how active consumers are in seeking information to help them in their decision making.

Henry Assael finds a number of significant differences between high-involvement, active consumers and low-involvement, passive consumers in-

---

IMPORTANCE OF VOLUNTEERS IN CONDUCTING RESEARCH*

Research is the foundation on which public relations and fundraising goals, objectives and activities should be developed. But lack of budget often intervenes.

Most nonprofit organizations have a resource which is readily available but usually overlooked for survey work—their volunteers. Naturally, this concept is unpopular among professional polling firms. They insist that only trained interviewers be used for any type of research. For complex subjects and sophisticated questionnaires this is true.

But many of the surveys needed for public relations or fundraising do not have to be complex or sophisticated. Usually they are trying to get baseline data or to identify knowledge levels, attitudes and opinions of a targeted audience. Many telephone surveys and intercept interviews can be done by volunteers so long as three things happen:

— The questionnaire is professionally constructed and tested;
— The volunteers are trained by a professional and have an opportunity to practice on one another;
— At least one professional is on the scene for supervision and problem-solving.

*From *Channels,* November 1982, reprinted with permission.

(*continued*)

Using volunteers accomplishes effective research and raises the involvement and knowledge levels of volunteers.

Other tips for volunteer-based surveys:

1. Unless you have an in-house research professional, it is *advisable to use a consultant for design, testing, training, supervision and analysis.* Money spent for these services will ensure the quality of the research while saving costs of professionals doing the interviewing.
2. Make sure your *interview instructions* for the volunteers *are simple and clear.*
3. *Don't expect volunteers to conduct interviews for more than 3 or 4 hours.* This can be a fatiguing exercise and you are better off with "shifts" of interviewers than with tired persons who have lost enthusiasm for the task.
4. As always, have on hand plenty of coffee, tea, soft drinks and snacks; and encourage the volunteers to take breaks and move around.
5. If several volunteers are conducting a telephone survey, *try to locate* them in one room. It might seem advantageous to separate interviewers, but they generally thrive on the busy and productive environment. . . . enthusiasm is contagious.

How many volunteers do you need? Multiply the time needed to complete an interview (in minutes) by the number of interviews, then add *3* minutes between each interview (for busy signals, refusals, breaks, etc.).

A hospital recently completed 450 12- to 15-minute telephone interviews using six shifts of eight volunteers. Each shift worked about 3 hours. Thus, in two consecutive afternoons and evenings, they accomplished a comprehensive public attitude survey about issues of importance to the hospital.

cluding how they obtain and evaluate information. Following is Assael's classification of the two types of consumers:

High-involvement view of an active consumer	*Low-involvement view of a passive consumer*
1. Consumers process information systematically.	1. Consumers learn information at random.
2. Consumers are information seekers.	2. Consumers are information gatherers.
3. Consumers represent an active audience for advertising. As a result, the direct effect of advertising on consumer behavior is weak.	3. Consumers represent a passive audience for advertising. As a result, the effect of advertising on consumer behavior can be strong.

4. Consumers evaluate alternatives before acting.
5. Consumers seek to maximize expected satisfaction. Hence they compare alternatives to see which one provides the most benefits related to needs and buy on the basis of comparisons of alternatives' attributes.
6. Personality and lifestyle characteristics are related to consumer behavior because the product is closely tied to the consumer's identity and belief system.
7. Reference groups influence consumer behavior because of the importance of the product to group norms and values.

4. Consumers act. Favorable attitudes may develop afterward.
5. Consumers seek some acceptable level of satisfaction and may choose on the basis of a few attributes. Familiarity is the key.

6. Personality and lifestyle characteristics are not related to consumer behavior because the product is not closely tied to the consumer's identity and belief system.
7. Reference groups exert little influence on product choice because products are unlikely to be related to group norms and values.[20]

Product Positioning

Positioning is a way to influence people in our communication-overloaded society. **Positioning** begins with a product, but it is not something you do to a product, it is how you influence the prospect—you position the product in the mind of the prospect.[21] This technique can easily be adapted by not-for-profits.

Your **target audience** is the individuals or groups you are trying to reach. Programs can be tailored to these audiences. One urban university defined its market segments, or target audiences, as students who lived no more than an hour away and who did not want to or could not afford to leave the geographic area, business people who worked in the downtown area, and women over age 35 who were interested in returning to school and needed individual attention.

Differentiated marketing is the way you treat different target groups. What works with one market segment may not work with another. Your research will help you identify these varying needs so that you can create the most effective messages to promote your product or service to each audience.

Generic product definition enables you to be more aware of your customer wants and needs. For example, a soap company may define its product as cleaning. In the not-for-profit field, a good example is the United Way. Until recently, most United Way organizations saw themselves as fund-raising and fund-allocating organizations. Today, however, many United Ways define themselves generically through mission statements that pledge them "to increase the organized capacity of people to care for one another."

Product research and development lets you evaluate the current product and consider possible changes. The fact that you see your product or service as desirable does not mean that your clients do. Have you "extended your line" recently (as the result of research, of course)? Should you de-market? Philip Kotler and Sidney J. Levy define **demarketing** as "that aspect of marketing that deals with discouraging customers in general or a certain class of customers in particular on either a temporary or permanent basis."[22] This is a strategy to fine-tune the client mix and, if necessary, reduce excess demand. Demarketing can be tricky, but especially so in a not-for-profit. What you demarket may be the pet project of a donor or volunteer. You also might double-check that you do not demarket inadvertently. One drug hotline discovered that by not having enough incoming telephone lines, it was discouraging callers. It took only one busy signal to turn a client away from the service—and not get the help needed.

Your product's **unique selling position** is what distinguishes it. Why is your organization different from others providing the same service? Is it size, location, or staff? Do you have a prestigious affiliation? Why should a client choose you? It is not uncommon for not-for-profits to try to be all things to all people. You would do better to find your market segment, decide how to reach and serve it, and then reinforce your unique selling position through communication.

Competition

Business marketers understand the word *competition* and know their competitors. Not-for-profit specialists have steadfastly avoided this concept and when forced to acknowledge it have been uncomfortable with it. Yet donors can choose where they want to contribute; volunteers can decide to which group they want to donate their time. Wherever there are choices, there is competition. You should know your competition's product, its advantages and disadvantages, as well as you know your own. Then you need to adapt the tools of competitive marketing—adjust your product, price, promotion, or distribution.[23] Can you offer a reduced membership or ticket price? What can you offer that the competition does not, and do you have a method of telling your audiences about it? Competition forces an organization to do what it does best and to do it efficiently and effectively. Why is this important? The 1983 General Electric annual report put it bluntly: In today's world, "winners and losers are clearly more definable. You're either the very best at what you do, or you don't do it very long."[24]

Shapiro adds a twist to the notion of competition in the not-for-profit world. He suggests that it may be possible to use cooperation for the same purpose as competition:

> Much could be accomplished through inter-organizational cooperation, especially in education and health care. If jealousies could be put aside, individual organizations could voluntarily restrict their activities to providing the services they are best able to provide. They could band together for those tasks which are more efficiently performed through joint effort than through individual action.[25]

Incentives and Promotion

There is one area of price marketing that not-for-profit groups are just beginning to use—incentives. For a small financial outlay, you can buy a tangible item to give donors or clients—something that will enhance your compaign or service use. One not-for-profit discovered that giving away T-shirts helped its solicitation efforts substantially.

Promotion is an area that not-for-profits tend to give too much emphasis. Do not promote just for the sake of promoting. Use research to choose your media and your channels, to target and differentiate. Leon Quera reviews the advantages and disadvantages of principal and supplementary media (see Tables 8.1 and 8.2). Understanding the limitations and benefits of each medium can facilitate selection of the appropriate channel for the target audience.

Location

The organization's location or distribution channels can be important to both resource attraction and resource allocation. The right location, says Shapiro, can make donation easier, can attract volunteers, can showcase the organization's commitment to an area, and can bring services to the areas that need them. In one sprawling southwestern city, for example, not-for-profits in the social service field share service centers in various outlying areas. The concept has worked so well that there are now discussions about an in-city service center. Not only do clients have a facility close to their homes, but they also like the convenience of having "one-stop/multiservices."

Evaluation

As we noted earlier, evaluation should be built into any marketing plan. Measuring techniques that can be adapted by not-for-profits include (1)

TABLE 8.1. PRINCIPAL MEDIA: ADVANTAGES AND DISADVANTAGES

Advantages	Disadvantages
Television	
1. Combines sight, sound, and motion attributes	1. Message limited by restricted time segments
2. Permits physical demonstration of product	2. No possibility for consumer referral to message
3. Believability due to immediacy of message	3. Availabilities sometimes difficult to arrange
4. High impact of message	4. High time costs
5. Huge audiences	5. Waste coverage
6. Good product identification	6. High production costs
7. Popular medium	7. Poor color transmission
Radio	
1. Selectivity of geographical markets	1. Message limited by restricted time segments
2. Good saturation of local markets	2. No possibility for consumer referral to message
3. Ease of changing advertising copy	3. No visual appeal
4. Relatively low cost	4. Waste coverage
Magazines	
1. Selectivity of audience	1. Often duplicate circulation
2. Reaches more affluent consumers	2. Usually cannot dominate in a local market
3. Offers prestige to an advertiser	3. Long closing dates
4. Pass-along readership	4. No immediacy of message
5. Good color reproduction	5. Sometimes high production costs
Newspapers	
1. Selectivity of geographical markets	1. High cost for national coverage
2. Ease of changing advertising copy	2. Shortness of message life
3. Reaches all income groups	3. Waste circulation
4. Ease of scheduling advertisements	4. Differences of sizes and formats
5. Relatively low cost	5. Rate differentials between local and national advertisements
6. Good medium for manufacturer/ dealer advertising	6. Poor color reproduction

Source: Leon Quera, *Advertising Campaigns: Formulation and Tactics* (Columbus, Ohio: Grid, 1973), 71–74.

return on investment (ROI), (2) market share, and (3) benefit/cost analysis. Paul Wagner explains how **return on investment** can be used:

Certainly one cannot simply follow a standard formula for developing ROI, but if a basic model of viewing inputs is used, with investments in an aggregate leading to a more substantial leverage of additional invest-

TABLE 8.2. SUPPLEMENTAL MEDIA: ADVANTAGES AND DISADVANTAGES

Advantages	Disadvantages

Direct Mail

Advantages	Disadvantages
1. Extremely selective	1. Often has poor image
2. Messages can be very personalized	2. Can be quite expensive
3. Little competition with other advertisements	3. Many restrictive postal regulations
4. Easy to measure effect of advertisements	4. Problems in maintaining mailing lists
5. Provides easy means for consumer action	

Point-of-Purchase Displays

Advantages	Disadvantages
1. Presents message at point of sale	1. Dealer apathy in installation
2. Great flexibility for creativity	2. Long production period
3. Ability to demonstrate product in use	3. High unit cost
4. Good color reproduction	4. Shipping problems
5. Repetitive value	5. Space problem

Outdoor Posters
(on stationary panels)

Advantages	Disadvantages
1. Selectivity of geographical markets	1. Often has poor image
2. High repetitive value	2. Message must be short
3. Large physical size	3. Waste circulation
4. Relatively low cost	4. National coverage is expensive
5. Good color reproduction	5. Few creative specialists

Transit Posters
(on moving vehicles)

Advantages	Disadvantages
1. Selectivity of geographical markets	1. Limited to a certain class of consumers
2. Captive audience	2. Waste circulation
3. Very low cost	3. Surroundings are disreputable
4. Good color reproduction	4. Few creative specialists
5. High repetitive value	

Movie Trailers

Advantages	Disadvantages
1. Selectivity of geographical markets	1. Cannot be employed in all theaters
2. Captive audience	2. Waste circulation
3. Large physical size	3. High production costs
4. Good medium for manufacturer/ dealer advertising	4. No possibility for consumer referral to message

Advertising Specialties

Advantages	Disadvantages
1. Unique presentation	1. Subject to fads
2. High repetitive value	2. Message must be short
3. Has a "gift" quality	3. May have relatively high unit cost
4. Relatively long life	4. Effectiveness difficult to measure

(continued)

TABLE 8.2 *(Continued)*

Advantages	Disadvantages
Pamphlets and Booklets	
1. Offer detailed message at point of sale	1. Dealers often fail to use
2. Supplement a personal sales presentation	2. May have a relatively high unit cost
3. Offer to potential buyers a good referral means	3. Few creative specialists
4. Good color reproduction	4. Effectiveness difficult to measure

Source: Leon Quera, *Advertising Campaigns: Formulation and Tactics* (Columbus, Ohio: Grid, 1973), 71–74.

ments in social improvement, the pyramiding theory can become operative and have a significant input on how financial resources are used in nonprofit institutions. Admittedly, the techniques for assigning values to the societal changes that take place are highly subjective, but thoughtful marketing executives can quantify the results in a way that most fair-minded Board members would find acceptable."[26]

Market share is a simple concept: How much of a given population do you serve? It becomes more difficult when no statistics on size of population are available. How many abused children are there in a state, province, or county? How many women plan to reenter the workforce in the next year? Because these and many other statistics are not readily available, you may need to use estimates and rough benchmarks for some calculations.

In **benefit/cost analysis,** the same problems arise. How do you quantify the benefit of enhanced client self-esteem? How do you quantify the cost of arthritis? However, using available information, you can make effective use of this evaluation method. Benefit/cost analysis forces you to sharpen your thinking about the important factors involved in a decision. Or, as Kotler notes, "It puts relevant data into what otherwise would be a wholly subjective act of decision making. It rests on the premise that organized ignorance is preferred to disorganized ignorance in making decisions."[27]

STRUCTURING A NOT-FOR-PROFIT FOR MARKETING

Once you commit to a marketing orientation, how do you fit it into an organization's structure? Depending on your organization, the first step may be to organize a cross-functional staff committee or a high-level volunteer committee, or both. *The support of the chief professional officer and the chief volunteer officer will be crucial to the introduction of marketing to your organization.* The committee(s) should look inward and outward when examining the organization's problems and marketing potential—as happens when a marketing audit is conducted. Preparation for the committee(s) may include readings, such as the literature cited throughout this book, and consultations with marketing specialists (both volunteer and paid).

If an organizationwide review of marketing is not possible, the communication and development specialists should conduct it or, if you are the only one with any interest in marketing communication, you should do it. Review marketing techniques; which ones can you use to improve your results and enhance your job performance? It may be a small start, but it will be worthwhile.[28]

SUMMARY

Everyone in an organization markets, whether he or she realizes it or not. Every telephone call that is answered, every letter that is written, every conversation that is held, says something about the organization. The trick is to take the existing marketing activities and integrate them into a comprehensive plan of action that supports an organization's mission. Marketing is not magic. It will not cure all ills for a not-for-profit. And, as Novelli so aptly put it, marketing is not a Hula Hoop, a fad, that will soon go out of style. It is, instead, a systematic, effective problem-solving tool—one that not-for-profits cannot afford to overlook as they go about educating, healing, helping, and improving their community and daily life.

NOTES

1. Adapted from Larry J. Rosenberg, "Master These 10 Skills for Marketing Career Success," *Marketing News,* 1 October 1985, 5.
2. James Gregory Lord, "Marketing Nonprofits," *Grantsmanship Center News,* January/February 1981, 56.
3. William D. Novelli, "Marketing: Competition for Social Service Communicators?" speech before the Social Service Section, Public Relations Society of America, Washington, D.C., 21 May 1981.
4. Philip Kotler, *Marketing for Nonprofit Organizations* (Englewood Cliffs, N.J.: Prentice-Hall, 1982), 8.
5. Ibid., 13–14.

6. These statistics are from *Enterprise* 3, no. 1, 1986, 14, (an employee magazine for Southwestern Bell Telephone).

7. Henry B. Hansmann, "The Role of Nonprofit Enterprise," *Yale Law Journal* 89 (April 1980), 835–901.

8. This discussion of differences between for-profit and not-for-profit marketing draws on material from Paul I. Hirt, "Newspaper Marketing: A Time for Reappraisal?" (Reston, Va.: International Newspaper Association, 1983); Christopher H. Lovelock and Charles B. Weinberg, *Marketing for Public and Nonprofit Managers* (New York: Wiley, 1984), 26–38; Kotler, *Marketing for Nonprofit Organizations,* Chapter 1; Benson P. Shapiro, "Marketing for Nonprofit Organizations," *Harvard Business Review,* September/October 1973; George Wasem, "Marketing for Profits and Nonprofits," *Bankers Monthly Magazine,* March 1975, in Patrick J. Montana, ed., *Marketing in Nonprofit Organizations* (New York: AMACOM, 1978), 31–37; Karen F. A. Fox and Philip Kotler, "The Marketing of Social Causes: The First 10 Years," *Journal of Marketing* (Fall 1980), 24–33.

9. Shapiro, "Marketing for Nonprofit Organizations."

10. Lovelock and Weinberg, *Marketing for Public and Nonprofit Managers,* 34.

11. John A. DiBiaggio, and Thomas M. Cooper, *Applied Practice Management: A Strategy for Stress Control* (St. Louis: Mosby Times Mirror, 1979).

12. Lovelock and Weinberg, *Marketing for Public and Nonprofit Managers.*

13. Novelli, "Marketing."

14. Ibid.

15. Lovelock and Weinberg, *Marketing for Public and Nonprofit Managers.*

16. Peter F. Drucker, *The Practice of Management* (New York: Harper & Row, 1954), 37.

17. Otto Lerbinger, *Purview,* a supplement of *PR Reporter,* 12 August 1985.

18. Gabriel M. Gelb, "The Uses and Misuses of Feedback," *Journal of Organizational Communication* 5, no. 4 (1976). For a discussion of inexpensive methods of marketing research, see Keith Gordon and Isabel Carr, *Low-Cost Market Research* (New York: Wiley, 1983).

19. Based on Lawrence N. Nolte, *Fundamentals of Public Relations* (Elmsford, N.Y.: Pergamon Press, 1974), 283–303.

20. Adapted from Henry Assael, *Consumer Behavior and Marketing Action* (Boston: Kent, 1981), 83.

21. Al Ries and Jack Trout, *Positioning: The Battle for Your Mind* (New York: McGraw-Hill, 1986).

22. Philip Kotler and Sidney J. Levy, "Demarketing, Yes, Demarketing," *Harvard Business Review,* November/December 1971.

23. James Gregory Lord, *Philanthropy and Marketing* (Cleveland: Third Sector Press, 1981), 15–22.

24. *1983 Annual Report,* General Electric Company, Fairfield, Conn.

25. Shapiro, "Marketing for Nonprofit Organizations."

26. Paul A. Wagner, "Marketing for NPOs—from a Practitioner's Point of View," in *Marketing in Nonprofit Organizations,* ed. Patrick J. Montana (New York: AMACOM, 1978), 49.

27. Kotler, *Marketing for Nonprofit Organizations,* 269.
28. For a more detailed discussion of ways to structure marketing within a not-for-profit, see Philip Kotler, "Strategies for Introducing Marketing into Nonprofit Organizations," *Journal of Marketing* 43 (January 1979). Another source for this topic is Arthur C. Sturn, Jr., "Institutional Marketing," *National Society for Fund Raising Executives Journal,* October 1979.

CHAPTER 9

Internal Marketing

Michael P. Quane, ABC*

> You must manage change or it will manage you.
> —*Edward Halleck*

Whether its task is to provide important background information needed by a sales force, to motivate support staff to get behind marketing efforts, or to communicate strategic change, internal marketing can make the difference between success and failure in an organization's total marketing efforts.

To put the internal-marketing function in perspective, however, remember that internal marketing is not any new magic potion or radical way of doing things. What we are talking about are basic communication skills used to stimulate support among its own people for a company's or institution's marketing strategy.

Although the tools are not new—internal publications, incentive campaigns, audiovisual programs, sales presentations—many organizations simply do not think of communicating their marketing efforts to one of their most important constituencies—their own employees. Many editors of internal publications, to ensure that the publications are "interesting," fill their employee magazines with stories about staff social news and people with unusual hobbies, forgetting that the company or institution has a product or service that it must sell if the organization is to stay in business. Employee publications are an excellent vehicle for reinforcing the sales effort, and yet some employee publications can be read cover to cover without the reader ever knowing what kind of business the company is in!

So again, when we speak about "internal marketing," we are not talking about any new formula or discipline. Rather, we are describing philosophical awareness, if you will, that an organization's communication efforts should support, internally as well as externally, the business the organization is engaged in.

---

*Michael P. Quane, ABC, is manager of marketing and communication at EAB in Long Island, New York. He is an accredited business communicator and a member of the board of the Marketing Council of the International Association of Business Communicators.

Figure 9.1. The importance of customer service is marketed to all Target Stores employees (50,000) through news stories, cover focus, and columns in the newsletter; through videotape programs and the company's C.A.R.E. Club at every opportunity.

Whether it is done by the marketing staff, the public relations department, corporate communication, employee communication, or a cooperative effort among any or all of these departments, internal marketing must be an integral part of the marketing mix. There is no room in a successful organization for independent empires that separate themselves from a company's or institution's basic reason for being. If the communication structure consists of individual departments, those departments must get together, for the good of the organization, to communicate the marketing effort internally.

If all this sounds a bit like preaching, that is because too many communicators harm themselves—and their profession—by not getting in step with the organization's business goals. This only reinforces the idea among many chief executive officers (CEOs) that communication or public relations departments are "fluff"—and thus expendable when times get tough. Robert Berzok, ABC, IABC chairman for 1986–1987, in his maiden speech on taking office in June 1986, put it well when he said, "We have to know as much about our business as the technical people do."

There are many fine examples of regular employee communication efforts that do not forget the organization's business goals. One internal publication that does an excellent job is *On Target,* the monthly employee publication of Target Stores, a division of the Dayton Hudson Corporation (see Figure 9.1). Produced by the Employee Communications Department, the publication, from its chairman's message to its employee profiles, does not let its readers forget that customers are what make the company profitable, and—not coincidentally, I am sure—it is. Target led all Dayton Hudson operating companies in revenue in 1985, and DHC as a whole reported record earnings.

While *On Target* provides an example of internal marketing integrated into an organization's regular, ongoing communication efforts, this chapter presents two case studies of exceptional situations that dramatize the need for internal marketing in communicating change—drastic, searing change—in an organization's strategic objectives.

CASE ONE: EUROPEAN AMERICAN BANK (EAB)

The two-year period between March 1984 and March 1986 was one of profound and traumatic change for European American Bank (EAB). During these years EAB experienced the following: a U.S. $132 million loss, one of the largest in banking history; a complete change in senior management; a reduction in staff by 25 percent; a move by most headquarters personnel from New York City to a suburban corporate center; and a fundamental change in the nature of its business, from an international financial institution to a regional, consumer-oriented bank.

Any one of these changes would have been considered major. Occurring together, as they did over a two-year period, they caused monumental morale and logistics problems, making complete and candid communication programs a necessity for survival.

Background

European American Bank was founded in New York City in 1968 by a consortium of six European banks with the goal of serving their customers doing business in the United States. As a "wholesale" bank, European American was successful in such areas as corporate lending, trusts, foreign exchange, and correspondent banking. In 1974 EAB became a full-service commercial bank when it purchased the failed Franklin National Bank, a 100-branch system based in Long Island, New York, which had met disaster when it entered the New York wholesale banking market. At the time, the merger was described as the "canary swallowing the elephant," since the three-branch European American immediately increased its assets from U.S. $2 billion to U.S. $8 billion.

While the move was justified as "solidifying the bank's American presence," many bank analysts questioned the merger. Indeed, five years later an article in the U.S. business magazine *Forbes* still called it "the most unlikely marriage since Mickey Rooney and Ava Gardner."[1]

The two areas never did blend completely, and EAB remained in actuality two banks with two separate corporate cultures. Many of the "corporate" people in the bank looked upon the branch system only as a source of funds for U.S. and international lending, considered the "glamor" areas of banking. The branch system did indeed post only marginal profitability, while the corporate people bragged that the bank did business with more than half of the Fortune 500 companies.

It was this attitude that contributed to the bank's later problems. In the recession of 1980–1982, many of the corporate loans went to nonperforming status, a large number of international loans went sour, and the wholesale diamond business, for which European Anerican had been the leading U.S. bank, plunged dramatically. Even with the economic recovery in 1983, many of these Fortune 500 companies, such as International Harvester and American Motors, were still in financial trouble, as were many developing countries. The diamond business did not really recover, even with the return of prosperity, and then came the oil glut, which caused loans to OPEC countries and to drilling companies in the U.S. Southwest to become shaky.

At the same time, the business with European subsidiaries in the United States largely dried up, as U.S. banking regulations changed and the shareholder banks opened their own American offices. In the meantime, the branch business on Long Island, while not a stellar performer because it was largely ignored, did hold its own, since the Long Island economy had been one of the few in the United States to come through the recession unscathed. With the problems in U.S. and international banking, however, it became apparent that disaster was imminent if EAB did not radically alter its course.

A New Strategy
In March 1984 EAB's board of directors brought in Raymond Dempsey (widely known as "the bank doctor," for turning Fidelity Bank in Philadelphia around) as chairman and CEO to replace the previous chairman, who had retired six months earlier. Dempsey identified a number of immediate problems:

> The bank was top-heavy with senior management: a chairman, two vice chairmen, a president, nine executive vice presidents, and 25 senior vice presidents in an organization with only 4,000 employees.
>
> The bank was overstaffed and inefficient, especially in the operations area.
>
> The bank's "core" businesses, U.S. corporate and international lending, were unprofitable for EAB.
>
> The bank was in a number of esoteric businesses—mergers and acquisitions, barter and countertrade, foreign exchange consulting— in which it could not compete with larger banks.
>
> A huge (one million square feet) and expensive, two-tower operations and corporate office center recently opened on Long Island was not attracting the outside tenants that had been expected to occupy 50 percent of the complex (and pay for its construction).

With the approval of the board, Dempsey began to chart a dramatically different course for EAB. He began to reduce and restructure the overpadded ranks of senior management, eliminating expensive "perks" for those who remained. He then sold off or eliminated unprofitable businesses including the European Desks, Mergers and Acquisitions, Foreign Exchange, and Consulting. An early-retirement package was offered as a way to reduce staff, especially in the operations area.

Then, in July 1984, in a remarkable gamble, he wrote off in one stroke U.S. $132 million in nonperforming loans to developing countries, diamond merchants, real estate developers, and oil companies.

Dempsey said he did this to "put the past behind us and start with a new slate." The move was a gamble because it might cause a run on the bank by nervous depositors. The gamble paid off when the run never materialized, largely because of some well-planned communication programs:

Dempsey announced the loan write-off in the context of initiating a new strategy of concentrating on the consumer and small-business markets on Long Island. Most of the press stories, based on Dempsey's availability for personal interviews, focused on the new direction rather than the loan write-offs.

Research showed that consumer depositors, buoyed by the knowledge that their money is insured by the U.S. Federal Deposit Insurance Corporation (FDIC), are slower to withdraw their funds from banks than corporations are. Unlike Chicago-based Continental Illinois, which was faced with similar problems, the bulk of EAB's deposits were from consumers. Moreover, most of these depositors lived on Long Island and thus were in agreement with the new strategy.

Before the announcement, large depositors were personally told the reasons for the write-offs and the new direction.

Since EAB was not publicly held, it attracted less media attention than it would have if a stock slide had occurred at the same time. Moreover, an injection of U.S. $80 million in new capital by the shareholders was announced simultaneously.

The announcement was timed for July, when business news is for the most part ignored.

To deal with the "white elephant" that the operations center on Long Island had become, Dempsey announced that most New York City employees would move there, resulting in savings both by eliminating much of the rent that was being spent in more expensive New York City locations and by filling the vacant space that was costing money.

Communicating the Changes Internally
As can be imagined, the bank's many difficulties created huge morale problems among employees. Many older employees felt insecure in their positions, and many younger, upwardly mobile ones felt that they would do better to move to more successful companies.

Internal communication was used extensively during the changes to explain the new strategy and to reassure employees about the company's eventual recovery. Soon after he arrived, Dempsey gave a frank interview to the employee publication, outlining his philosophy of banking and the immediate changes he was planning.

Then, before the write-offs, the chairman held a series of meetings with all departments to explain the changes and the new strategy. He candidly answered all the questions, no matter how tough.

With each new development—and there were many, as various businesses were dropped or new moves to Long Island were announced—the chairman issued a bankwide report to all employees, explaining the reasons for each action.

Those employees scheduled to move to Long Island were informed personally in a letter from Human Resources. Those in New Jersey or Manhattan who found it difficult to move were offered financial assistance for a household move to Long Island, assistance in commuting (interest-free car loans or stipends for public transportation) or were offered a generous separation package if they decided to leave EAB's employ.

While the previous management had been remote from the rank and file, Dempsey initiated many social events for employees, such as picnics and receptions, at which he was available to talk with employees at all levels. Working conditions and employee areas like the cafeteria were greatly improved, reinforcing Dempsey's position that the bank was now healthy and ready for growth.

While change in an organization is always trying, employees who remained at EAB took on a spirit of "let's get on with it" as the organization moved back into profitability.

Dempsey had promised that with the write-offs behind it, EAB would be profitable in each succeeding quarter. As each quarter of 1985 proved the truth of the promise, morale grew better and better.

Communicating the New Strategy Internally

As we have mentioned, under the old regime EAB's branch system had been regarded as a poor stepchild to the more glamorous corporate areas. This had been true as much in self-image as in outside perception, and much had to be done to get branch personnel to believe that they were now the ones who would really "drive" the bank.

A number of steps were taken to bring this about:

1. Salaries for branch personnel were brought to a level that was competitive with those paid by other area banks.
2. A refurbishing of all branches was announced, with new furnishings, landscaping, and other improvements.
3. A commitment was announced to spend considerable funds on a new automated teller machine system to improve service.
4. Incentive programs were started, rewarding employees who brought in the most new individual retirement account (IRA) de-

posits, automated teller machine (ATM) card applicants, and so on. Prizes included trips to Hawaii and the Caribbean, as well as cash incentives.

5. Recruitment "bounties" were given to employees who brought in new teller applicants.

6. A new graphics and corporate color scheme was developed that was more consumer-oriented, replacing the old corporate maroon and ivory with a brighter green and white logo.

7. "EAB" rather than "European American" was highlighted, reflecting the fact that the international side of the business was no longer the bank's most important area.

8. A new publication, *Branch Update,* debuted in June 1985. First a monthly, and then a weekly as incentive campaigns tooled up, this simple, breezy newsletter kept branch personnel aware of developments important to them.

9. The monthly employee publication, *EAB People,* concentrated more on branch business news.

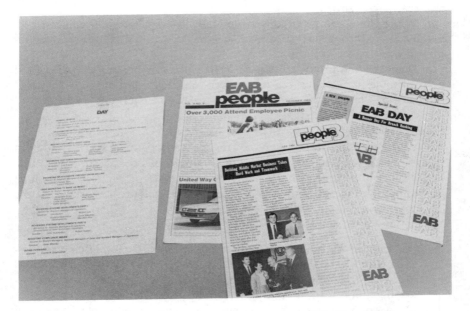

Figure 9.2. The EAB identity was featured on all materials, from the upgraded employee publications to the new periodicals, the advertising, and the customer materials. New graphics and corporate identity were reinforced through these publications and other employee materials.

10. *Branch Marketing Notes,* a publication that had been issued fitfully in the past, was given a new look and issued more frequently. It alerts branches to new products, changes, and other developments.
11. An all-day seminar for every branch manager and assistant manager was held on a Saturday to explain the new direction and other developments designed to help the branches improve their business. This seminar was featured in a special issue of *EAB People* that was devoted to "EAB Day."

EAB's new graphic identity will have an ongoing role in communicating the new strategy. According to one EAB advertising professional

> Most companies change their graphic image when they change their corporate direction. The repetitive use of "EAB" down the side in many of our ads and publications will solidify "EAB" in the public's mind rather than "European American Bank." Over time, the full name will get smaller and eventually disappear. By that time, we think no one will know it's gone.[2]

The corporate communication structure also was changed to reflect the new direction. Under the previous management, public relations had been a unit of the marketing group, which reported directly to the chairman. Though part of marketing, public relations had always operated independently and from a separate location. Under the new structure, public relations joined the marketing group physically as well as philosophically, becoming the Marketing Communications Unit. The marketing group became part of the Branch Banking Division at EAB Plaza, on Long Island. While those in the communication field who are jealous of their identity might see such reorganization as a problem, it communicated, as much as anything else, that the branch system was now the major area of the bank. What was the result of the bank's new strategy (and its communication effort)? EAB posted a U.S. $22 million profit in 1985 and, as of the end of 1986, had increased its profits in each successive quarter. Nothing demonstrates the success of good communication better than a healthy "bottom line."

CASE TWO: ALLSTATE INSURANCE COMPANY

> Communications strategy must be developed in concert with the overall business strategy.

This quote comes from Donald F. Craib's acceptance speech when the chairman and CEO of the Allstate Insurance Company received the award for "Excellence in Communication Leadership" from the International Association of Business Communicators in May 1986 in Kansas City, Missouri. The fact that Craib's remarks were teleconferenced from London is an indication of the communication benefits of advanced technology. The teleconferencing arrangements also point up the importance of the communication process at Allstate, one of the giants in the insurance industry in the United States. The key role of communication in Allstate's overall business strategy became especially apparent during the years 1983–1985, when Allstate embarked on a major, top-to-bottom reorganization program.

Craib and Richard Haayen, Allstate president, realized from the beginning that a major change in a company of Allstate's size (40,000 employees) and geographic breadth (4,000 offices throughout the United States), would require a well-planned communication strategy.

In 1982, when Don Craib took charge of Allstate, he realized that, although the company had an enviable profit record, its industry was "mature," with limited capacity for growth. In order to grow and compete, the company would need to become leaner—more efficient and more responsive to changes in the marketplace.

What was different between Allstate's approach to restructuring and the way most companies tend to operate was the company's decision to develop a comprehensive strategy for communicating change before undertaking any actual changes in the company itself. As Craib explained:

> We knew that the communications effort would have to involve top management in a very visible way. We knew that we would have to use every communications tool available and reinforce our basic messages at every opportunity. We knew that employees viewed managers and supervisors as the most credible communicators of all. And, finally, we knew that the communications effort would have to work both ways—that we would have to encourage a participative environment where dialogue was not a buzzword, but a reality.[3]

Allstate began by initiating a communication skills training program for *every* manager and employee, and within two years every manager and employee had gone through the program. Next the company introduced "growth teams"—groups of a dozen or so employees drawn from different departments at every field office. These "growth teams" were brainstorming circles, charged with finding ways to increase Allstate's market share and sell more insurance. By involving people from nonsales areas in these "growth teams," the company reinforced the message that every employee was involved in supporting marketing strategy.

To stress the importance of dialogue, Chairman Craib and President Haayen began "hitting the road" in what they termed "upward communication sessions" at Allstate's regional offices. Meeting with 15 to 20 employees at a time, from all levels and departments, they not only transmitted the company's strategies but also learned what was on employees' minds. Said Craib, in describing the sessions (which have become part of an ongoing program), "It's no holds barred, and I can tell you the questions get pretty pointed." The sessions are videotaped and distributed to Allstate locations around the country, added Craib, and managers are told: "If you aren't listening to your people, you should be."[4]

The "growth teams" and "upward communication sessions" were part of an effort to establish a more communicative culture within the company.

Figure 9.3. Employee publications and other communication efforts are used by Allstate Insurance to encourage closer employee identification with the company and its objectives. To focus on the importance of each employee to the company, existing publications were upgraded and issued more frequently and a life insurance publication and a management magazine were started.

To strengthen the new culture, formal channels of communication were also used to communicate information about the new direction.

One of the ways in which Allstate ensured that the company's communication programs were in step with its overall strategy was the creation of a communications board, composed of top operating executives and communication professionals. The board discussed communication strategy, evaluated publications, and suggested new uses of communication media that board members thought necessary.

While some communicators might consider a group like the communications board an infringement on their area of expertise, in fact it gives communicators one of the benefits most sought in a corporate environment: access to senior management.

Buck Williams, Allstate's communications director, said that the company's publications were realigned to reflect the new emphasis on sales:

> Formerly, each of the six major departments had its own magazine. Under the new strategy developed by the Communications Board, three departmental magazines were discontinued and the all-employee magapaper, *Allstate Now,* was upgraded and its frequency increased from six times a year to monthly. A new publication, *Allstate Life,* was introduced to demonstrate the new emphasis on life insurance products, and an employee annual report, *Perspective,* was produced to do what the title said, put the restructured company into perspective.
>
> In addition, a management magazine, *The Bottom Line,* was initiated to provide this key group with a communication vehicle to clearly outline company strategy. The magazine for the insurance agents, *Contact,* was also given more four-color pizzazz, to demonstrate the importance of the sales force to the company's success.[5]

Williams noted that the company's weekly videotape program, *Intercom,* was also revamped to highlight corporate changes more effectively and to address employee concerns more directly.

Allstate measures the effectiveness of its communication programs in two ways: by surveying the level of credibility among employees and by surveying the level of information that employees believe they are receiving from the company through the various information channels. Responses to these surveys indicate that the company is achieving its objectives.

Perhaps the best way to gauge the effectiveness of a company's communication programs is to look at the proverbial bottom line: Allstate's profits rose from U.S. $475 million in 1982 to U.S. $555 million in 1983 and to U.S. $660 million in 1984. Judged by that criterion, communicators at Allstate have certainly done an effective job, and they can take pride in the fact that despite the upheaval of change, they helped their company achieve success in its strategy of growth. As CEO Craib put it:

Allstate has become a more communicative company—more productive, more competitive, and more participative than ever. In a mature market . . . in an industry struggling with major problems . . . Allstate is thriving. I think it's because our strategy is on target, and because our employees understand that strategy.[6]

SUMMARY

The lesson to be learned from these two case studies is that communication professionals must be in step with the overall goals of the organization. Whether you work for a corporation, government agency, or not-for-profit organization, whether you work in marketing communication or public relations, as a communication professional you must be concerned about getting the organization's message across to the people who are going to make the organization a success or a failure—the people who work there.

The examples given involved crisis situations. But internal marketing is just as necessary when things are going well. For example:

When Barbara Findley, ABC, joined the Barnes Group, Inc., in Bristol, Connecticut, in 1985, as manager of corporate communication, one of her first assignments was to arrange visits by the CEO to the company's facilities around the country. The purpose of the visits was to present personal employee annual reports, which had always been given only to management-level employees.

Findley suggested that hourly workers be included because they had just as big a stake in the company's financial report. Some senior executives criticized this position, saying that hourly workers were not interested and would not understand the CEO's message.

Findley persisted and the CEO took her advice. He was gratified by the response: By their questions and attention at the meetings, the hourly workers demonstrated intense interest in the performance and direction of the company.[7]

Internal communication cannot work in a vacuum. Anyone involved in this discipline must ask the key question: "What am I doing to make my organization a success?"

NOTES

1. *Forbes,* 9 July 1979, 98.
2. Personal interview with EAB advertising professionals, February 1986.
3. Donald F. Craib in a speech teleconferenced to the international conference of

the International Association of Business Communicators in Kansas City, Missouri, May 1986.
4. Ibid.
5. Personal interview with Buck Williams, communications director, Allstate Insurance, June 1986.
6. Craib.
7. Personal interview with Barbara Findley, ABC, manager of corporate communication, Barnes Group, Inc., November 1986.

CHAPTER 10

Charting Audience Trends

Roberta Resnick, ABC*

Breathe a big sigh of relief . . . you have your new programs off the ground. Now you can sit back and relax. As the French are fond of saying, *Plus ça change, plus c'est la même chose.* The more things change, the more they stay the same. Right? Never more wrong—though it may have been true in the more leisurely past, when people's attitudes, needs, and expectations were less sophisticated. In those days changes were so gradual that they did not noticeably affect the communicator's ability to "read" audiences. If you came close to giving your audience what it wanted, you claimed success and followed up as necessary. "Keep up the good work," said everyone, including your boss.

But in today's marketplace, your audience changes rapidly in lifestyles, in demands, in needs, and in expectations. Attitudes change more slowly than these other characteristics, but they do change. What satisfied audiences yesterday may fail to meet their needs today. A miss is as good as a mile . . . and even a strategy that is right on target at the beginning may veer off course a few months later.

When this happens, what has gone wrong? Perhaps a new competitive product, service, or program has reached the marketplace and is diverting your consumers. Significant organizational events—a layoff, a takeover or consolidation battle, downsizing, or an abnormal increase in competitive pressure—may have caused a dramatic shift in employee attitudes, needs, or concerns. Then again, the shift may simply be the result of audience boredom with a program that has become too familiar and comfortable, that has failed to keep up with the times.

---

*Roberta Resnick, ABC, heads her own communication consultancy, Roberta Resnick & Associates, in Don Mills, Ontario, Canada. She is an accredited business communicator and a member of the board of the Marketing Council of the International Association of Business Communicators.

CHANGING ATTITUDES, BEHAVIOR, PERFORMANCE

People, whether employees or prospective customers, change constantly. Marketing communication is designed to tap those changes for the organization's advantage ("Buy my product," "It's not just for breakfast anymore," "Drive safely," "Buckle up!" "Work smarter/harder/faster," "Understand our position," "Give to my charity," "Use my hospital," "Vote for my candidate").

Our role as communicators is to bring about creative change in behavior or performance and, ultimately, in attitudes that enhance campaign, program, and organizational objectives. Once we have launched the campaign or introduced the program, we must analyze results and continue to monitor change. These activities help ensure that the key communication strategies—advantages and benefits—of the campaign or program reflect the changes that will inevitably occur in the audience or the key target market. When do the responses peak? How long before they slump? What factors in our particular marketplace are influencing those responses? How do we adjust our approach to keep results on track with our objectives?

It is imperative to monitor change in our target audience to make sure our primary messages or motivational programs meet ever-changing individual and group needs, attitudes, and expectations.

STAYING TOO LONG WITH A "GOOD THING"

There are a number of examples where competent marketers have simply stayed too long with a good campaign. A case in point:

> Radio City Music Hall, one of New York City's major institutions and tourist attractions, turned its first profit in 30 years in 1985, by adding the music and the musical stars of the 1980s to its traditional "family" entertainment. Alternating the Rockettes and first-run, G-rated feature films with Madonna and the Grateful Dead, Radio City Music Hall made a significant comeback; it now accounts for more than half of all concert tickets sold in the New York City area.

One wonders why it took management so long to recognize the major change that had occurred over the years in who actually selects and *purchases* entertainment. Teenagers and young adults now make those decisions and attend events in peer groups; to a great extent, entertainment ceased to be a family activity in the 1960s.

Another notable example:

> The U.S. National Safety Council and its original Safe Driving campaign featured photographs of automobiles horribly mangled in accidents that no one

could (or did) survive. At first, these ads caught the public's attention and were successful in scaring people into driving safely. But research conducted well into the campaign revealed that, eventually, the photographs were perceived as too awful to think about. People simply could not bring themselves to identify with those situations and concluded, "That can't happen to me," "I only drive close to my home," or "I don't drive that fast." Thus, a campaign designed to encourage drivers to be careful resulted in a rejection of the basic premise.

Even though campaign managers knew that their audience—the general public—emotionally rejected the application of twisted metal to their driving habits, the campaign continued for several more years. Only recently did the old campaign give way to more current public concerns: use of seat belts and prevention of drunk driving (the latter largely the result of efforts by Candy Lightner and the Texas-based Mothers Against Drunk Driving, or MADD). Drunk driving causes death on a nation's streets and highways; using seat belts has statistically been proven to save lives.

These newer campaigns involve and motivate the public, because people can identify with—and take action on—helping to reduce their own risk of death and destruction: "I can wear my seat belt," "If I'm driving, I won't drink." Yet, these campaigns do not and will not change behavior until the very action becomes part of the fabric of our society. For that reason, both use of seat belts and the degree of impairment from alcohol become critical aspects of automobile accident investigations by the police, as well as part of the media reports on them. In addition, seat belt laws, where enacted, need to be enforced constantly and consistently.

Public information campaigns for the use of seat belts and against driving while under the influence of alcohol are periodically geared up to address specific patterns of public behavior—travel during holidays, long weekends, and summer vacations. In Toronto a seasonal spot-check program empowers police to stop motorists at random and suspend licenses immediately if they find alcohol impairment. The program has been so successful in reducing highway accidents during holiday periods that it has been extended for the entire calendar year. Public support of the program, called RIDE (Reduce Impaired Driving Everywhere), has grown over the past few years, so that the additional personnel and equipment required to conduct these spot-checks are now available. Despite this change in emphasis from periodic to permanent program, continuous marketing of the program to the public is still required, to ensure that people continue to heed the need for care and caution in both their drinking and driving habits.

High school students in a number of small Ontario towns are making news by running their own campaigns to reduce drunk driving among their peers. Thus, continuing publicity reflects the changes that are taking place in attitudes about drunk driving.

BETTER LATE THAN NEVER

A number of business organizations, presently engaged in restructuring their diversified and far-flung operations for today's marketplace, are looking at their publications as a reflection of that change.

Gulf & Western, Beatrice, Transamerica Corporation, and AT&T are only a few of the companies that recognize not only their employees' changing attitudes toward their jobs and the company but also the need to compete for employees' reading time. As a result, a number of publications are being redesigned in both content and appearance to address both issues: holding together increasingly diversified parts of the organization, thus unifying their respective employees, and competing with consumer magazines for readership by using similarly attention-getting format and design.

The news and feature stories in commercial newspapers also are reflecting changes in target audience attitudes and sensitivities, particularly in sections that once were called "The Women's Page," then "Life," "Lifestyles," or "Modern Living." News about social events, recipes, and homemaking has given way to in-depth discussion of such modern issues as sexual harassment, child and adult abuse, wage and salary inequities between men and women, responsibility for child care in a two-career family. These topics appeal to men as well as women.

INCORPORATE THE NEW, BUT KEEP YOUR PROGRAM'S INDIVIDUALITY

Does that mean we all have to aim for total redesign in appearance and content to make us look like the magazines our readers pull off a newsstand or drop into their supermarket carts? Certainly not. It does mean, however, that we must continue to keep our eyes and ears open for the changes affecting our audiences that could and should be reflected in the work we do. Taking the pulse of an organization usually plays a key role in implementing a *new* communication program. Yet it may be even more essential in critically evaluating *existing* programs to see how they are meeting the objectives on today's agenda.

Most communicators are extremely sensitive to their mandate to keep published news as current as possible. But there are other key communication programs that, once designed, implemented, and running smoothly, tend to be forgotten by communicators and top management. What is the communicator's role in adjusting these programs, some of which are maintained by administrators and coordinators outside the communicator's domain, to better meet the audience's changing reactions and needs?

Campaigns, both internal and external, fall into two major categories: those which are always underway, like safety and suggestion programs, and those which receive annual or periodic attention for a fairly limited period of time, such as product and service promotions and fundraising events wholly or partially sponsored by the organization.

Whatever their duration or value, campaigns in both categories must be marketed or "sold" regularly to target audiences. Such marketing requires strategic planning and the application of these strategies to tactical communication, programs, or events to achieve desired results: increased sales, enhanced image, greater participation, fewer accidents, more ideas, increased contributions to charity, or whatever.

Monitor the results the program was designed to obtain. When results show that an ongoing program is slipping, rejuvenate it with a new promotion to your target audience or change it to adjust to any changes you find in your audience's attitude, needs, or expectations. Market it as a "new, improved" edition.

CONTINUING CAMPAIGNS: THE CASE OF THE ORGANIZATION'S SAFETY PROGRAM

There is nothing like a serious accident to make safety a high priority in an organization. All manufacturing operations—and a number of service organizations—place a high priority on safe working conditions and habits. Accidents cost money in terms of lost time for affected employees; they also may increase the organization's workers' compensation expenses. At the very least, lost-time accidents may mean poor inspection reports by governmental agencies such as the Occupational Safety and Health Administration in the United States or a Provincial Labour Department in Canada. No wonder, then, that safety is a primary management responsibility and concern.

Before designing, redesigning, or changing the communication program, review the existing safety program, asking the following questions:

How long has the safety program been in force?

When was the last time management made an issue of it? Most likely, it was just after the last major accident!

How frequently is a major promotion conducted to "sell" safety to employees?

Does the program include reminders? incentive contests or awards?

Are the reminders and incentives boring? When were they last changed?

What is your organization's or plant's standing in the workers' compensation safety rating list for your industry and location? The lower your organization's standing, the higher its workers' compensation assessment is likely to be.

How do your employees react to the program emotionally? Do they respond positively? Do they like it? Do they care about safety?

Is management aware of the results achieved with the current program?

If the program has been in effect for longer than three years, chances are it needs a new approach and a brand new selling campaign for employees. Just as marketing campaigns (new-product launches, special promotions, television commercials, and the like) eventually wear out and become tiresome through continued repetition over a period of time, employee programs become stale from familiarity. Employees lose interest, and accident rates increase. Even safety incentive contests lose their effectiveness: the higher the accident rate, the less likely anyone is to win the prizes or awards associated with the safety program. The results the program was originally designed to achieve can no longer be obtained.

Suppose a major accident occurs, even in the midst of a successful, positive, popular safety incentive campaign. The tendency may be to look at what is wrong with the campaign, rather than to search for basic flaws in the system.

Perhaps your organization employs a number of people for jobs requiring few, if any, recognized skills. If their tasks include operating equipment that could be dangerous to the employee, two consequences are possible: someone could get hurt, or an employee could refuse to work at a job he or she perceives as dangerous. In the United States and Canada, the employee can legally walk off the job and take others along.

One way to monitor what is happening in the organization is to read accident reports prepared by an injured employee, those who were working near him or her, the line supervisor, and the safety inspector from the regulatory agency. One communicator who read the file on an accident saw this statement by a supervisor: "I told her not to do that (place her hands near the cutting edge of the knives at her station)." The 17-year-old employee had just lost two fingers of her left hand, ostensibly because she had failed to follow instructions. However, no formal training procedures for the injured girl's job existed, nor was there any written guidance to help a line supervisor make sure that a new employee knew how to operate the equipment safely.

The communicator concluded that it was impossible for anyone to judge whether people were being properly trained, because nothing was documented. It seemed more likely that experienced employees were passing on bad habits to new people. From this conclusion came an entire program, with the full support and participation of plant management, to document proper machine operation including specific training instructions and safety precautions. The instructions were not only distributed to people new on the machine but also served as guides for on-the-job training by line supervisors. A training log recorded both the training time spent with each new employee and the distribution of instructional materials. All formal off-the-job training courses also were recorded. The company remains liable for safety in the work environment, of course, but there is now documented uniformity in on-the-job training activities. Now everyone can sit back and relax, right? Not yet.

CONTINUING CAMPAIGNS: THE CASE OF THE SUGGESTION PROGRAM

Suggestion programs are the forerunners of quality circles. Although the problem-solving exercise is less involving for participants than for those in a quality circle, suggestion programs offer some distinct advantages. They are open to everyone in an organization (all of whom have an opportunity to earn extra cash and receive official recognition), they require less training on the part of administrators, and they are considerably less threatening to line and middle-management people.

They do, however, demand a high degree of management commitment, and, like other employee programs, they periodically lose their "oomph" as ongoing motivators and thus lose their potency as interest generators. They will need redesign or rejuvenation and ongoing promotion.

Employee suggestion programs are important not only because they tap the knowledge and observations of the people closest to the actual work, but also because they are an excellent source of information about malfunctions in company systems or procedures, negative supervisory attitudes, and the quality of a variety of services paid for or supported by the company (cafeteria, dispensing machines, and the like). They serve as an avenue for complaints from people who might otherwise never speak up. Thus they are often a prime souce of information about changing employee attitudes, expectations, and needs.

Successful suggestion programs incorporate a number of key elements:

They are promoted regularly throughout the organization, though only partly by official recognition of those who earn both large and small awards.

As big a fuss as possible is made over those who have earned big awards and who thus have made the most important contribution to operational improvements.

They are perceived by both participants and nonparticipants as fair in their evaluation and acceptance of ideas.

Key management people serve on the coordination and review committee, thus communicating that management places a high priority on employee input.

Replies—both acceptances and rejections—have an upbeat motivational tone, and decisions are communicated as quickly as possible.

Participants are kept appraised of the status of their submissions when evaluation time is longer than is normal for the system.

The program is periodically boosted by hefty increases in cash awards and organizationwide campaigns to increase awareness and participation.

Complaints submitted through the program are handled as quickly and seriously as are employee-suggested solutions to operational problems.

Communicators can help maintain top company performance on these key elements by making sure that activities respond to employee attitudes and needs. Here are some key steps:

1. Check the program regularly. If the number of suggestions declines, it may be time to look for a new way to market the program to employees.
2. Ask to read employee suggestions to get a feel for the kinds of problems that line employees are identifying.
3. Better yet, offer your help in preparing replies. Some standard replies are demotivational ("This is not a new idea!"). You can play a major role in drafting responses that maintain individual pride and dignity even when ideas are rejected by the committee.
4. Look for ways to add "hoopla" to reminder campaigns and to increase recognition of award winners.
5. Plan special events, with trumpets blaring and balloons flying— anything to reaffirm, indirectly, the value of the program to both employees and the organization.
6. Be the conscience of the local committee and coordinators by emphasizing fairness in evaluations, speed of replies and supportive tone in letters, particularly if you have nothing to do with them.
7. Redesign, on a regular basis, the drop boxes and the forms used for the program; make sure the rules and regulations are up-to-date on the nature of current awards.

After each major boost to the program, review the results and monitor them for numbers and for content. Many employee suggestions relate to safety, providing valuable information about possible flaws in the existing safety program. Others may deal with quality improvements, which can be related to other efforts throughout the organization.

Adjust the suggestion program to include a bonus award for safety or quality suggestions that relate to current priorities, such as zero defects. If, for example, your basic suggestion award is U.S. $50, add a $25 bonus for good ideas for safety or quality improvements. That bonus award communicates the organization's emphasis on the "problem of the year" and tends to focus employee creativity on that problem. Your programs are unified without a major upheaval, and you have a new aspect for each program that can be marketed to employees.

Use the information you get from the employee suggestions as critical feedback for where programs, systems, or procedures may be off target. When something is not working right, employees will spot it. Their suggested solutions may not be the answer, but they will have highlighted an important need *from their perspective*. Therefore, rejected suggestions are just as important as accepted ones because they pinpoint problems and identify employee attitudes toward their work environment. *Now* can you sit back and take it easy? Nope.

WEAVE SUPPORTIVE CONCEPTS THROUGH MANY PROGRAMS

There are many ways to skin a cat, says the old cliché. A communication program designed to fill one specific information need also can reinforce another existing communication program, like safety.

Almost all employees believe that quality is their competitive advantage, and not only because, as communicators, we tell them so . . . and frequently. They truly take pride in achieving that high level of quality. Similarly, they can be emotionally devastated when a major production problem affects the finished product.

Everyone knows that mistakes are unavoidable, but you try to keep their nature and number small in order to minimize their impact on the organization. In a food-processing operation, for example, procedures are stringently followed to make sure production anomalies are caught in the plant, before the product reaches the marketplace. The same is true in other industries with less potential for injury or illness.

When you manufacture durable goods, or even some kinds of consumer packaged goods, you can often put each of your products through tests that reveal the efficacy and quality of each unit before it leaves the plant. With canned food, however, once the food is sealed in cans at the rate of 200 to 300 cans per minute, the only way to see what has happened in each can is to open it and examine the contents. That gives you 100 percent quality assurance, but it leaves you nothing to sell, because you have destroyed it all. So canned foods are tested by sampling, directly off the production line and at various stages thereafter. Finished product leaves the plant only when the samples have survived an incubation period of storage at extremely high temperatures for up to 10 days. This precautionary procedure simulates the reaction of the sealed cans to 12 to 18 months of storage in warehouses, local retail stores, and the consumer's pantry.

The canned fruit and vegetable packing season in Canada lasts only as long as it takes to harvest each fresh crop. During this time, canneries run 24 hours a day: two work shifts of 10 hours each, with the remaining four hours devoted to cleaning the equipment for the next day's run.

One year, toward the end of the tomato harvest, a major Canadian processor discovered a problem with the entire pack of the most popular-sized can of one of these seasonal products. The company knew that the problem did not affect every can, but the only way to ensure product quality was to remove all the sealed and labeled cans from every carton and check the integrity of each can by putting it through nondestructive tests. Morale throughout the plant plummeted to rock-bottom, even among seasonal employees.

How incredible, thought the communicator, that people with little in common except the end result of their labor could feel so universally demoralized by having, literally, to redo the work. The thought lingered for a long time.

Several years later, the time came to use the information gained during that experience. The production line seemed to be producing more "anomalies" than ever—not large ones, as in the incident with the entire seasonal pack, but a succession of small ones. Management began to seek solutions to these problems. One possibility was to initiate a communication program to feed back crucial production information to hourly employees. How well had they done on each shift and with each case of food produced over that period of time? It was information they had never before received, and no one could be sure they wanted it. But it seemed essential to group performance: how can you work more effectively today if you do not know how well you did yesterday?

Middle management at the plants—managers, superintendents, line supervisors—were extremely resistant to the idea: "It's just too complicated," "They won't understand it," "They don't care." Thinking back to the low morale when an entire pack had to be reconditioned, the communicator knew damn well they did care. However, designing a feedback program that meant something in easy-to-understand terms was a different matter.

With the support of the president and the vice president of manufacturing, the communicator appealed to the industrial engineering manager. Could they develop a formula, based on four or five major production elements, that could interpret specific data in terms of plus or minus 100? If employees saw 100, for example, it would mean they had done well; 102, extremely well; 99 or less, something had gone wrong. However, that "something" had to be under *their* control, not management's.

"Why not factor in safety and quality, too?" the industrial engineer suggested, explaining that the results could be adjusted downward for major and minor accidents and for product segregations (major) and holds (minor) that meant additional testing and checking before the finished product could be released to prime stock for distribution.

"What a terrific idea," said the communicator. "And suggestions relating to quality improvements can earn more than other types of ideas accepted in the suggestion program!"

The communicator met with each management group to get additional suggestions for adjustments to the formula as outlined, since each operation was unique in type of product, equipment, labor assignments, and processing of raw materials. Each plant would have a 6-foot-by-4-foot blackboard that could be easily updated and would be imprinted with an explanation of the formula and the point penalties. Managers at the company's three plants remained unconvinced it could work, but they grudgingly agreed to make sure that the information was posted daily for each of the shifts involved.

The program was promoted in advance to employees through bulletin board announcements. Other elements in the initial marketing campaign included an employee contest to name the program, with the winner to receive a television set as a prize. Interest—evidenced by the number of submissions—ran high, and a management committee selected the name "Pipeline." The winner was announced in the employee publication at the start of the program, and posters and payroll stuffers were prepared to promote the program to hourly employees. The record boards went up, and the feedback information was posted. Hooray! The program was launched.

Early reactions from the management group at one location, however, continued to be negative: "No one is looking at *your* board." "Don't worry," said the communicator. "It'll take some time for them to get used to it and to understand what they're seeing." Three weeks later: "No one is looking at *your* board!" "Where did you put the board?" the communicator asked. "Down by the time clocks." "Good. I think I'll go down and take a look at it myself," the communicator ventured. "You won't see anyone looking at it."

Sure enough, no one was. The board was indeed mounted in the same area as the time clocks, but off in a corner where there was no natural traffic. Employees would have to walk out of their way, lean over several pallets loaded with cases of product, and then walk back to the time clocks to punch in or out.

The board was soon relocated on a high-traffic wall in the same area, and by the time people got into the habit of looking at it, plant managers had claimed the program as their own. They even made sure the critical data were posted during the hectic 20-hour production days of the fresh-vegetable packing season.

Remember, the program may be right on target, but results may be affected by external elements. Before you replace or adjust the program, make sure you check all elements related to its implementation. If you cannot physically follow through yourself—as the communicator at the canning plant did—make sure the program does not get torpedoed by its detractors, who may subconsciously arrange for it to live up to their expectations instead of yours.

Certainly, now, you can sit back and accept congratulations! Well, not quite yet.

In a union environment, consideration must be given to the concept of "perking" a program, as opposed to paying for performance. Essentially, everyone is expected to produce first-quality results. If special rewards are made for alert and careful effort, which can rightly be considered a condition of employment, there is a danger that hourly workers will perform well and be on their toes only if there is something extra in it for them. Once you begin awarding that something extra, people can come to expect good performance to be followed by extraordinary rewards, when, in truth, you are simply emphasizing the high standards you consider routine.

A few months after the "Pipeline" feedback program was underway, two of the three plant managers—both fully aware of potential consequences and increased expectations—decided to add a small "perk": free coffee for everyone responsible for a production rating of 100 or better.

The manager of the third location decided to carry on with the program as designed for as long as possible, even though the probable need for periodic "perking" had been discussed at the initial meetings. Eventually, feedback through first-line supervisors began to indicate that employees at this plant thought the comparison between night-shift and daytime production was unfair; management was setting up "unhealthy competition" between two groups operating under totally different circumstances. According to the feedback, employees thought the night supervisor was deliberately being made to look bad.

The competition between shifts and between product lines was exactly what top management was after. One of the initial objectives of the program was to instill a "we can do better than they can" attitude on the part of those in different groups. However, no one anticipated that any individual would be singled out as the "fall guy." So the night supervisor was asked about any discomfort he might be experiencing as a result of an unfair comparison. "No," he said, "the reasons for any production shortfalls on my shift are fully documented in the daily log, and my boss knows that most of them are beyond my control. I don't have a problem, but it's kind of interesting that my people think I do."

When the third plant manager finally decided to "perk" the program with free coffee for 100-plus production ratings, he included a challenge to employees in his own newsletter, which was produced regularly and posted on the plant bulletin boards. "Have a coffee on me . . . *please*," he wrote. "I'll be happy to pay the tab." The implication that he was personally paying for the coffee was deliberate—and effective, even though everyone knew the company would absorb the expense. For a number of weeks, the manager was challenged by groups of employees to "get ready to pay up" for *tomorrow's* results. Employees put their best effort into their work simply to collect a free cup of coffee.

When developing an incentive program, remember that the rewards do not have to be substantial. They just have to be there. In fact, modest perks can be extremely cost-effective: the cost of coffee for 35 to 50 people is nothing compared to the expense of rechecking product that fails to meet production standards.

THE CONTINUING PROGRAM: THE CASE OF PERSONNEL ACTIVITIES

Chances and improvements in existing organizational systems and programs often have to be marketed, first to management and then across the organization to employees. This is particularly true of personnel programs because of their profound effect on everyone in the organization.

American Express Canada was considering a change in its existing performance appraisal program that enabled employees formally to evaluate their managers and supervisors on predetermined management skills. This upward evaluation program had been extremely successful for two or three years, but personnel people began to pick up signals of "wear-out." They decided to experiment with a major change in emphasis for the performance appraisal process with a control group of six to eight people from one department.

At the conclusion of the pilot project, the participating employees, who were very enthusiastic about the new program, volunteered to present it to senior management. They made their own videotaped commercial and expanded the presentation with videotaped role playing of performance appraisal discussions. The department manager and supervisor played the roles of employees, and the staff took the management roles. The new program is based on a "win/win" philosophy of negotiations and is explicitly geared toward helping employees analyze their own career goals and objectives. The concluding segment of the presentation to management was formatted as a live game show that revealed that six of the eight people in the pilot group had made career changes within the company and were highly motivated and enthusiastic.

The communication and personnel departments at American Express Canada assisted the control group with technical aspects of the presentation, but made no effort to make it slick or professional. The individual enthusiasm and creativity exhibited by this group resulted in a sales presentation of almost unprecedented credibility. As a result, every vice president in the organization accepted the new program, primarily on the basis of the presentation.

Selling ideas for key employee program changes to management may require the same marketing magic you use to reach other target user or participant audiences.

THE PERIODIC, OR REPETITIVE, PROGRAM

Rarely does a target audience rise up to make its views as clearly or as widely known as "old Coke" drinkers did when the Coca-Cola Company replaced its traditional product with "new Coke." In most instances, you have to dig for information about audience response to a given event or project. Much of the information you seek can be found in a careful analysis of the results of the program or in openly questioning a random sampling of the target audience. This is true for ongoing programs as well as those for limited campaigns such as United Way campaigns, quality-improvement campaigns, product promotions, and direct mail efforts, which can be measured in terms of actual results. United Way campaigns may draw the same reaction from you as they do from many of your audience: "Oh, no, not again!" The path of least resistance is to do what you have always done: take key canvassers to United Way agencies to see how the money is used, feature touching photographs of children and old people in your publication, and so on. If that is your approach, check results for the past few years. A noticeable pattern of reduced employee contributions, or even a plateau in donation levels, is a signal that something new and dramatic is called for.

Since the objective of the campaign is to increase contributions, a historical pattern of decline or plateau signals a need for more punch in the introduction of the program in order to arouse audience compassion and cause either a response from more people or an increase in levels of giving from those who normally respond to such an appeal. Look at previous campaigns analytically and at each proposed one creatively. And do not hesitate to get sample opinions from your audience about what might appeal to them. Better yet, ask what they think will motivate **their colleagues** to participate.

Zero defects and other quality-improvement campaigns should be built on results of quality-control information from the production line. Make sure you have access to this information. When each product cannot be checked before it reaches the marketplace, feedback from customers will tell you what you need to know about the success of an internal quality campaign. Monitor customer contacts with your organization (telephone calls, letters) that communicate satisfaction or dissatisfaction. Discuss this feedback with manufacturing and marketing personnel to make sure you have as realistic a picture of the situation as possible. Then get ready to market your recommendations for changes and improvements to the appropritate manager or management group.

Marketing promotions for products or services should include evaluation procedures for analyzing results of each promotion. Take the initiative in analyzing the results of each promotion. Do not wait for others to do it. Marketers are usually working on the next promotion before the final results are available from the last one; they are mentally tuned into the future, not the past. Yet problems may arise before a promotion is completed: supplies of premium items may be depleted, redemption houses may be slow in responding to consumer inquiries, consumers may not understand contest rules and regulations or the length of time it takes to choose and inform winners. Prizes may fail to reach winners, or the individual preferences relating to prizes may require additional special handling. A million things could go wrong, and many do.

Everyone involved in promotions should be aware of problems that may be encountered in the follow-up and conclusion stages, so the next promotion can be modified or changed to avoid them. The purpose of promotions is to increase sales of products or services through *satisfied* customer participation. Marketers are doomed to repeat mistakes unless someone (you?) takes the initiative to call their attention to the need for change.

Direct mail pieces, to internal and external audiences, usually produce straightforward results: recipients either respond or they do not. But you might get a greater response next time by avoiding phrasing that may be perceived as negative or irritating, by emphasizing more persuasively your organization's ability to fill a potential need, or by pleading a better case for your organization's need for funds or volunteers. Why not propose a follow-up inquiry to a random sampling of nonrespondents, using their answers to develop future mailings? Or plan a similar mailing to some of those who *did* respond, asking what prompted them to take positive action?

REVIEWING QUALITATIVE RESULTS

Results analysis may not be appropriate for some special programs, particularly those designed primarily to honor or motivate employees, either as individuals or as a group. Extraordinary milestones, like the one-millionth customer served or product manufactured, also fall into this category. When you plan an event to celebrate or recognize employee contributions to the organization's success, follow-up analysis usually relies on qualitative data, primarily feedback from the people involved. A successful one-time special event might generate such employee enthusiasm that both verbal and written feedback will be voluntarily forthcoming. Even with unsolicited feedback, though, ask as many participants as possible about their reactions to these events. They may, and probably will, provide valuable ideas for making the next event even better.

The same thing is true of long-service recognition, whether the recognition occurs regularly in a workplace ceremony, in your publication, or through an annual dinner or special evening. With ongoing programs like employee recognition, solicit the information you need from the people who are honored at these events. If your organization has a Quarter-Century Club or similar group, contact people who have been in it for some time to see if the program, or agenda, has become too predictable and routine. If the group includes an unusual number of "old-timers," you may want to perk the agenda to include special recognition or participation for those at the upper end of the service scale, in addition to welcoming the newcomers.

For a repetitive program, take the time to analyze carefully and completely the results of each event. Be prepared to measure how good or bad the results were in terms of previous history and reasonable expectation. What made it successful, or why did it miss its mark? What can you learn from participants or attenders to make the next event more memorable and enjoyable?

EVERY CONTACT WITH YOUR AUDIENCE IS POTENTIAL FEEDBACK

Letters from consumers inform marketers of the impact and progress of new product launches and promotions; letters from internal sources provide general reactions to employee-oriented programs or messages. Your organization may already be receiving comments for "Letters to the Editor," "Speak Up" programs, or a question-and-answer column for the publication. These communications are audience reactions to both the climate of and the events within your organization. Positive and negative reactions to policies, systems, procedures, and programs will tell you something about how well you are doing in your own communication and special-events marketplace. They provide top management with information about how well they are doing, too.

When these responses indicate a lack of understanding about what the program or system is designed to do, they may be pointing out a need for clarification or expansion. Alternatively, they may reflect a general dissatisfaction with a program that is beginning to wear out.

How can you determine which solution is called for in any given situation? Listen, question, analyze, and interpret information from as many sources as you can.

Communication channels already operating to elicit informal employee feedback on a wide range of subjects, at the employee's discretion, are excellent sources of information about the remaining vitality or efficacy of other programs in force. These channels include department meetings where supervisors and managers encourage their people to speak up and informal lunch meetings with the president or another top executive, where randomly selected employees can ask questions and obtain immediate answers.

> A major Canadian financial and travel organization holds regular "Let's Talk" sessions with groups of 15 to 20 employees and the president. Brown-bag lunches reinforce the informal nature of the get-together, and participants are encouraged not only to ask questions but also to raise complaints and offer suggestions for discussion and response. Not all subjects can be fully explored during these sessions, but all are investigated and responses made later and distributed widely. The communicator sits in on every session with each group, ensuring appropriate follow-up and contributing to accurate interpretation of the meaning and implications of the questions asked or subjects broached.
>
> The program is open to all employees, management and clerical, in mixed groups, though supervisors and their subordinates never attend the same session. The program has been successful enough to survive two different presidents, the one who initiated the program and his successor. The discussions turn up vital information about management systems, supervisory attitudes and skills, major acquisitions or divestments, general operational activities, incentive and recognition programs, performance appraisal and objective setting, and, yes, communication programs.
>
> As a result of this feedback, programs and operations are under constant review and are continually adjusted to keep them in tune with organizational and individual needs. This may sound as if everything undergoes continuous upheaval, but that is not at all the case. Rather, operational and program improvements are triggered by members of key audiences at all levels, who will eventually see the impact of their contributions in progressive stages over the long term. Now, that is really keeping your finger on the pulse of audience response!

This kind of information about audience response is available at any given time through a number of existing feedback channels. You need only tap them regularly for updates.

BACK TO BASICS

It is important to go back periodically to your original research—to the information that helped you start the program in the first place. These data represent a benchmark for follow-up surveys, audits for new quantitative measurement, or new focus groups for updated qualitative data. Any of these research methods will enable you to identify and measure the extent and duration of changes that have occurred in the audience since the program began. Look for key indicators to help you outline the action or adaptation you believe is required to fill new needs or expectations.

A word of caution, however. Be careful not to mistake a change in the composition of the target audience for a change in attitude; your solution will be way off base. A dropoff in participation or interest may indicate not "wear-out," but a lack of understanding about the program's objectives on the part of the audience. Investigate further: the program might be revived simply by providing information about its purposes to the new people who have joined the organization since the program was launched.

FEEDBACK FROM WALKING AROUND

. Is anything in the organization off-limits to inquiry and suggestion on the part of the communicator? Not really. Communicators have extraordinary mobility and a wide range of personal contacts in their organizations. Keeping your sensitive antennae alert and drawing reasonable conclusions from what you see and hear can make you extremely valuable as ombudsperson, facilitator, or expediter. But make careful use of the opinions and observations that come your way. If you sit on them or in any way abuse them, you will lose not only your sources but also your credibility as a conduit.

Managers manage by walking around, by being available to their people. Communicators also get valuable information either by deliberately making themselves available or by just being there. For many employee groups, accessibility is the key to feedback; many people will not write letters to the editor, submit suggestions, or participate actively in a feedback group. But they may respond to impromptu, open-ended questions that seek their opinions of policies, programs, procedures, informal communication, publications. Do not take just one person's opinion; ask around, and look for a pattern. If someone tells you something that indicates a program is failing to do its job, chances are you will get similar feedback from others. And do not let anyone tell you to ignore the comments of "chronic complainers." They just may be the ones willing and able to verbalize the thoughts of others who lack the opportunity or courage to speak up.

If the verbal feedback can be quantified, go back and carefully analyze the results, patterns, and audiences for a given program. If it has outlived its usefulness, design a new program and launch it with pizzazz. But be careful about publicly "burying" a program, because someday you may find it necessary to revive it. It may be wiser simply to let an existing program become dormant while you market a new one. We regularly add new channels to our communication network: a computer bulletin board provides faster distribution of information than the management newsletter; a telephone news hotline for employees in the field supplements traditional announcements or bulletin boards. You do not give up one for the other; rather, usage alters the emphasis.

MONITORING A COMPANY SAFETY PROGRAM: A CASE HISTORY

A major Canadian food company operates several plants within 20 miles of one another in southwestern Ontario. Employee safety at each location has always received some management attention, but the programs were rarely promoted, except for low-key activities at the company's can-manufacturing operation. Employees at the can plant, which was only 10 years old, had achieved an enviable record of 2 million work hours without a lost-time accident, when tragedy struck.

During a night shift, three men were cleaning equipment in preparation for the next day's production when a flash fire broke out and engulfed two of them, killing one almost immediately. The second man lingered in the hospital for several weeks before succumbing to burns. The third man escaped serious injury, but the fire had started so quickly that he could remember almost nothing about it.

Investigation of the accident by the company, the Provincial Department of Labour, and the Provincial Fire Marshall's Office revealed that the men had been following undocumented but generally accepted standard procedure, using a Class A flammable solvent to wash down the equipment. Even a single spark of static electricity could have ignited the solvent.

In fact, a much larger problem was disclosed by the accident investigation: a number of highly flammable chemicals were being used everywhere in the can-making operation. Many of these and other potentially dangerous chemicals were discovered in an audit of the company's other plants. In almost every case, the chemicals were being handled without awareness of their hazards on the part of those who used or stored them. Up to now, employees had simply been lucky.

The company launched an all-out safety program for every location. The program included: specific safety guidelines and procedures for handling all volatile materials, emergency evacuation procedures for each location, special safety instructions for skilled workers who used welding equipment, lock-out procedures for equipment repair to make certain that machines could not be activated while electricians and machinists were working on them, safe vessel-entry procedures, and "hot work" permits that made sure fire alarms were inactivated during any repairs that created enough heat to set them off and then made sure the alarms were reactivated.

The Quality Assurance Department (QA) obtained safety precautions and medical-treatment instructions from all suppliers of chemicals, no matter how benign the chemicals seemed. QA also was made responsible for ensuring that all members of top manufacturing management approved the acquisition of any new chemicals so that proper storage facilities could be arranged and safety instructions for their use could be issued.

Handouts were prepared and distributed to all full-time employees and to the hundreds of seasonal people hired each summer. The handout material included a form that each employee signed to acknowledge that he or she had read and understood the safety rules and regulations. The signed acknowledgement became a part of each employee's personnel file.

Tens of thousands of dollars were spent to update firefighting and emergency breathing equipment and to install emergency showers, eye baths, stretchers, and first aid centers wherever necessary. Structural posts were painted red to identify locations of fire extinguishers, and maps were posted in every department to show everyone, including visitors, the fastest evacuation route in an emergency. For the first time, production was interrupted for regular fire drills, and emergency committees were established to take head counts in order to make sure everyone was outside the buildings.

Within six to eight months after the fire, the company had in place a model safety program that was being emulated by other companies in the area and by all the other production facilities of the multinational parent corporation. The program included an employee incentive program, announced by the president and promoted through bulletin board announcements, the employee publication, and letters to employees' homes. Safety Bingo was designed to reward employees for working safely and for keeping safety uppermost in their minds. For each week of accident-free operations, numbers were drawn for employees to record on Safety Bingo cards. Cash prizes were awarded to those who completed their cards according to bingo rules (horizontal, vertical, corner-to-corner, and so on).

More than any other element of the program—employee handouts, safety training, evacuation education and practice—the Safety Bingo program generated individual interest and involvement. Crowds gathered for the drawings that resulted from safe operations, and employees who were absent for both a drawing and the posting of drawn numbers were likely to rush to the personnel office on their return to find out if their numbers had been drawn. Winners were publicly announced, congratulated, and rewarded. The number of accidents, both major and minor, declined.

It would have been easy for management to sit back then and turn its attention to other problems. But after more than a year of intensive activity on a single program, new habits of awareness had become ingrained in the management group. Safety Bingo maintained its efficiency for yet another year, at which time accident rates started rising, and offhand comments from line employees began to reflect a growing boredom with the incentive program as it stood.

Plant management correctly read this change in attitude and decided to perk the program. They requested a new contest design, with higher cash awards. And they inaugurated the new contest with all the hoopla associated with the original.

Thus the valley of response in the wear-out phase was turned into another peak—but another valley is always just down the road. Regardless of the composition of the employee group or the innovation built into the program, you can expect that up-and-down pattern to continue forever, unless the program is ignored and permitted to plateau permanently on the down cycle. Everything wears out, and communication incentive programs are no different from the television jingle that was so clever last year but eventually became an irritation.

Now can you sit back? Sure. But do not get too comfortable. There is probably something else out there crying for a change. Better keep an eye out for it.

SUMMARY

1. Monitor changes in your target audience to ensure that your message remains on track.
2. When results on a continuing program begin to slip, promote it again, perk it, or change it.
3. Read accident reports to make sure management is not neglecting an area of your safety program.
4. Remain alert to any potential problem in program or system implementation by keeping tabs on your audience. Read between the lines of Suggestion Program submissions for clues to what is working and what is not.
5. Adjust a program concept that seems to have lost its impact only after you have checked the collateral elements. The program itself may be fine, but something may have gone wrong in presentation, or too many new people may not understand it.
6. Program perks can be modest and cost-effective. You do not always have to push for a big reward.
7. Market your ideas to management and "sell" them to employees. Find the magic that makes a program or event memorable and motivating.
8. Analyze results for repetitive or recurring programs carefully and

completely. In-depth measurement will help you discover improvements that can be made in the creative content and effectiveness of the next event.

9. Use every possible channel to keep yourself up-to-date on audience attitudes and expectations: existing programs, letters, "Speak Up" and "Let's Talk" programs, focus groups, surveys and audits, and just walking around.

10. Do not try to perk a program that has outlived its usefulness. You need not bury it publicly; just let it become dormant.

CHAPTER 11

Selecting the Right Media for the Audience

James Colin Charles Pritchitt*

Targeting audiences is an area in communication where the "80/20 rule" of business frequently applies. That is, 80 percent of the time and effort can be spent on targeting only 20 percent of the audience, whereas 80 percent of the audience can usually be reached with only 20 percent of the total effort.

This is one of the reasons why management can become disenchanted with the productivity of its communication group, particularly with public relations consultants. Efforts to reach the (sometimes obscure) wider audience can take ever-increasing amounts of time, and the communication task can become nonproductive.

To maintain productivity, communicators should continually check to ensure that the "easy" part is being done well and that most of the target audiences are getting the right information.

Another major point often overlooked in targeting audiences is that target groups may overlap. There is a tendency to think in terms of specific publics—employees, stockholders, neighbors, the financial community, suppliers, customers—whereas membership in these groups may overlap. The danger is that as groups overlap, a message aimed only at one group also will be received by people in other target groups. Properly handled, this should not be a problem, but anyone who tries to give conflicting information to specific groups and believes that they are isolated targets can end up in trouble.

So it is vitally important to ensure that messages to all target audiences are consistent. Certainly, specific messages can be emphasized in communications to certain groups and played down in communications to other groups. However, a company that sends a message to the investment com-

---

*James Colin Charles Pritchitt is managing director and chief executive of the Sydney public relations firm Corporate Communications Pty, Ltd., Neutral Bay, NSW, Australia. He serves as an Australian National Coordinating Councillor for the International Public Relations Association and is a member of the Public Relations Association of Australia.

munity that it has achieved record profits and is expecting even better things in the future should not be surprised to find that union negotiators are using this information in their dealings with the company.

The first step for communication at any level is to determine the message and define the audience. Only when this is done can the medium, or mix of media, be selected. It is essential to start by listing the proposed points that you would like to communicate and then the publics with which you wish to communicate. By putting this information in the form of a simple grid chart, you can check off the points you wish to make with the various publics. This will help you to select the media and also to ensure that there are no oversights or omissions.

MEDIA SELECTION

Broadly speaking, media can be classified into two groups:

Group 1: Mass Audience or Special-Interest Media

Newspapers

Radio

Television

Magazines—consumer

Magazines—special-interest

Magazines—work-related

Commercial newsletters—special-interest and work-related

Group 2: Do-it-Yourself Media

Newsletters and magazines produced by a company

Direct mail pieces

Exhibitions and displays

Seminars

Outdoor advertising

Sponsorship of special events (sports competitions, art fairs and festivals, health fairs, community and civic events, floats in parades, and so on)

Competitions

Open houses and organizational tours

Participation in local events

Company audiovisuals

Sponsorship of educational films/display material

Speeches
Company reports
Personal contact
Joint promotions
Government achievement awards

Group 1 consists of mass media and special-interest media that are already in existence. To be successful in using these existing media, you must know who uses them and how they operate.

Group 2 consists of avenues that you create in order to reach the group with which you want to communicate. In most cases, the cost of presenting a message this way is considerably higher than when you use existing media. Therefore, it is essential that you have a clearly defined picture of who your audience is and how it can best be reached.

In most cases, to be cost-effective, a great deal of your effort will be directed toward Group 1 media, but some campaigns will require you to create your own media. Do-it-yourself media are usually used because the existing media do not reach the audience you want; because the existing media do not provide the ideal environment for your message; or, as often happens, because these media cannot, in isolation, carry your complete story.

USING EXISTING MEDIA

Prominent in the list of activities for almost every communication program is production of stories that are intended to be used by media of one kind or another. With Group 1 media, messages will be directed toward several different audiences at the same time, which means that in order to reach them all, you will have to select several different media.

For example, a story about a new product development may need to be directed not only to consumers but also to company shareholders, in order to ensure their continued confidence and support; to potential retailers, in order to ensure distribution; to raw material suppliers, in order to ensure ongoing supply; to the business and financial community, in order to ensure continued support. The story may need a few changes in emphasis, depending on the style and content of the medium and the interests of the target audience, but it will still be the same basic story. For example, information about the funds allocated for marketing support is not something to communicate to consumers, but it is of vital interest to retailers.

Choosing the media to convey a message is a fascinating business, as it involves tapping into the lifestyle of your prospective audience. A useful skill to develop is the ability to see yourself as the type of person you are trying to reach. It is this skill that is honed to perfection by the editors of the mass media in which you want your material to appear. Imagine yourself in your audience's shoes—picture what they eat, where they live, whether they are homeowners or apartment renters, their social life, how they spend their leisure time, the type of pressures with which they have to cope, their self-expectations, the impact on them of peer pressure and peer approval, the items on which they spend their discretionary income, the personal qualities they would like to think they have. If you do this well and begin to feel what it is like to be a member of your audience, you will better understand which type of media your audience is most likely to respond to and how to structure your message to make it noticeable.

This approach avoids the waste of effort in targeting information to media that will not reach the right audience. You may have heard a communicator boast of getting a company that is in business-to-business sales on the radio. But if that radio program airs in mid-morning, how many business people will be listening?

Readership Profiles

If a fairly precise media selection is required, you will need to use information on readership profiles and circulation size of magazines and newspapers, plus similar data (including time slots available) for television and radio audiences. An important point to check when considering reading profiles of special-interest publications, especially those distributed to a mailing list, whether paid or not, is whether the recipients actually *read* the publication. Many companies simply consider it politic to support their trade media by subscribing, even though they actually get their information from other sources.

At this stage you can compile a media list on the basis of audience size in your target group and suitability of environment for your message. At times you will need to commission your own research. To be useful, research must be conducted properly by a fully qualified and experienced research company, as discussed in previous chapters.

Quality May Outweigh Numbers

In advertising, the cost efficiency of media selection used to be based on cost per 1,000—the cost of reaching 1,000 members of your specific audience. While this is still a useful measurement, it must be balanced with other considerations, such as timing. Time of exposure to the medium is very important, as it affects not only the likelihood of your target audience's being exposed to your particular message but also the amount of time and attention that they devote to it.

A fortnightly publication may be useless for a news announcement, but may present an excellent opportunity to repeat the message at later dates or to correct any bias that the daily news media may have introduced to the story. A weekend or weekly publication is usually read at a more leisurely pace than a daily and possibly in more relaxed surroundings. However, a message read over a weekend, may not encourage a business decision. Still, company newsletters mailed to employees' homes are read outside company time by a large audience, including family and friends.

Choosing the "Right" Media

Let us assume that you have a message about your client or your organization and you have identified the groups you want to reach. In the context of existing mass media and special-interest media, consider the following checklist:

Can your target audience be reached by mass media, and, if so, do you know which publications or broadcast programs?

Will your message appear in the sort of company you want it to keep? For example, you may know that large numbers of your prospective audience read *Playboy,* but that magazine may not be the right environment for a message about your organization's financial position.

Will the media you have chosen allow you to present your message as often as is necessary to inform your audience adequately?

Will these media reach enough members of your audience, or will you have to reach some of them by other means?

If broadcast media are the better way to reach your chosen group than print, can you present a story that has sufficient news value for radio or adequate visual material to get exposure on television?

Is your audience so widespread that a shotgun approach—presenting your information to every medium that could conceivably want to use it—is acceptable?

Are you being too narrow in your media selection? For example, builders can probably be reached through a feature or news story in one of the special-interest publications, but it is well to remember that builders also are consumers. It is sometimes possible to reach such a special-interest audience through consumer media. If you can think of an angle that has some implications for a wider audience than, say, just the builders, then maybe the story can be given to a newspaper or general-interest magazine and reach your builder at the same time.

The "angle" approach can be a very effective backup to trade-magazine exposure because most people believe, rightly or wrongly, that information in general consumer media is less likely to present commercial bias than that in a trade publication.

Consider whether the story has more than one angle. It may well be that you can present different versions to different publications. For example, a new factory planned for a major corporation will provide news stories for national and metropolitan business media, local press and broadcast media, and construction, finance, and engineering publications. Each version would require only a modest amount of rewriting.

Sending one story out everywhere and hoping for the best is not the best way to get results, however.

The Mass or Special-Interest Media as Target Audiences

How you go about presenting your material to your chosen media is very important and will depend on your understanding of the media and journalists. Thus, the media become target audiences themselves. This does not mean that knowing a journalist will get your story printed. It simply means that if a journalist knows that you are truthful and reliable, your story will have a better chance of being considered than if you are unknown or, worse, known to exaggerate or make light of the truth. It also means that you will know what the journalist looks for in a story and you can prepare your message accordingly. By giving the journalist exactly what he or she wants, you increase your message's chances of being used.

Working with the mass media can take many forms: media releases; exclusive stories; interviews; bylined articles; or, increasingly popular, the official "leak." The method by which information is given to a journalist is often overlooked. Even courier-delivered or telexed information can wind up on the wrong desk or even at the wrong address, so it is essential to check that your material has been received—but do so sensitively, without pushing.

Promises about exclusivity should not be made lightly. Give an exclusive only if you believe it is the only way to get your material presented, and abide by your promise. Do not give the same material to another reporter, and *never* promise an exclusive and then give it to someone else as well. Editors and reporters *never* forget a broken promise.

CREATING YOUR OWN MEDIA

Along with considerations about how best to reach your prospect, producing your own media carries with it a heavy budgetary responsibility. Creating your own media costs money, and this fact must be weighed very carefully against the likely results and the return on the company's investment. Consider just two examples other than newsletters among the many avenues available.

Direct Mail

It is not hard to identify groups of people for whom direct mail campaigns can be very effective, but doing so is worthwhile only if your list is relevant and up-to-date. Lists can be bought from direct mail houses, in which case you will not normally have prior access to them, which makes it difficult to know just how good they are. Many are very poor.

An added danger of the "outside" list is that your message could be delivered to people who do not wish to receive unsolicited mail and who would discard your message as "junk mail."

If possible, it is better to compile your own mailing list. You might hire students to work on this under your guidance, using your own sources, business and professional directories, telephone directories, electoral rolls, remodeling applications approved by local governments, or whatever other sources are relevant. When you compile your own list, you control and plan the makeup of the target audience.

Exhibitions

Participating in trade or public exhibitions and seminars or even mounting your own is another way to reach special-interest audiences. Sometimes an exhibition is held in conjunction with a seminar, conference, or festival, but often it is something you can organize and promote on your own.

Large regional shopping centers can usually give you some idea of the demographics of their customers. Some even have data for different days of the week, and your displays can be geared to reach the desired audience.

Many events such as exhibitions can be used both as a medium and an opportunity to attract the interest of other media. For instance, a speech is aimed at the audience that attends, but it also can be the subject of a news release intended to reach a wider audience. Printed copies of the speech, or highlights, can be distributed to selected audiences, and the speech can be summarized in internal publications.

AND DO NOT FORGET . . .

At the end of a project or activity, review other opportunities. This is an aspect that is frequently not fully explored because of the rush to get on with the next project. Whenever the printed word is available, no matter what the format, consider the wider distribution. News releases give your organization's point of view on an issue and can be sent to a number of audiences other than reporters. They can go to politicians, industry groups, shareholders, and even competitors, if you believe it will help your position. Press clippings are a useful means of getting messages to other audiences through a single direct mail activity. Annual reports are better off in the hands of your publics than collecting dust on a shelf in a storeroom.

Create the communication channels and then keep them open through regular use without reducing their effectiveness through overuse. And never underestimate the importance of personal contact. A list of opinion leaders and the people or organizations that affect your organization's operations should be developed, and regular contact maintained.

CHAPTER 12

Promotions and Special Events: Integrating Public Relations into the Marketing Mix

Carole M. Howard, APR*

When Ford Motor Company launched the Mustang in the 1960s, Lee Iacocca, then general manager of the Ford Division, worked with his public relations team to develop promotion plans that culminated in a remarkable coup: the car was featured simultaneously on the covers of both *Time* and *Newsweek* magazines. Said Iacocca: "I'm convinced that *Time* and *Newsweek* alone led to the sale of an extra 100,000 cars."[1]

When the Reader's Digest Association decided in 1985 to counter the perception that its magazine was out of step with the times, it sent selections from its private collection of Impressionist paintings on a tour of the United States and Europe as the first step in a campaign to show that it was a contemporary, world-class publishing company. The tour did change attitudes. The art critic for London's *Financial Times* said the exhibit "certainly surprised me. To judge by it, the collection as a whole must equal or surpass quite a few well-established art museums."[2] The tour also resulted in enhanced corporate visibility and new advertising customers for *Reader's Digest* magazine.

When the Hershey Chocolate Company agreed to let its Reese's Pieces candy be featured in the 1981 film *E.T., The Extraterrestrial,* sales of the tiny candies soared as *E.T.* became the top-grossing film of all time.[3]

Such dramatic sales results and glowing testimonials can turn public relations practitioners into avid marketers overnight, since such cases are highly visible demonstrations of the value of our craft to the corporate bottom line. John O'Toole, chairman of the board of Foote, Cone & Belding, said, "Advertising is salesmanship in print."[4] The same view can be applied to a well-planned special event. Yet while many organizations are broadening their traditional public relations activities to include successful events,

---

*Carole M. Howard, APR, is vice president and director of public relations and communications policy, Reader's Digest Association, Inc., Pleasantville, New York. She is coauthor of *On Deadline: Managing Media Relations,* and is accredited in public relations.

others overlook legitimate opportunities to promote their products and services with these valuable communication tools.

As Paul Solman and Thomas Friedman have observed, "A product without marketing is not unlike an army without weapons."[5] So too, a marketing plan without an active promotions and special-events effort is likely to waste a vital part of its potential ammunition.

Public relations limited to such traditional functions as employee communication, speech writing, media relations, and advertising may have a difficult time documenting its contributions. With responsibilities broadened to include marketing communication and promotions, you can not only take advantage of your public relations skills but also produce results that make a direct, measurable contribution to your organization's or client's sales. For a charitable organization, special events can provide a platform to reaffirm the importance of its cause, raise funds, and broaden its volunteer and donor base. Further, announcing a new product, unveiling a modern office building, or hosting an image-building event can be professionally stimulating and newsworthy, as long as you direct your messages to the right audience via the right media at the right time.

BE AWARE OF YOUR OPPORTUNITIES AND RESPONSIBILITIES

Special events are staged occurrences, so you usually control the timing. Held to promote good news, they let you take the offensive (proactive role), rather than the defensive (reactive role). Because they tend to have a casual, party atmosphere, they encourage person-to-person dialogue between the participants and your organization's or client's executives. They can be an especially useful tool for cementing relationships with key reporters and editors. To be effective, however, they should be more than cheerleading events; they should be planned for that strategic moment that helps you tell and sell your story. Only then will they be profitable in terms of improved public opinion, increased sales, and positive news coverage.

Three steps are crucial to getting the most effective results from special events. First, work closely with the marketing specialists so that everything you do supports the sales plan; second, clearly state your information objective and evaluate every idea by whether or not it helps meet that objective; third, keep lists that can be updated to track progress and responsibility for all activities. Think constantly in generalities, but at the same time live in details.

Michelangelo is said to have counseled a young artist, "Perfection is made up of details"—sage advice for communication professionals. A shortage of coat hangers and umbrella stands on a wet winter evening can bring chaos to a first-class event; lack of ashtrays and no-smoking sections can turn happy guests into dour complainers. Special events are a perfect example of the old adage that the difference between success and failure depends more on the last 5 percent of effort than on the first 95 percent.

TEAM UP WITH MARKETING

Special events can be an important component of the marketing mix if they support the marketing plan and are measured against its objectives. The events are significant not as ends in themselves, but as planned, integrated parts of the overall marketing effort. Everything you do should fit together, sending mutually reinforcing messages to your key audiences. Follow the lead of the Coca-Cola Company, which knows, as *The Wall Street Journal* succinctly put it, that "what it sells is not just flavored water but a carefully marketed image."[6]

Similar to an employee publication or news conference, a special event must have a specific purpose, be directed to a specific audience, and be part of an overall plan. It must be managed like any other part of the business. And it must support the organization's marketing and sales objectives.

For example, a cocktail party to announce a new product may be an enjoyable event for all involved. But it may cost less—and serve overall marketing goals better—to make demonstration units available to selected reporters whose media reach specific end-user markets. Apple Computer, Inc., practiced this hands-on promotion technique dramatically when it offered potential buyers home demonstrations on its new Macintosh personal computers, backed by a U.S. $10 million advertising campaign with the theme, "Test drive a Macintosh." The resulting first-person testimonials, combined with announcement extravaganzas that *Fortune* magazine labeled "event marketing,"[7] resulted in valuable publicity for Apple's new products.

Similarly, use of celebrities can help sell your product or service. But it can backfire if the celebrities are so well known that their fame overshadows your product or message or so involved in their own causes that they neglect to mention your organization. AT&T once arranged for an Olympic star to appear on a television talk show to promote a sports event it was sponsoring. With the exception of the logo on the athlete's jacket, AT&T got no visibility or credit.

Gimmicks also can be counterproductive—and costly. Targeting your message to your customers' needs and presenting your product's or service's strengths clearly is paramount. Burger King Corporation learned this lesson the expensive way in 1986, when its U.S. $40 million "Search for Herb" campaign failed to build sales, win significant numbers of new customers, or clearly position the fast-food chain's image. "If I had been selling, 'Herbs,' I'd probably be a multimillionaire right now," said Jay Darling, president of Burger King. While the campaign got great visibility for his company, "it didn't work hard enough in extolling the virtues of our products."[8]

Whether your organization or client sells directly to consumers, relies on volunteers, or markets through wholesalers or retailers has a major impact on the way you plan your special events and frame your message. Take care not to become isolated from your customer base, as Gordon S. Bowen, executive creative director of Ogilvy & Mather, cautioned advertising people who "begin moving in sushi circles and lose touch with Velveeta and the people who eat it."[9]

CONSIDER INTERNATIONAL CUSTOMS

Equally sensitive are local customs when you are planning a special event outside your own country. Public relations practices and marketing-communication activities differ throughout the world. Knowledge of language, religious observances, local culture, and media practices are indispensable. In some areas the government controls access to the news media, press associations are the only avenue for news conferences, and "publishing fees" must be paid in order to get a release printed. You also should be briefed on business customs. You will need to understand government relations, trade concerns, local-content laws, import restrictions, and technology-transfer issues before you plan a publicity effort outside your own community or organization headquarters. As *Forbes* put it bluntly, "There are two ways to market products in Japan—their way, or not at all."[10]

Local customs also will affect your choice of mementos to be given away at your special event. A small digital clock might be perfect in the United Kingdom but be received with dismay in Asia. Similarly, colors have religious connotations in several countries. Graphics also must be chosen with care, since symbolic abstractions in one language can be hex signs in another.

If you are a novice, it is well worth the investment to hire an in-country public relations firm with expertise and experience in your industry. Local nationals not only give you valuable insights into the local scene but also help you avoid the resentment that may be felt toward a product or company headquartered elsewhere.

DEVELOP A MASTER CHECKLIST

Once the announcement is a "go"—even before you have a firm date—develop a master checklist of all activities that need to be undertaken. This overall listing will spawn a number of more detailed "to-do" lists for many of the entries. But the master list will serve as a control device. Be sure to include the following:

1. *Guests:* Customers? Federal, state, provincial, local government officials? Community and business leaders? News media—local, national, and trade? Other VIPs? Employees? Spouses? Financial and security analysts? Distributors or suppliers?

2. *Type of occasion:* News conference? Lunch, dinner, or reception? Local customs on food and alcohol? Budget restrictions?

3. *News-media relations:* Press kit materials? Sound and lighting facilities for electronic media, typewriters and telephones for print media? Transportation to site?

4. *Date and time of announcement:* Conflicting events such as a holiday or an election? Best time for the local news media? Availability of key participants?

5. *Site of announcement:* Your organization's headquarters or local manufacturing plant for the new product? On-site or in a hotel or commercial establishment? Ease of accessibility for guests and news media? Fire and other emergency exit procedures?

6. *Main theme:* Expansion of your organization into a new business or service? Upgrade of current product or service line? Announcement of new product or international venture?

7. *Speakers:* Your organization's executives? Top federal, state, provincial, county, or regional official? Mayor or other local official?

8. *Bad-weather plan:* For an outdoor event, alternatives if it rains or snows?

9. *Invitations:* Written or by telephone? Special arrangements with typing pool? RSVPs required? Separate for news media? For head table or VIP guests?

10. *Mementos:* Appropriateness? Cost? Different ones for media and VIPs? In keeping with theme? Time to engrave or personalize? Place on tables if meal, or distribute as guests leave?

11. *Travel arrangements:* Hotel and travel reservations for your organization's executives? Fruit basket or similar welcome gift in rooms? Other VIPs? Spouses? The media? Preregistration courtesies? No-smoking room preference? Floor preference? Billing arrangements? Late checkouts?

12. *Collateral materials:* Exhibit? Printed program? Brochure about
your organization? Place cards at table setting? Name tags? Reserved table signs? "Working media only" sign outside news conference room?

It is a good idea to ask others who will be involved to review the master
list to see if you have omitted anything or overlooked local customs if you
are moving into a new area of the country or the world. Establish an information objective and budget, assign responsibility for each of the activities, develop an overall timetable, and set specific due dates. Then oversee
implementation on a day-to-day basis.

PLAN FOR NEWS LEAKS

Integral to your planning should be the knowledge that your plans very
likely are not going to be kept secret until announcement day. New product
announcements are especially vulnerable to rumors. If the product is significant—in terms of technology, prestige of the company, number of potential jobs, new strategic direction, or geographic expansion for your organization, for example—count on a leak occurring. Sales people boasting
to customers, planners carelessly chattering about their work in a bar or
restaurant, a hotel visited to evaluate conference facilities—all provide ample opportunities for the news to slip out despite precautions.

There is a basic reason for keeping a tight lid on your news before
announcement day: You very likely cannot afford to alienate the news media and lose the free—and probably positive—publicity they will give you.
Except in rare cases, reporters will not cover a special event or product
announcement as news if they believe that too many of their readers or
viewers already know about it. Leaks also can embarrass your sales force
when customers hear the news from the media rather than their account
executives.

IBM is experienced at guarding its business plans. It has to be, since
mere speculation about the introduction of a new product can dry up orders
for existing ones. As one means of protecting its secrets, IBM shows different versions of unannounced computers to software developers and dealers to keep people in the dark about the final choice.[11] That strategy is
backed by IBM spokespeople, who are experts at ducking queries about
unannounced products. If you are involved in planning such an event, keep
ready for immediate use an approved noncommittal statement such as, "We
do not discuss future products until we are ready to make a public announcement," in case a reporter calls seeking your comment on rumors.

CHOOSE THE BEST TYPE OF EVENT

Coming up with ideas for special events is relatively easy. The hard part is narrowing the field to those one or two that will best meet your marketing objectives with an appropriate investment of money and time. The right kind of event will bring attention to your organization or client, communicate its style, and provide an attention-getting platform for your marketing message. It also should be a creative and cost-effective means of achieving a specific marketing goal.

Avoid limiting your recommendations to traditional activities such as news conferences and cocktail receptions. Make sure your event is different from those of your competition. Consider product fairs, breakfasts with your customers, community sponsorships, or outings to cultural or sports events if there is a tie-in to your organization or client. You should strive for unusual, memorable, and, if possible, unique ideas. Heed the advice of the late fashion designer, Coco Chanel: "Fashion changes, style remains."

Following are examples of successful events that can offer inspiration and ideas to other communicators. Some were sponsored by multinational corporations, others by smaller organizations; some were expensive extravaganzas, others modest local events. Central to the success of each event is a concentration of resources on sending specific messages to clearly defined target audiences.

Corporate Support for the Arts

American Express has been a leader in tying contributions to the arts to its marketing program. It underwrote a traveling retrospective of paintings by Grandma Moses and sent the Alvin Ailey Dance Company to Japan. In both cases, the familiar blue American Express logo went along for the ride. Said Susan Bloom, vice president for cultural affairs, "We prefer to deal with special projects, mainly because of the visibility to American Express. The Medicis did not give away their money without being acknowledged for it."[12] Similarly, Mobil Corporation is not bashful about tying its philanthropy to its marketing goals. "The choice of (art) exhibitions we underwrite is very much oriented to the company's objectives," said Sandra Ruch, Mobil's manager of cultural programs and promotion. "In the process we also bring something to the public." For example, with a new plant in New Zealand and a desire to continue good relations with the government there, Mobil sponsored the "Te Maori" art show at New York City's Metropolitan Museum of Art.[13] The show later traveled to museums in St. Louis, San Francisco, and Chicago, drawing thousands of viewers, dozens of news stories, and a great deal of goodwill for the company. In addition, other sponsors, such as Bechtel Corporation in San Francisco, signed on for specific shows.

However, you need not be a corporate giant to tie your marketing effort to the arts. Even without bountiful budgets, organizations can take their cue from these events. Displaying the best of local artists' work in your lobby or cafeteria on a rotating basis can do much to demonstrate community involvement—especially if you give a reception for civic, business and cultural leaders to launch the exhibit and invite reporters from local newspapers and radio and television stations to cover it.

Narrowly Focused Communication

Sometimes success is achieved by targeting efforts to a very select audience. Flair Communications of Chicago created a promotion for Beatrice Foods, which wanted to improve its image and sales among black Americans. Beatrice recognized 100 leading black businesswomen and then counted on these opinion leaders to pass along its message. "We are using them as a means to spread information to their communities; the impact of the promotion will filter down to their associates and friends," said C. Roy Jackson, Flair director.[14] In a similar narrowing of focus, Adidas now targets its promotional activities less on the end users of its sporting goods than on the administrators of important sports federations and national Olympic committees that control contracts with national teams. "If we hadn't done that, we would have paid more for less," said Chairman Horst Dassler. Adidas, the largest sporting-goods manufacturer in the world in 1985, has made its trademarks ubiquitous at major sporting events.[15]

Sports Events

Sponsoring sports events can be beneficial to marketing efforts. Anheuser-Busch, Inc., has transformed Budweiser into one of the most familiar trademarks in the world and increased its share of the beer market through aggressive sports promotions, ranging from local softball tournaments to the Olympic Games. With detailed marketing approaches to demographic segments, it sponsors local events in major U.S. cities and small towns. On one summer day in 1985 in New York City, for example, Anheuser-Busch simultaneously sponsored two disparate events: the Battle of the Corporate Stars for 250 business executives and a rodeo where black cowboys displayed their riding skills to a crowd of 5,000 people. In Texas, one of the biggest beer markets in the United States, the company sponsors local events such as parades and fiestas.[16]

Also emphasizing a connection with the sporting world—but targeting a smaller audience segment—the United Kingdom's Pimm's Cup has become almost the official drink at major U.S. polo events as it directs its sales message to drinkers who like to look and feel sophisticated. The U.S. connection is a natural extension of the company's marketing efforts in the

United Kingdom, where for years the British have served Pimm's Cup at three traditional and prestigious sports events: Wimbledon tennis matches, the Royal Ascot horse races, and the Royal Henley regatta.[17]

The Ken Venturi Guiding Eyes Classic is an outstanding example of how a not-for-profit organization melds fundraising with fun. Each June sighted and blind golfers team up in a unique golf tournament in Westchester County, New York, that in nine years has raised more than U.S. $1.6 million for Guiding Eyes for the Blind. "We run the special event the same way you run a successful business—finding volunteers who are specialists and then taking advantage of their areas of expertise," said tournament director William C. Heyman. "We appeal to local organizations and companies with a natural connection to golf and concern for blind people. That way our fundraising and their marketing goals are mutually supportive."[18]

Anniversary Celebrations

Anniversaries can be useful pegs for special events that generate media coverage and increased sales. Steuben Glass used its elegant store on New York City's Fifth Avenue for a "Fifty Years on Fifth" exhibition that resulted in extensive print and broadcast coverage. "Based on current advertising rates, the publicity about 'Fifty Years on Fifth' is equivalent to more than U.S. $400,000 in advertising space," according to Eugene Ritchie, vice president–public relations and advertising. "The exhibition also realized dramatic increases in the New York shop traffic."[19] This idea could be adapted by almost any organization with an anniversary to celebrate. A hospital could promote six decades of improvements in healthcare. A restaurant could feature dishes from the past for a special month of celebrations. A retail store could present fashion shows featuring changing clothing tastes over the decades.

Trade Shows

Trade shows can be cost-effective platforms from which to launch new products, generate sales, and introduce executives to the media. The right trade show can put your company or client in direct contact with customers who would otherwise remain unreachable. Since they have frequently traveled great distances to get there, visitors are guaranteed to constitute an interested audience. In addition to the usual reasons for participating in trade shows, many companies like AT&T have a further objective: covering the cost of trade show participation by direct sales off the exhibit floor or following up on leads generated by trade show attendance. Moreover, reporters from the trade press are in attendance, looking for news to cover.

Figure 12.1. This poster design featuring Stevie Wonder was selected from entries submitted by nearly 1,500 teams of copywriters and art directors. It became the focal point of a scholarship program to spur student ideas for anti-drunk-driving campaigns.

Hands-on demonstrations of your products can be effective if they are attractively displayed in a booth or conference room. As one wag put it, "A picture is worth a thousand words, and a product demo is worth a thousand pictures." Try to arrange media interviews at your exhibit if it is not too crowded and has a seating area.

Contests

Contests can stimulate interest and publicity if they are well targeted. *Reader's Digest* appealed to advertising agencies' creative pride in 1985 by sponsoring a design contest for a poster that would become the theme of a U.S. $500,000 "Don't Drive and Drink Scholarship Challenge" for high school students. Nearly 1,500 teams of copywriters and art directors responded. The winning poster—a picture of blind rock star musician Stevie Wonder beneath the headline, "Before I'll ride with a drunk, I'll drive myself"—was distributed to 16,000 high schools to help spur entries for another competition, seeking the best student-developed programs for combating drunk driving. The contest resulted in widespread media coverage and a changed image that surprised some observers. *USA Today* headlined, "Wonder of Wonders: Stevie Wonder Is the Star of a New Poster for Reader's Digest."[20]

Charity-Related Marketing Campaigns

The restoration of the Statue of Liberty to celebrate its 100th birthday in 1986 brought widespread participation and credibility to cause-related marketing efforts tying sales to donations for charitable efforts. Hundreds of companies and suppliers actively sold products with promises that some of the proceeds would be contributed to the restoration or paid a fee for a license to produce official Statue of Liberty souvenirs, from clothing to coins to chocolate.

For the most part, sponsors and other companies involved in promotions say that the benefits have turned out to be as large as expected. For example, when Kellogg offered to make a U.S. 50-cent contribution to the Statue of Liberty restoration fund for each two box tops returned from Kellogg's Corn Flakes and Crispix cereals, it received 175,000 replies.[21]

GUIDELINES FOR CONDUCTING A SPECIAL EVENT

As you begin to implement your special event, here are some guidelines that may be helpful:

Write down the objective(s) for your event. Be sure that the objectives support the organization's marketing and sales goals and that they are agreed to in advance by everyone involved, including your CEO. The written plan should include both the key message and the target audience. Before making any decision, evaluate it against the objectives.

Carefully define your publics and the reasons for including them in your target audience. For educational institutions, for example, it may be more crucial to attract alumni and major contributors than faculty or legislators, depending on the objectives for the event.

Circulate a proposed invitation list well in advance to people who can provide counsel on who should be included. In some communities the sheriff or chairperson of a local regulatory agency can be as influential as the mayor or county commissioner. Marketing and sales people should be given the opportunity to invite major customers to the main announcement event or to concurrent local ceremonies if the event is a news conference restricted to the media. Reporters should be carefully chosen for their interest in the product or news, ongoing coverage of your industry, employment with local media, or ability to reach your target audience.

If your event takes place outside your own country, allow enough time for your materials to be translated into the local language. Although most business and media people with whom you will deal understand and speak English, it is a courtesy to provide written materials in their own language. Arrange to have your business cards and those of your executives translated into the local language and size. Similarly, when addressing your message to the U.S. Hispanic population, use a Spanish vocabulary accessible to Mexicans, Cubans, Puerto Ricans, and Latin Americans. Even if fully conversant in English, most Hispanics think—and make buying decisions—in their native language.

If your company's stock is traded publicly, consider the financial community in your planning. Reporters frequently call security analysts and market experts for an outside, "objective" evaluation and for quotable comments to include in their story on a major corporate announcement. Thus it is advantageous to make sure that financial analysts who follow your company and industry are fully informed about your news, preferably on announcement day. You can either have copies of the press kit delivered to financial analysts or arrange a separate restaging of the news conference for them. (It is normally not wise to invite reporters and security analysts to the same event. Their interests are different, and they deserve individual attention.)

It is usually good politics as well as good public relations to invite the governor of the state or province, or the mayor or chief county official, to make a few brief remarks. Try to limit remarks by politicians to a five-minute official welcome, rather than scheduling them as the keynote address. This will enable you to keep control of the length of the program and the main message the audience takes away from the event. Provide speakers and spokespersons with solid background information, and conduct practice sessions to rehearse speeches and sharpen interview skills.

Avoid getting involved in distracting clerical tasks that can be delegated to others, such as making travel arrangements or hotel reservations for VIPs. However, maintain enough oversight to reassure yourself that details are being taken care of. Pay special attention to news media materials.

If your organization or client has an advertising or promotion campaign under way, look for opportunities to use its theme or creative materials during your event so that you can reinforce its sales message to your target audience. When AT&T announced its first personal computer in 1984, all promotional materials—from press kit to advertising, including dais banners at simultaneous news conferences and customer seminars from San Francisco to New York—carried the theme, "Watson, watch us now!" Within the company the theme was reinforced in everything from articles in the employee newspaper to bumper stickers distributed to all employees.

If a tour is part of the program, time it and walk the route with a group the same size as that which will take the tour on announcement day. Keeping a group of people together and rounding up stragglers can be time-consuming enough to destroy a schedule.

Severely limit the number of officials introduced individually or allowed to speak as part of the announcement ceremony. Such so-called obligatory recognition is boring to the audience and is not normally required. To have public officials or key executives feel they are getting VIP treatment, you can reserve a separate table for them at the lunch, provide them with special mementos, or have the CEO thank them personally after the event.

If a meal follows the announcement, arrange for "Reserved for Press" tent cards on tables nearest the podium or head table. Do not assume that reporters will stay for the meal because they are attending the news conference. Ask them for separate RSVPs to the news conference and the lunch or reception invitations.

Discuss the meal schedule with the caterer in exhaustive detail, specifying serving times and forbidding any clearing of tables while speeches are in progress. Many a first-class occasion—and potential television or radio coverage—has been ruined by the clatter of dishes.

Review and update checklists often. The ball can take odd bounces, and you must always keep your eye on it. Conduct frequent meetings at which everyone involved shares progress reports. If the committee members are physically separated, issue written status reports and make periodic telephone conference calls.

Try to have a separate workroom at the announcement site for storage of press kits, mementos, and other office materials such as typewriter or word processor and blank news-release paper, in case you have to revise the release at the last minute. If your event is taking place at a commercial establishment, ship these materials well in advance.

Understand that the primary focus of reporters' and customers' questions will be on how your product or service is different from the competition's and how it helps your *customers* meet *their* objectives. Make sure your spokespersons phrase the news from the viewpoint of the consumer, not of your company. Choose—and keep repeating—one or two key selling points that make your product or announcement newsworthy, unique, and of value to the buyer (making his or her life easier, richer, or more rewarding).

Make sure the head table and news conference are physically arranged so as to photograph well, to help ensure maximum exposure for your message. The lectern should carry your organization's logo, not the hotel's. If the drapes behind the staging area have a busy pattern or inappropriate color, put a portable screen or curtain behind the speaker or an attractive sign with your theme or organization's name. All visuals should be simple, with copies included in the press kit. View the staging through a camera's eye—literally, if necessary.

Find the nearest public telephones so that you can inform media representatives of their location. Arrange for at least one line for the exclusive use of your organization's executives, the governor or other top government officials, and their aides.

Set up a reception table with at least one staff person available to direct guests to coatrooms and restrooms, to control access to private telephones, to take messages, and to provide other logistical support. Give this person photographs of the individuals who should get special care and attention if he or she does not already know them.

Assign someone to help handle press kit distribution, requests for private interviews, and other courtesies extended to reporters. You can have a first-class news kit folder and also save money by using a photograph or drawing along with your organization's name and event theme—but not the date of the event—on the cover. That way you can produce the kits before a final date is set to avoid overtime printing charges and keep your last-minute duties to a minimum. You also can use the folders for follow-up promotion activities.

Immediately before the event, prepare a final, detailed chronology of every activity related to announcement day. Include arrival and departure times of your organization executives and other VIPs, limousine arrangements, and the agenda timed to the minute. Give copies to everyone involved—including limousine drivers, the hotel catering manager, and the person at the guest reception table.

Prepare a separate package of materials for executives involved in the program. Include the press kit and the detailed agenda as well as main copy points, a questions-and-answers sheet covering information that may come up, a list of officials and reporters deserving personal attention, potential local concerns, and each executive's itinerary and schedule (with a reminder of the times each should be available for separate media interviews if any will be arranged).

Coordinate the agenda and schedule closely with the press secretaries or aides of government officials who are participating in the program. Inquire about security or other necessary arrangements.

Arrange for setup time and personally inspect all the facilities the night before and the day of the event. Test the sound and lighting arrangements for television and radio. Arrange for separate distribution of the announcement kits simultaneously with or immediately after the news conference to reporters and important customers not attending the event. Only in rare cases should you allow advance distribution, which decreases chances of in-person attendance.

Do not forget employees. Distribute announcement materials internally on the day of the event so that your employees hear the news first from you rather than from the local newspaper or radio or television news. They can be highly motivated sales people if kept informed. When AT&T launched the Merlin communications system at a morning news conference in 1983, the news team repeated the announcement at a rally that afternoon for all employees involved in the product introduction.

Monitor the evening's television news programs. Arrange for videotapes of television shows and audiotapes of radio coverage. Get copies of the daily newspapers. Within 24 to 48 hours, provide your top executives and marketing clients with samples of initial news coverage of the event as well as a videotape of the full news ceremony, if you made one. Consider preparing a separate, shorter version for showing to employees and the board of directors or trustees.

A month or so after the event, when most news accounts have been gathered (though trade-magazine coverage may take several more months to appear), prepare a summary for your organization's officers and board that includes information objectives and a brief analysis of how they were met, with selected samples of news media coverage. Include a review of disparate reaction by region, country, or type of publication; compute the equivalent advertising funds that would have been spent to buy the space given to the news coverage; evaluate the positive or negative opinions of reporters, customers, and market and financial analysts as revealed in the news coverage, and recommend follow-up media efforts to build on positive stories or to counter negative reaction.

Translate your experiences into recommendations and techniques that will be useful in the future. Solicit advice from all departments that contributed. Whether you share this report widely with others or confine it to those involved in the project does not matter. The crucial point is to record ideas—especially constructive criticisms—while they are fresh in your mind.

SUMMARY

Advertising guru David Ogilvy said that his objective was not to write advertising that was creative but rather to write copy that would make people *buy the product*. "When Aeschines spoke, they said, 'How well he speaks.' But when Demosthenes spoke, they said, 'Let us march against Philip.' "[22] Although aimed at copywriters, that counsel is equally appropriate for communicators planning special events. Your objective is not only to entertain but also to pass on concrete information that will help sell your organization's or client's product or service. As Reader's Digest Association, Inc., chairman and CEO George V. Grune put it, "Good public relations people are selling all the time."[23] Just as advertising that promises no benefit to the consumer does not sell products or services, neither do special events without clear marketing messages send away convinced customers. Yet special events can be an integral part of your marketing mix if they are carefully planned and well packaged.

NOTES

1. Lee Iacocca, with William Novak, *Iacocca: An Autobiography* (New York: Bantam Books, 1984), 72.
2. Sir David Piper, "Rare Impressions Blow a Refreshing Breeze," *Financial Times,* 23 January 1986, 11.
3. Robert M. Finehout, "Products in a Supporting Role," *Public Relations Journal* (August 1985), 32.
4. John O'Toole, *The Trouble with Advertising* (New York: Chelsea House, 1981), 16.
5. Paul Solman and Thomas Friedman, *Life and Death on the Corporate Battlefield* (New York: Simon & Schuster, 1982), 101.
6. "Profoundly Changed, Coca-Cola Co. Strives to Keep on Bubbling," *Wall Street Journal,* 24 April 1986, 1.
7. Bro Uttal, "Behind the Fall of Steve Jobs," *Fortune,* 5 August 1985, 20.

8. Quoted in Brian Moran, "Herb Helped BK Visibility, but Little Else," *Advertising Age,* 24 March 1986, 1.
9. Quoted in "Now Hear This," *Fortune,* 14 October 1985, 11.
10. "When in Japan . . . ," *Forbes,* 10 March 1986, 153.
11. "Businesses Struggle to Keep Their Secrets," *US News & World Report,* 23 September 1985, 59.
12. "Corporate Culture," *Manhattan Inc.,* September 1985, 149.
13. Ibid., 150.
14. "Promotion and PR not Lost on Market," *Advertising Age Thursday,* 19 December 1985, 30.
15. Bill Abrams, "Adidas Makes Friends, Then Strikes Deals That Move Sneakers," *Wall Street Journal,* 23 January 1986, 1.
16. Richard W. Stevenson, "How Anheuser Brews Its Winners," *New York Times,* 4 August 1985, F1.
17. "Pimm's Cup Rides with Polo Set," *Advertising Age,* 29 August 1985, 6.
18. Personal interview with William C. Heyman, April 1986.
19. Kate Bertrand, "Glassware Ads Reflect Image of Quality," *Advertising Age Special Report,* 9 May 1985, 18.
20. *USA Today,* 14 January 1986, D1.
21. Martin Gottlieb, "Statute of Liberty's Repair: A Marketing Saga," *New York Times,* 3 November 1986, 1.
22. David Ogilvy, *Ogilvy on Advertising* (New York: Crown Publishers, 1983), 7.
23. Comments by George V. Grune, chairman and CEO, Reader's Digest Association, Inc., during a press interview, January 1986.

Glossary

accidental sampling A nonprobability survey research method that relies on chance, the survey subjects being at the same place, at the same time, as a researcher. Not statistically valid.

added value The "extras" an organization puts on a product in the form of packaging, services, customer advice, financing, delivery arrangements, warehousing, and so on, that people value.

advertisement A paid public notice in print or on the air. Broadcast advertisements are called *commercials*.

attitude survey A study that measures all aspects of work life, from employee perceptions about benefits and compensation to job satisfaction and organizational communication. Also called *climate study* or *employee relations study*.

augmented product *See* added value

audit A periodic study of an organization, its products or services, and the attitudes of its key audience(s) toward the image it projects, intentionally or unintentionally.

benefit/cost analysis A method of weighing the cost of a promotion or marketing communication campaign against the benefits that will result from increased sales, increased use, or the development of new markets.

cluster sampling A probability survey research method in which successively smaller groups within a large population are randomly selected until a sample of manageable size is obtained.

communication audit A way of measuring employee and management perceptions of the effectiveness of an organization's communication messages and message-distribution channels.

content analysis A method of studying media coverage of a company or individual by analyzing stories (focusing on adjectives, adverbs, and verbs) and their contexts and determining whether the report is favorable or unfavorable.

demarketing Discouraging customers in general, or a specific group of customers, from buying or using a product or service on a temporary or permanent basis.

demographics The characteristics of survey respondents or of an audience: age, sex, race, educational level, occupation, and so on; also, the questions that seek this information.

differentiated marketing The promotional, marketing, or communication campaigns that are created to "sell" the same product or service to different segments of the same market or to different markets.

downsizing Reducing the size of the organization, the size of staff, the size of product or service offered, to make the organization more efficient and profitable.

focus group Five to 10 people selected to participate in guided discussions to obtain an indication of consumer attitudes and behavior toward a product, service, or organization.

gatekeepers The internal and external "guardians" or arbitrators that determine how an organization will be perceived by its target audience.

image study A method of measuring how key audiences perceive an organization compared to how the organization wants itself perceived.

involvement study A method of measuring how much thought and effort individuals exert before making a decision. Low-involvement decisions include impulse purchases and commitments; high-involvement decisions include a home purchase or selection of a college.

law of similar response The way in which the attitude and action of the message sender calls forth a similar attitude or action from the message recipient.

life-cycle analysis A forecast of the life of the product or service from its introduction through growth and maturity to decline.

marketing The management process of identifying, anticipating, and satisfying customer requirements profitably.

market share The overall sales of product or service, or the clientele served by a not-for-profit, as a percentage of the potential total market.

market penetration The percentage of the total possible market that could be reached for a product or service.

multidimensional scaling Paired comparisons that help researchers create three-dimensional models to position an organization or its products or services, or to help it identify its place in potential consumer's minds.

nonprobability sampling Methods of sampling that are based on chance or personal knowledge rather than on mathematical selection. (*See* accidental sampling)

point-of-sale (point-of-purchase) Promotional or advertising materials displayed in the area where a product or service is sold.

positioning Defining the position in the market that the product or service is intended to fill; for example, the audience targeted by Lincoln as an upmarket automobile.

PRIZM (potential rating in ZIP markets) A United States registered trademark of Claritas for a market segmentation database system that identifies demographic and lifestyle characteristics by ZIP codes.

probability sampling The selection of research subjects according to mathematical guidelines that allow each member of the population surveyed to have an equal opportunity to be selected.

psychographics The psychological and sociological influences that affect purchasing attitudes and patterns, for example, preferences for colors, foods, and sports and attitudes about such topics as religion, politics, and parenting.

publicity Information about a product or service that is issued as news or feature material.

purposive sampling A nonprobability survey research method that relies on the researcher's knowledge of characteristics of the population being surveyed. Subjects are selected on the basis of this knowledge and of the purpose of the study.

qualitative research Research that studies opinions, attitudes, and feelings toward an organization, product, or service.

quantitative research Research that provides statistical information about an organization, product, or service.

quota sampling A nonprobability survey research method based on selected characteristics of the population being surveyed that are considered important to the study, for example, age, sex, race, ethnic background, education.

ratings points The "share" that a station or network has of the percentage of homes with television or radio stations tuned to that station or network.

sample A special subset of a population selected to meet key criteria, such as age, sex, residence, and education, in numbers representative of the whole group, as a basis for measuring attitudes and opinions of the broader group.

simple random sampling A probability survey research method that involves drawing a sample from the entire population, so that every member of the group has an equal chance of being selected.

Starch survey A method of testing print advertising for consumer recall of copy content, product, or organization, compared to recall of other advertising in the same medium.

store traffic A measure of the number of consumers entering a store or shopping in a particular department or specialty section.

stratified sampling A probability survey research method in which the population is divided into small, homogeneous groups for more accurate representation.

survey research A method of measuring attitudes and opinions of a group of people.

systematic random sampling A probability survey research method in which the sample is selected from existing lists of names.

target audience The individuals or groups an organization is trying to reach as potential customers or clients.

unique selling position The features or benefits that set your organization's products or services apart from the competition.

vulnerability relations The alleged or actual weaknesses in an organization, its products, or its operations that can affect its relationships with its publics.

validity The reliability of the testing methodology; the reliability of the resulting research data.

Resource Groups

Advertising Research Foundation
3 E. 54th Street
New York, NY 10022

American College of Healthcare
  Marketing
5530 Wisconsin Avenue, NW
Suite 917
Washington, DC 20815

American Marketing Association
250 S. Wacker Drive
Suite 200
Chicago, IL 60606

Asian Mass Communication
  Research and Information
  Centre
39 Newton Road
Singapore 1130 Singapore

Associacion de Ferias
  Internacionales de America
(Association of International Trade
  Fairs of America)
PO Box 257
Lima 18 Peru

Association Européenne
  de Marketing Financier
(European Financial Marketing
  Association)
16 Rue d'Aguesseau
F-75008 Paris, France

Bank Marketing Association
309 W. Washington Street
Chicago, IL 60606

Biomedical Marketing Association
505 E. Hawley Street
Mundelein, IL 60660

Council of Sales Promotion
  Agencies
176 Madison Avenue
New York, NY 10016

Direct Marketing Association
6 E. 43d Street
New York, NY 10017

European Direct Marketing Associ-
  ation
Fuchsenbergstrasse 15
CH-8645 Jona/SG, Switzerland

European Marketing Academy
c/o EFDM-EIASM
Rue Washington 40
B-1050 Brussels, Belgium

Federation Internationale
  du Marketing
(International Marketing
  Federation)
30 Rue d'Astorg
F-75008 Paris, France

**Financial Institutions Marketing
  Association**
111 E. Wacker Drive
Chicago, IL 60601

**Insurance Marketing Communica-
  tions Association**
175 W. Jackson Boulevard
Room A-1251
Chicago, IL 60604

**International Exhibitors
  Association**
5103-B Blacklick Road
Annandale, VA 22003

**International Association of
  Business Communicators**
Marketing Council
870 Market Street
Suite 940
San Francisco, CA 94102

**International Newspaper Advertis-
  ing and Marketing Executives**
Box 17210
Dulles International Airport
Washington, DC 20041

**Life Insurance Marketing
  and Research Association**
8 Farm Springs
Farmington, CT 06032

Market Research Society
15 Belgrave Square
London SW1X 8PF England

**Promotion Marketing Association
  of America**
322 Eighth Avenue
Suite 1201
New York, NY 10001

**Public Relations Society
  of America**
845 Third Avenue
New York, NY 10022

**Technical Marketing Society
  of America**
KB Building #609
3711 Long Beach Boulevard
Long Beach, CA 90807

Additional Readings

Advertising Age
220 E. 42d Street
New York, NY 10017

Adweek/National Marketing Edition
49 E. 21st St.
New York, NY 10010

American Demographics
PO Box 68
Ithaca, NY 14851

Business Marketing
Crain Communications
740 Rush Street
Chicago, IL 60601

Campaign
Marketing Publications Ltd.
22 Lancaster Gate
London W2 3LY England

Channels
PR Publishing Company, Inc.
Dudley House
Box 600
Exeter, NH 03833-0600

Communication Briefings
806 Westminster Boulevard
Blackwood, NJ 08012

Communications Concepts
Box 1608
Springfield, VA 22151

Communication World
International Association
   of Business Communicators
870 Market Street
Suite 940
San Francisco, CA 94102

Consumer Attitudes and Buying Intentions
(Contemporary Research Centre Ltd.)
Conference Board of Canada
255 Smyth Road
Ottawa, ONT K1H 8M7

Dartnell Sales and Marketing Newsletter
4660 Ravenswood Avenue
Chicago, IL 60640

Dartnell Sales and Marketing Executive Report
4660 Ravenswood Avenue
Chicago, IL 60640

Direct Marketing Magazine
224 7th Street
Garden City, NY 11530

Incentive Marketing
633 Third Avenue
New York, NY 10017

Journal of Advertising Research
3 E. 54th Street
New York, NY 10022

**Journal of International Marketing
and Marketing Research**
European Marketing Association
18 St. Peters Steps
Brixham, Devon
England

Journal of Marketing
Texas Tech University
Lubbock, TX 79409

Journal of Marketing Research
250 S. Wacker Drive #200
Chicago, IL 60606

Madison Avenue
369 Lexington Avenue
New York, NY 10016

**Management and Marketing
Update**
Rydge Publications Pty, Ltd.
72 Clarence Street
Sydney, NSW 2000
Australia

Marketing
777 Bay Street
Toronto, ONT M5W 1A7

Marketing
22 Lancaster Gate
London W2 3LY England

Marketing Communications
50 W. 23d Street
New York, NY 10010

Marketing News
250 S. Wacker Drive #200
Chicago, IL 60606

Marketing Research Society Journal
Marketing Research Society
15 Belgrave Square
London, SW1X 8PF England

Marketing Review
American Marketing Association
  (New York Chapter)
420 Lexington Avenue
New York, NY 10170

Marketing Trends
A. C. Nielsen Company
Nielsen Plaza
Northbrook, IL 60062

Marketing Week
Centaur Communications, Ltd.
60 Kingly Street
London, W1R 5LH England

Marketplace
R25 Caxton Ltd.
Roosevelt Park
PO Box 48985
2195 Johannesburg, South Africa

Market Research Facts and Trends
Maclean-Hunter, Ltd.
Maclean-Hunter Building
777 Bay Street
Toronto, ONT M5W 1A7

Medical Marketing and Media
7200 W. Camino Real #215
Boca Raton, FL 33433

Motivational Marketing
411 Richmond E., #102
Toronto, ONT M5A 3S5

Potentials in Marketing
50 S. 9th Street
Minneapolis, MN 55402

Public Relations Quarterly
44 W. Market Street
PO Box 311
Rhinebeck, NY 12572

Public Relations Review
10606 Mantz Road
Silver Spring, MD 20903

Quarterly Review of Marketing
Marketing House Publishers, Ltd.
Moor Hall
Cockham, Maidenhead, Berks SL6
  9QH
England

Research for Marketing
R10 University of South Africa
Bureau of Market Research
Box 392
Pretoria 0001, South Africa

Social Science Monitor
10606 Mantz Road
Silver Spring, MD 20903

Index